BRENDAN BEHAN

When Brendan Behan died in 1964 the legends were already thick about him and have gone on growing since: the roaring boy, the tosspot, the incurable drunk; the dishevelled, incoherent caricature of a nineteenth-century 'Paddy', at home again with oaths and stories in every bar between Stratford East and San Francisco—but never at home with himself; the tousle-headed, toothless Caesar of more words than work whose plays *The Quare Fellow* and *The Hostage*, and his book *Borstal Boy*, brought him an international reputation when he no longer had the talent or constitution to support it.

Here is an account of the whole Behan with an emphasis on his anonymous youth as a writer and revolutionary: Brendan, the spoiled grandson of eccentric, scheming Granny English who owned a block of Dublin tenements, spent most of her life in bed, sent the boy running for pints and took him to drunken funerals at the age of six; Brendan, the son of parents who instilled in him an early love of music and literature; Brendan, the failed revolutionary at sixteen, sent as a courier to Liverpool by the I.R.A. and promptly arrested for carrying home-made explosives— remanded in Walton jail, virtually excommunicated by the Chaplain and viciously beaten up by two warders; Brendan, the Borstal Boy exiled in Suffolk, and the inadequate gunman sentenced to fourteen years by his own courts on his return to Dublin.

His middle years were spent in the euphoric literary atmosphere of post-war Dublin and Paris. Ulick O'Connor has researched the shadowy part of Brendan's life in great detail: his friendships with writers as different as Donleavy and Camus, his little known Gaelic poetry and hitherto unknown play *The Landlady*, his superb short stories published in various little magazines and the events which led him up to the London production of *The Quare Fellow* which subsequently launched him on his garrulous decline.

Brendan Behan

Ulick O'Connor

CORONET BOOKS
Hodder Paperbacks Ltd., London

Copyright © 1970 Ulick O'Connor
First published in Great Britain
by Hamish Hamilton Ltd 1970
Coronet edition 1972

Printed and bound in Great Britain for
Coronet Books,
Hodder Paperbacks Ltd,
St. Paul's House, Warwick Lane,
London, EC4P 4AH
by Hazell Watson & Viney Ltd,
Aylesbury, Bucks

ISBN 0 340 16260 0

BRENDAN BEHAN

ACKNOWLEDGMENTS

I am very grateful to the many people who helped me in the preparation of this book. Eric Lasher originally suggested the idea. Axel Goodbody did much industrious and persistent research. Earnan de Blaghad Og gave me invaluable assistance with the translations: his renderings of Brendan's Irish plays *An Giall* and *An Ciosach* are the ones used in this book. David Tomkin was available at a moment's notice to help. Eilish Ellis and Dick Timmins also helped with research. Joseph Hone was an able and careful editor.

I am particularly grateful to Soto Grande on the Costa del Sol where I had some months of perfect conditions while I was writing parts of the book. Also to Señora Enrequeta Salvecchi of Chez Enrequeta, Torreblanca, and David Fitzgerald and the staff of the La Touche Hotel, Greystones. Doctors and specialists whom I consulted were most generous with help and advice. As always I am grateful for the help and superb courtesy of the National Library in Dublin, and its Director Dr Henchy.

Finally, I am grateful for the help given me by Miss Rita Lorrigan and Mrs Mollie Dobbyn who typed a major part of the MS for me. Miss Norah Mackey, Miss Betty Newsome and Miss Sarah Compston worked on the second half of the MS. My grateful thanks to Rory and May Furlong, Sean Furlong, Brian Behan, Beatrice Behan, Mrs Kathleen Behan and the late Stephen Behan. I would like to acknowledge especially the help given by the following: Liam Brady, Denis O'Dwyer, John Sheridan, Michael Traynor, Frank Cahill, Mick Murphy, Paddy Kelly, Charlie Joe Gorman, George Jeffares, Dr Dave McSweeney, the late Patrick Kavanagh, Tom Langan, Edward Daly, Capt Sean Feehan, Conall Gogan, Sindbad Vail, Dick Flaherty, George

Kleinsinger, Peter Arthurs, Milton Machlin, Allen Churchill, William Lipschitz, Norman Mailer, Perry Bruskin, Jim Downey, Nick Lynch, Desmond McNamara, the late Eoin O'Mahony K.M., Alan Simpson, Carolyn Swift, Sean O'Briain, Richard Walshe, Dept of Phoenetics, University College, Jimmy Bourke, Mrs Evelyn Bruce, Dr Terence Chapman, Sean McBride, S.C., Mrs Teresa Byrne, Niall Tobin, Anthony Havelock Allen, Eamonn Andrews, Dr Kevin Nowlan, John Ryan, Dr Olaf Lagerlöv, Mr and Mrs Tom Nisbet, Dr Ivor Browne, Leslie Mallory, J. P. Donleavy, Detective Officer Hanrahan, Detective Officer Donegan, Don McDonald, Kenneth Allsop, David Nathan, Norma Nathan, Seumas Sorahan, Fred O'Donovan, Dr Norman Moore, Bernardine O'Neill, Marilyn Roberts, Carlos Kenny, Ultan O'Neill, Martin Quearney, Sean McCann, Judge Kenneth Deale, Ernest Woods, S.C., Seamus Brady, Dr and Mrs Monk Gibbon, Dr Garry O'Connor, Jean Reid, Godfrey Quigley, Daniel Farson, David Astor, John Montague, Alun Owen, Jack Holland, Micheál O hAodha, Dr Harris Tomkin, Riobard MacGorain, Marcus Bourke, Norma Jessop, Olive Reid and Pat Crowley.

I wish to thank the following publishers, newspapers and magazines for permission to quote from copyright material: Hutchinson & Co. Ltd. for extracts from Brendan Behan's *Borstal Boy* and *Brendan Behan's Island;* Methuen & Co. Ltd. for Brendan Behan's *The Hostage* and *The Quare Fellow;* Heinemann & Co. Ltd. for extracts from Dominic Behan's autobiography; and Neville Spearman Ltd. for J. P. Donleavy's *The Ginger Man;* the editors of the *Daily Mail, Daily Telegraph, Guardian, Irish Times, Journal American, New York Times, Observer, Sunday Telegraph, Sunday Times* and *Die Welt;* and the proprietors of *Envoy* and *The Bell.*

Allsop, Kenneth: *The Angry Decade*. Peter Owen.

Behan, Brendan: *Borstal Boy*. Hutchinson.
Brendan Behan's Island. Hutchinson.
Hold Your Hour and Have Another. Hutchinson.
Confessions of an Irish Rebel. Hutchinson.
The Scarperer. Hutchinson.
The Quare Fellow. Methuen.
The Hostage. Methuen.
Moving Out and A Garden Party. Proscenium Press.
Brendan Behan's New York. Hutchinson.

Behan, Brian: *With Breast Expanded*. MacGibbon & Kee.

Behan, Dominic: *Teems of Times and Happy Returns*. Heinemann.
My Brother Brendan. Frewin.

Brinnin, John Malcolm: *Dylan Thomas in America*. Dent.

Burca, Seamus de: *The Soldier's Song*. P. J. Bourke, Dublin.

Camus, Albert: *The Myth of Sisyphus and other essays*. Hamish Hamilton.

Caulfield, Max: *1916*. Muller.

Carney, James: *Mediaeval Irish Lyrics*. Dolmen Press.

Connolly, James: *Labour in Irish History*. Three Candles.

Coogan, Tim Pat: *Ireland Since the Rising*. Pall Mall Press.

Corkery, Daniel: *The Hidden Ireland*. Gill & Son, Dublin.

Cronin, Anthony: *The Life of Riley*. Panther.

Cross, K. G. W.: *Scott Fitzgerald*. Oliver & Boyd.

Deale, Kenneth: *Memorable Irish Trials*. Constable (this contains an excellent account of the trial of Bernard Kirwan who was the original 'Quare Fellow').

Delaney, Shelagh: *A Taste of Honey*. Methuen.

Dillon, Myles: *Early Irish Literature*. University of Chicago Press.
        (with Norah K. Chadwick). *The Celtic Realms*.
        Weidenfeld & Nicolson.

Dostoevsky, Fyodor: *The Devils*. Penguin.

Douglas, Lord Alfred: *Oscar Wilde*. Icon.

Ellman, Richard: *Yeats: The Man and the Masks*. Faber.

Fairfield, Letitia: *The Trial of Peter Barnes and others*. Wm. Hodge.

Fitzgerald, F. Scott: *Short Stories. Vol. 4*. Penguin.

Fitzgibbon, Constantine: *The Life of Dylan Thomas*. Dent.

Flower, Robin: *The Irish Tradition*. O.U.P.

Gaucher, Roland: *The Terrorists*. Secker & Warburg.

Genet, Jean: *The Miracle of the Rose*. Blond.
        Funeral Rites. Blond.

Gwynn, Stephen: *Oliver Goldsmith*. Butterworth.

Heidegger, Martin: *Being and Time*. Blackwell.

Holland, Vyvyan: *Son of Oscar Wilde*. Rupert Hart-Davis.

Hyde, Dr Douglas: *The Religious Songs of Connacht*, Vols 1 and 2.
        Gill & Son, Dublin.
        The Love Songs of Connacht. Gill & Son,
        Dublin.
        The Life of Raftery. Gill & Son, Dublin.
        (Ed.) *Songs Ascribed to Raftery*. Gill & Son,
        Dublin.

Irwin, Wilmot: *Betrayal in Ireland*. Hutchinson.

Jeffs, Rae: *Brendan Behan: Man and Showman*. Hutchinson.

Jullian, Philippe: *Oscar Wilde*. Constable.

Kavanagh, Patrick: *Tarry Flynn*. New English Library.
        Collected Poems. MacGibbon & Kee.

Kavanagh, Peter: *Lapped Furrows*. The Peter Kavanagh Hand
        Press.

Larkin, Emmet: *James Larkin*. Mentor.

McCann, Sean: *The Wit of Brendan Behan*. Frewin.
        The Wit of the Irish. Frewin.
        The World of Sean O'Casey. Four Square.
        The World of Brendan Behan.

MacErlean, Rev J. C.: *Poems of David O'Bruadair*, parts 1, 2 and
        3. Irish Texts Society.

Mann, Thomas: *Doctor Faustus*. Secker & Warburg.

Marowitz, Charles (with Tom Milne and Owen Hale): *The Encore Reader*. Methuen.

(with Simon Trussior): *Theatre at Work*. Methuen.

Maud, Ralph (ed.): *Poet in the Making: The Notebooks of Dylan Thomas*. Dent.

Merriman, Brian: *Chuirt an Mhean Oiche* (The Midnight Court). Dolmen Press.

Murphy, Gerard: *Early Irish Poetry*. O.U.P.

Saga and Myth in Ancient Ireland. O'Lochlainn, Dublin.

Neeson, Eoin: *Poems from the Irish*. Mercier Press.

The Civil War in Ireland. Mercier Press.

Neligan, David: *The Spy in the Castle*. MacGibbon & Kee.

Nolan, Kevin B. (with Desmond Williams): *Ireland in the War Years and After, 1939–51*. Gill & Macmillan.

Norman, Frank: *Fings Ain't Wot They Used t'Be*. Secker & Warburg.

O'Conaire, Padraic: *The Woman at the Window*. Mercier Press.

O'Connor, Frank: *Kings, Lords and Commons*. Macmillan.

O'Hegarty, P. S.: *A History of Ireland Under the Union, 1801–1922*. Methuen.

O'Sullivan, Maurice: *Twenty Years a-Growing*. O.U.P.

O'Sullivan, Seamus: *Mud and Purple*. Talbot Press.

Payne, Robert: *The Life and Death of Lenin*. W. H. Allen.

Pearse, Padraic: *Collected Works*. Phoenix Publishing Co.

Pearson, Hesketh: *Bernard Shaw*. Collins.

Pirandello, Luigi: *The Merry-Go-Round of Love*. New American Library.

L'Umorismo.

As You Desire Me. Samuel French.

Maschere Nude.

Right You Are! (*If you think so*) *and other Plays*. Penguin.

Twentieth Century Views. Prentice Hall.

Ransome, Arthur: *Oscar Wilde*. Methuen.

Russell, Leonard: *English Wit*. Hutchinson.

Simpson, Alan: *Beckett and Behan*. Routledge, Kegan Paul.

Starkie, Dr Walter: *Luigi Pirandello*. Dent.

Thody, Philip: *Jean Genet*. Hamish Hamilton.

Thomas, Dylan: *Miscellany 2*. Dent.

Turnbull, Andrew (Ed.): *Letters of Scott Fitzgerald*. Bodley Head.

Unamuno, Miguel de: *The Tragic Sense of Life*. Macmillan.

Vittorini, Domenico: *The Drama of Luigi Pirandello*. University of Pennsylvania Press.

Wilde, Oscar: *Epigrams*. The Peter Pauper Press.

Williams, Desmond: *The Irish Struggle, 1916–1926*. Routledge, Kegan Paul.

Yeats, W. B.: *Autobiographies*. Macmillan.
　　　　　　　A Vision. Macmillan.
　　　　　　　(Ed.) *The Oxford Book of Modern Verse*. O.U.P.

Magazines:

Points, numbers 11, 12, and 15. Paris 1949–51.
　　　　　Short Story Anthology. Paris, 1951.

The Fianna (Files).

Comhair.

The Wolfe Tone Magazine (Files).

The Irish Socialist (Files).

The Irish Democrat (Files).

The Bell.

Envoy.

CHAPTER ONE

THOUGH later on he liked people to think he was, Brendan Behan was not in the true sense of the word a slum-boy. His grandfather on his father's side had been a painting contractor. His mother's family owned two grocery shops, and had come from a line of strong farmers in County Meath. Brendan's parents were a genteel family come down in the world. They lived in a house that could be classed as a tenement, but this was because his grandmother owned a string of these houses and let them have the rooms without payment.

Stephen Behan, Brendan's father, was a well-educated man and claimed to have studied for the priesthood. Lacking the spur of ambition and perhaps disturbed at his mother's second marriage after her first husband died, he slipped easily into the life of a housepainter, where he cruised along without exerting himself and on subsidy from his mother.

John Kearney, Brendan's maternal grandfather, the grocer, died at forty-three leaving six children. One of these was Brendan's mother, Kathleen, who was then aged nine. As she grew up, there was little money in the house. But there was a tradition of learning, ballads, music and poetry. Her brother Peadar wrote the Irish National Anthem and afterwards became stage manager of the Abbey Theatre.

Before she met Stephen Behan, Kathleen had been married to a Jack Furlong from Belfast, who died in the influenza epidemic of 1917. As a young widow she obtained a clerkship from the Dublin Corporation where she met Stephen Behan. They were married in 1922. She had two sons, Rory and Sean, by her former husband. Her first son from her second marriage, Brendan, was born on February 23, 1923. When she went to live in

14 Russell Street off the North Circular Road, some of the other tenants called Kathleen 'Lady Behan'. Her gentility clung to her.

Russell Street was on the perimeter of the Georgian slum area in Dublin. From it, you looked up along Fitzgibbon Street, a short Georgian thoroughfare with massive mansions on either side (they were tenements), to the high glory of Mountjoy Square, one of the great Dublin squares, two sides of which were still in a state of good repair in the 'thirties. The houses in Russell Street were smaller than those in Fitzgibbon Street or Mountjoy Square, but with their neat classical doorways, red-brick facings and slender eight-pane windows, they had the distinctive marks of Dublin domestic Georgian architecture.

Some of the houses in Russell Street were privately owned and occupied by their owners. Others were rented out in floors or rooms, with a mixture of clerks, tradesmen and working men living in them. At the end of the street there was an elegant mansion in which the manager of the Phoenix Bottling Company lived, and in houses almost directly opposite the Behans, a civil servant, a master baker and a fortune teller lived. On the other hand, a prostitute plied her trade from a room directly under the Behans, and a travelling man next door kept his donkey in the room with him until, after many attempts to eject him, the house had finally to be demolished around him.

In the Behan family there was a general awareness of culture, literature and music, that would have been rare enough even among the better-class families of the city. Stephen Behan read both French and Latin. Often in the evening, after tea, he would settle his four boys down into the big settle bed and read them selections from his favourite authors: *The Pickwick Papers*, the novels of Zola and Galsworthy, the short stories of Maupassant and Pepys' *Diary* were among the books the Behan boys had read to them as young children. 'Da would act each part as he came to it in the dialogue', Rory, Brendan's half-brother, recalls. 'He was marvellous at *The Pickwick Papers*, doing all the parts with real relish. He read the preface of *John Bull's Other Island* to us so often that Brendan knew it off by heart by the time he was twelve. Another author he read was Marcus Aurelius. One day, after Da had given us extracts from the *Decameron*, I wanted to see what went on between the covers of the nice Moroccan leather book he read from. I stole it and was reading it in the back yard when Ma caught me. She took it from me and we all firmly believed ever since that she burnt it.'

On other nights 'Da' played the violin for them, the third and fourth movements of *Poet and Peasant*, perhaps, or a cut-down version of Humperdinck's *Hansel and Gretel*, which he illustrated with his own narrative, making it a mixture of music and acting. Their mother brought them up on a variety of ballads, Irish history and hatred of England. She had a vast repertoire of songs of all sorts besides ballads and could sing for hours without stopping—music-hall favourites, songs from Viennese operettas, and hymns and slow Irish airs which had been handed down to her by her mother and her Gaelic-speaking grandmother.

Kathleen Behan was a fiend for fresh air, and as she took her children on walks round the city, she would point out where Sheridan, the playwright, was born (she always referred to him as 'Richard Brinsley'), the houses of Shaw, Swift and Wilde, and the places where the city's revolutionaries were born or executed; Robert Emmet, Lord Edward Fitzgerald, Wolfe Tone, romantic-looking Protestant patriots in high collars and cravats with aquiline profiles, who epitomized the nobility of a cause which still required heroes to die for it. She had a store of unlikely knowledge and would quote them passages from 'Richard Brinsley's' plays, tell them local legends that were still extant about Swift when he was Dean of St Patrick's Cathedral, or sing them versions of poems she had set to music, like Kingsley's poem beginning:

> When all the world was young, lad

and Housman's

> With rue my heart is laden

which she had joined together and sang to an air of her own.

It was like having a mixture of Marie Lloyd and Speranza (Oscar Wilde's mother) for a teacher. Kathleen could have been a successful music-hall artiste with her brilliant blue eyes, Titian hair and gift for arousing gaiety and laughter in whatever company she was in. She sang with verve, was a master of facial expression and could create laughter and pathos in her listeners by an actress's gift of being able to vary the pace and pitch of her voice to suit the different moods of her songs.

Besides Kathleen and Stephen, Brendan's older half-brothers, Rory and Sean Furlong, filled the house with literature. Sean was a Socialist and subscribed to the Left Book Club, from which he received books by Clifford Odets, Shaw, Pushkin, Eugene O'Neill and Orwell, while Rory had a taste for avant-garde literature, which he satisfied by clipping out the critical columns of the *Irish Times* and later in buying in soft covers the books which had been recommended there: Samuel Butler, Hemingway, Scott Fitzgerald, J. B. Priestley and Graham Greene, were some of the authors in the parlour library as Brendan was growing up. Brendan in fact had a private education on his doorstep. He was able to read at three, could recite Robert Emmet's mammoth dock speech at six, could play Ravel's *Bolero* on the mouth-organ and had written newspaper articles before he was twelve. His recitations were all the more remarkable because he had a pronounced stammer. Once he got warmed up, in a recitation however, the stammer vanished.

As a very small boy he seems to have been confident in his future. One of his hobbies was following funerals. He would fall in behind the hearse and trot after it with the mourners to the graveyard, observing the whole ceremony with careful scrutiny. He liked the style; the top hats of the hearse drivers, the nodding black plumes on the horses; then the ritual round the grave, the priest in vestments scattering holy water and chanting the Latin Psalms.

One day he noticed a single horse drawing the hearse instead of the usual resplendent four. As he fell in behind it, he remarked to his little girl friend, Teresa Byrne, who was with him: 'What a lousy funeral. When I'm dead they'll come from all over the world for mine.' Stung by his vanity, Teresa replied: 'There won't even be a "Rustler" there.' ('Rustler' meaning somebody from Russell Street). 'Rustlers won't be able to get in on the edge of the crowd', Brendan replied firmly.

Even at this age he had begun to drink. His Granny had given him the taste for it. Teresa Byrne remembers him going out regularly to get pints for her aunt in a can, drinking half of it before he returned, and filling the can up with water to cover the deficiency. When her aunt used to remark that Mr Gill was giving a very poor pint, 'the cheeky bugger would go back and make Mr Gill fill up the can again'. Teresa remembers that at ten Brendan was often merry from drink. 'He would stick his head round the snug door of the pub and say to the oul' ones, "Give us the froth off your pint", which they usually did and more.'

As a child he read everything he could lay his hands on. He had a passionate appetite for books. One day his father found him up in bed reading the back of a tram ticket, which he had picked up off the floor. He could sing ballads for hours. He taught the other children in the street to sing patriotic songs, swam and played football with them and one day launched his tiny frame from the top of the thirty-foot lock-gates at Cross Guns Bridge, with his 'coach', 'Chuckles' Malloy, down on his knees begging him not to do it.

By the time he was nine, he was writing letters to his friends in verse. One day, as a result of a joke he played on her, he got Teresa into trouble with the nuns, and wrote her a poem of apology. He had written an Irish essay in Gaelic for her and had included derogatory references to the morals of the nuns in the middle of it, which she hadn't noticed, not being very good at the language she was writing the essay in.

> Teresa I am sorry
> If I got you bashed in school.
> It was a stupid thing to do
> And I feel an awful fool.
>
> I was really raging
> When I heard you went to the pics
> With, of all the eejits,
> Snotty-nosed Paddy Fitz.

I think you were awfully decent
Not to give my name.
Not even to your Da or Ma,
But shouldered all the blame.

Oh, what can I do now, love,
To restore our happiness?
Will I go across to Gill's pub
And to your Ma confess?

Actually, Teresa,
I've just got two and six
So will you stop sulking in the parlour
And go with me to the flicks?

I'll take you to the Drummer
To the ninepenny cushion seats,
And that will leave me with a bob
To get you oranges and sweets.

To give this its proper ending
I'll wind up with yours for ever, Brendan.

He was an exceptionally good looking child and his mother was
always hearing comments on that 'beautiful boy of yours'. He
had coal-black hair, large blue eyes, perfect teeth and ivory white
skin. He was the darling of the oul' ones, especially his Granny
English, who lived up the road in Fitzgibbon Street. After
her first husband, Brendan's grandfather, died, she had
married a Patrick English. When he died some years later,
she devoted the accumulated profits of a double widowhood
to the property market, with such success that she was
a flourishing landlord by the time Brendan was growing up.
She collected the rent from five houses in Russell Street and
owned one enormous Georgian tenement in Fitzgibbon Street
nearby.

Mrs English was a handsome woman, very well preserved and,
until the day of her death, had raven black hair, which she wore
close to her head in the Victorian fashion. In her house in
Fitzgibbon Street, she remained most of the day in bed, not
from any physical disability, for she was as nimble as a goat,
but merely because she found it was a convenient place from
which to transact business. Nor were visitors ushered into her

presence expected to show surprise if they found her son, Paddy, who was in his thirties, asleep in bed beside her with his cap on. Here she would hold court for the neighbours to bring her choice bits of scandal, hoping, no doubt, that if the day came when they were short of rent, Mrs English would not forget it to them. She relished the control she exercised over other people's lives. Brendan was her declared favourite, little 'Bengy' as she called him. He alone had the right of admission to her sanctum without advance notice. He would spend hours up there with his Granny, gorging himself on dainties and taking occasional sips from the jugs of porter he used to carry from Gill's pub at the corner to her bedroom. Mrs English had a dislike of nourishing food and baths, and together they connived to resist the efforts of improving relations who endeavoured to make her wash and eat like another Christian. Gleefully, she would order quantities of spiced meats and tinned delicacies and scoff them in secrecy with her grandson, while they chuckled together over the defeat of the common enemy.

Whenever she went out, Bengy accompanied her. They made a curious pair, the despotic old lady and the talkative little boy with his knowledgeable comments on matters well beyond his years. When she held her conferences in the morning, at which all sorts of feminine information were poured into her ear, little Bengy was allowed to sit in the middle of the gathering. On one occasion she decided to install an aged crony in the Hospice for the Dying, a hospital near Harold's Cross on the south side of the city. She, Brendan and the crony set out for the Hospice, only to return, plus crony, at midnight the same day, the three of them roaring drunk. On the way home, a passer-by seeing Brendan, said: 'Isn't it terrible, ma'am, to see such a beautiful little boy deformed?'

'How dare you?' said his Granny. 'He is not deformed. He's just drunk.'

Brendan acquired his taste for spirits from his Granny as well. When he was eight, she fed him whiskey: 'It'll cure the worms', she told his mother, when Kathleen complained that Brendan was coming home 'woozy'. He knew what it was to be inebriated

19

well before he was in his teens. An I.R.A. friend, Tom Langan, remembers him, aged twelve, dancing around the Parnell Monument in O'Connell Street, as tight as an owl after a party where there was a supply of free drink. His mother never forgave Granny English for plying Brendan with drink, and attributed a lot of his problems in later years to her early influence. But Stephen and Kathleen were largely in Mrs English's grip. They were subsidized by her at a period when the country was almost bankrupt from the combined results of the Civil War and world depression. Without the help they got from her, they would have had difficulty in keeping going.

The worst thing his Granny and the other women could have done for Brendan was to have spoiled him. 'To have made a god of Brendan', Brian, his brother, was to recall in later years, 'was to destroy him as surely as sticking a knife in his back. He would never brook any argument as to what he did or where or when he was to do it.' Throughout his life he was to have an all-consuming desire for notice. If he didn't get it he was likely to resort to any stratagem to do so. Early on, his father noticed this tendency and though later on Stephen was to ascribe many of Brendan's failings to it, to some extent the fault was the father's as he did little to discipline his family in their formative years.

Brendan was a very good-looking child and was usually very even tempered. But he had another side. Because he was the golden boy, he always wanted his own way. There was a vicious streak in him side by side with the personality of a sensitive little boy. I remember finding him one day with a little boy half his size up against the railings and the child nearly throttled. We pulled him off, but Brendan still wanted a go at the child who had angered him. Another time I discovered that he had tortured a dog which had bitten him a few minutes before. He played a dastardly trick on one of our neighbours in Russell Street. He put sacks over the windows of her room so that when she woke up she thought she was blind. She didn't know whether it was night or day until someone opened the door three days later and let the light in. Brendan was also very jealous of any of the other children who managed to attract his Granny's attention. He didn't want his position to be usurped. Once he discovered that Seamus (his younger brother) had scrounged a penny from the Granny. Brendan rushed up the stairs, grabbed Seamus and threw him down shouting, 'She is my Granny, not yours'.

Besides the cultural advantages Brendan inherited from his parents, the indigenous tradition of Dublin played a major part in his development. It is difficult to explain the Dublin working-class in terms of other urban proletariats. Their use of the English language, for instance, transferred directly to print, has provided dialogue for two major writers, Joyce and O'Casey. Even their swearing was more than mere cursing; it was an orchestration of words, used musically with a sense of the rhythm of language to improve the effect of their sentences. Words choicely chosen gave them the same pleasure that others might get from food or drink. Catastrophe, accrued from the cruelty of their condition, they turned into tales which dredged it of its degradation. There were few situations so frightful that they couldn't derive laughter from them. The inevitable they defeated by derision.

It would not have been true to say that the average Dublin docker of that time was an opera fan, or that the labourers carried Shakespeare in their pockets. But Shakespeare was known and respected in working-class Dublin and recited often at pubs and parties. *Bel canto* arias were sung in pubs as an approved and recognized turn and among tradesmen especially it was not uncommon to find in a tenement room a small library of Dickens, Shaw, Shakespeare and some of the Russian authors, which were read and re-read over again. Through the Church, they learned to use symbol as a means of survival. Working-class Dublin filled the churches, not only on Sundays but during the liturgical seasons and feasts throughout the year. In the Crucifixion and Resurrection they encountered promise of existence beyond earthly agony. Among the incense and candles, the swell of the Latin chant, the sensuous swing of chasubles, purple for pain, green for joy, black for death, they discovered that imagination could provide an anodyne against the worst that poverty and injustice could do to them.

From the Dublin docks to the North Circular Road up the north side of the Liffey was a vast area of palatially-built houses. They were of the special Dublin Georgian type, seventy feet high, long slender windows with eight panes, and iron-work balconies, massive classical doorways, and with exquisite moulded ceilings and fireplaces inside. They had begun to fall into decay after the aristocracy had moved south of the river and back to the country when the Act of Union was passed in 1800. At the turn of the present century, the area had become a mass of gaunt cliff-like palaces, grossly overcrowded with families who had neither heat nor proper sanitation. In 1913 a Government inquiry reported that there were over 20,000 families occupying one room each in these tenements, and that the conditions there were worse than Delhi or Calcutta. Though Russell Street was on the perimeter of this area and indeed many of its inhabitants would have looked down on the slum-dwellers further in, their vocabulary had much in common. These were the sort of phrases Brendan would hear in daily conversation as he was growing up:

'A shut mouth will catch no flies.'

'If you didn't go to school, you must have met the scholars on the way back.'

'Isn't the weather very changeable? You wouldn't know what clothes to pawn.'

'Carry on with the coffin, the corpse will walk.'

'You're the flower of the flock, the heart of the roll.'

'He had a face like a plateful of mortal sins.'

Russell Street shared the tenement penchant for nicknames that is a feature of the Characters in O'Casey's plays: Joxer, Paycock, Fluther, Needle, Covey.

One family alone in the street had fourteen nicknames attached to it: 'Drummer Doyle, the Dandy Doyle, Jewels Doyle, Woodener Doyle, the Dancer Doyle, Elbow Doyle, Altarboy Doyle, the Hatchet Doyle, Coddle Doyle, the Rebel Doyle, Uncle Doyle, the Shepherd Doyle, the Hurrah Doyle, the Porternose Doyle.'

When he was six, Brendan was sent to William Street Convent, where Sister Monica, the head nun, advised his mother that 'she was rearing a genius' when Kathleen told her she was worried because some of the neighbours had complained that Brendan was bold. After this he attended the Christian Brothers at St Canice's in Brunswick Street till he was fourteen. One day, his

English master sent for Stephen. Had his father given Brendan any help with his essay, he wanted to know. He showed Stephen the copy book. The essay was entitled 'French Influence on British Culture in the Renaissance'. Stephen was astonished when he read it but said that, as far as he knew, it was Brendan's own work.

Stephen's sarcastic turn of humour undoubtedly influenced his son. Once when the boy was reading John Mitchell's *Jail Journal* he came across the phrase 'Dublin, city of genteel dastards'. He asked his father if the author didn't mean bastards, and Stephen replied: 'No son, he didn't. You see, you're born a bastard; you can't help that. But you've got to work at being a dastard.' 'Rosy' Behan as he was known in the trade had a reputation for repartee and fanciful tales. Once he was standing at the counter in a public house when a man sneered at him for being 'a spoiled priest' (one who hadn't finished his course for the priesthood). The man happened to be a former Christian Brother. 'At least,' replied Stephen, 'I was put out for adultery. You were expelled for stupidity.'

At fourteen Brendan left school and decided to follow his father's trade as a painter. 'After all,' he would say later on, 'I was almost born in a paint-pot.' He became an apprentice at Bolton Street Technical School, where he was paid 6/- a week. There is no doubt that he should have gone to secondary school, but his father did little to press him. Brendan wanted to be in funds for a change and have a few spare shillings for drink.

In later years Brendan was to express his resentment that Stephen didn't do better for him in the way of education. But what Stephen had given his children was of greater value to them than a formal education could have been: the fruits of an artistic temperament. It was because of this, handed on by their father, that Brendan, Dominic and Brian became writers. Stephen had avoided responsibility and had chosen a maverick life, rather than settle down in the straight-jacket of middle-class existence, and having made this choice himself, he was too fair a man to demand that his sons do otherwise. In later years, whenever his sons spoke bitterly of their lack of opportunity,

Stephen would remain silent. It was his secret. His stoicism helped him keep it.

At the back of his mind too, Stephen must have had expectations that he would benefit from his mother's will. Through his father, her husband, some of her property was his by right, but when she died in 1935, she left it to her son by her second marriage, Paddy English, who slept with her nightly in the same bed.

Rory, the eldest of the family and Stephen's stepson, understood him better than any of the others. Though he has never written a line, Rory is in some ways the most artistic in temperament of the whole family—sensitive, quizzical, detached. Once Stephen said to him, after there had been a slight coldness: 'Did I ever treat you and Sean different from the rest?' 'No', said Rory, 'You treated us all with the same sublime indifference.' Stephen gave a delighted grin and turned away. He knew what Rory meant. There was no offence, but in an oblique way, praise. When Stephen died two years ago, and for a good while afterwards, Rory would leave the room with a catch in his throat whenever he found himself talking of Stephen, the father who had treated all his family with 'sublime indifference'.

Though the Behans had come down in the world, they had relations who lived in comfortable middle-class surroundings. The family, for instance, always had free tickets to Dublin's Queen's Theatre, which was rented for most of the year by P. J. Bourke's company. Actor and impresario, he was married to Kathleen's sister. Brendan was an early and frequent theatre-goer. He was to write about this later:

> Rory and Sean, my stepbrothers and I, looked around the parterre in a weakness of adoration, wishing there was someone there to tell the people to point from us to the stage and at the centre, glorious against the lights, a strapping lad from Kildare in his lawn shirt and velvet breeches, and to say, 'See those three kids there, and see your man there, the O'Grady, the Colonel that's after telling off the other rat of an English officer on the Court Martial? Well, he's their Uncle.'

As little boys, dressed up in their Sunday best, Rory, Sean, Brendan and Dominic would go out to the Kearneys' red-brick house in the sedate suburbs of Clontarf, take tea and cakes, and come back with pocket money from their relations.

Mrs Furlong, Kathleen's mother-in-law by her first marriage, held musical evenings at weekends in her house on the North Circular Road, where her daughter Evelyn would play the piano, accompanied by Stephen on the violin, and Kathleen, Rory, Brendan and Emily, Evelyn's sister, would sing ballads, and musical comedy airs.

Mrs Furlong, who later lived in Kincora Road, Clontarf, was another remarkable Granny of Brendan's. She was a woman of ferocious revolutionary outlook who combined ardent Catholicism with an admiration for Communists and anybody else who caused trouble for the English. She had a picture of Archbishop Mannix, the patriot Irish churchman, on her wall side by side with a photo of Lenin. Her ambition was to blow up the English, one which, as we shall see, she later took decisive steps to fulfil. She was often within an ace of blowing herself up, because the beds in her house frequently harboured bombs, revolvers and ammunition left by vagrant revolutionaries who had to vamoose in a hurry. Rooms in her house were called after Irish patriots. There was a Tone Room, a Robert Emmet Room, a Davis Room. Granny Furlong's blend of Catholicism and Socialism was reciprocated in the Behan household. The atmosphere of the house was Socialist-Republican. When the Spanish Civil War broke out, and those who opposed Franco were denounced from the pulpits, the Behans took the Republican side.

Kathleen Behan saw nothing inconsistent in being a Communist, a Catholic and a Republican at the same time. She was and is an ardent Catholic. It was she who saw to it that the children had a religious upbringing. Brendan, she recalls, was 'a very fervent little boy' and would never go out without saying his morning prayers. He was a weekly communicant until he went to jail in England in 1940 and found himself excommunicated for I.R.A. activities. During periods of fervour, he would get up early in the morning to go to Mass and Communion before having his breakfast and going to school. He devoured the lives of the Saints, which he borrowed from the library or found about the house, and had a bent for religion which none of the rest of his family, except his mother, showed.

Stephen had ceased to go to Mass after a religious crisis as a young man but he had no wish to influence the rest of the family to his way of thinking. He told Kathleen to tell the children when they saw him in bed on Sundays that he had been up at six for early Mass and had gone back to bed again. He was too fair a man to be anti-clerical and too humble to be an atheist. He was fond of quoting Voltaire's last words: 'Now for the great secret.' Once I asked him did he believe in a Creator and he replied:

> I didn't come into this world of my own volition and I won't go out of it of my own volition, unless I take my own life away, which I have no intention of doing at the present moment.

CHAPTER TWO

I gave up my boyhood
To drill and to train
To play my own part
In the Patriot Game.

Dominic Behan

FROM the age of sixteen to twenty-two, with the exception of six months, Brendan Behan was to spend his life in prisons of some kind. From February 1940 to December 1941, he was in Hollesley Bay Borstal, in Suffolk, England. In May 1942, he received a sentence of fourteen years at the Special Criminal Court in Dublin and was detained in Mountjoy Prison, Arbour Hill Barracks and the Curragh Camp until July 1946. These sentences were as a result of activity with the Irish Republican Army, popularly known as the I.R.A. The I.R.A., when Brendan became associated with it in the 'thirties, was an illegal revolutionary organization which operated underground in Northern Ireland, the Irish Free State and England. Its aim was the establishment of an independent all-Ireland Republic.

There were two types of I.R.A. men. First there were disenchanted guerrillas, veterans of the Anglo-Irish War of 1919–21, who had refused to accept the treaty with England, or the cease-fire in the subsequent Civil War. Then there were younger members who had joined in the intervening years, and who were mostly from artisan or working-class backgrounds. They were victims of the lack of opportunity in the new State, creaking from the results of the Civil War, where social progress had been slow and a futile economic war with England which had magnified the effect of the world depression in the 'thirties. These young men had refused to join the emigrant boats

27

leaving every day from Dun Laoghaire and the North Wall. They stayed at home determined to be on the spot when the war up North began. For them, this was where the source of Ireland's trouble lay—in the partition of the country. If the British were to clear out of the six north-eastern counties, then an all-Ireland Republic could be declared and the new dawn promised by the revolution would come at last. They were often the pick of their class, idealists unable to give up their ties with the homeland, even though to stay at home meant poverty and lack of opportunity. They leaned on the cultural environment their organization brought them in touch with, something which helped to compensate them for their lack of education. The majority were bilingual in Gaelic and English; they had a knowledge of Irish music and poetry. Besides having read Russian and German revolutionary writings, they were often well read in the classical literature of these countries.

The typical I.R.A. man was above average in looks, was of sensitive temperament, and was religious. That some of them perpetrated acts that were regarded by many fair-minded people as outrages, seems hard to reconcile with their background. But it was so. They were revolutionaries They felt obliged to employ the methods of revolution.

The I.R.A. owed its survival in the 'thirties to the dual nature of the Irish revolution. In the years 1919–21, an improbable blend of parliamentarianism and terrorism had given birth to the new State. Parliament had triumphed finally but the terrorist element, deeply rooted in the national tradition, had never been totally eradicated. Throughout the nineteenth century, terrorism had manifested itself at different levels from Whiteboys, Ribbonmen, Invincibles and Fenian dynamitards to private enterprise groups who lay patiently in wait, armed with buckshot, for a shot at local tyrants.

It was nihilism born of the frustration and suppression of a class whose intelligence might have leavened the community, had it not been submerged in smoke-filled cabins or the anonymity of a tenement room. This nihilism had been channelled into an effective force by a revolutionary of genius, Michael

Collins, who evolved a formula of terrorist tactics and guerilla warfare, which for the first time in history succeeded in ejecting a colonial power from an occupied country. But Collins realized the limitations of his technique and was prepared to compromise for limited objectives. Other sections of the I.R.A. were not prepared to compromise and they continued on in bitter resistance to successive governments in the new State.

By the time Brendan Behan became associated with the I.R.A. in the 'thirties, it had been weakened by internal dissensions. It had no Michael Collins or anyone approaching his genius. Its chief of staff was Sean Russell. Russell had ability of a sort, he had been director of munitions on Collins's general headquarters staff, but he was of fanatical disposition and narrow outlook. His two interests in life were Religion and Revolution. He was a daily Communicant. 'Sean was able to convince himself that the operations he carried out were justified on the grounds that he was a soldier obeying orders even though he had given the orders himself. He would then go to Communion', is how one detective described his character. Russell lacked a sense of humour and had none of Collins's magnetism. He could inspire others, but he was not really a leader. Perhaps his greatest fault was that he was unable to delegate authority. His adjutants were seldom capable people. Under his leadership, the I.R.A. was to have a brief notoriety because of the bombing campaign in England in 1939–40. Subsequently it degenerated rapidly under increased pressure from the Irish government and lack of support from the Irish public.

The Behan household was impregnated with the spirit of Republicanism. There was Kathleen with her endless tirades against England, and her brother, Peadar, the poet and stage-manager of the Abbey Theatre, who kept alive his dislike of the enemy he had fought against in 1916. On the wall of his room, he had pinned a map upon which he followed with glee the various defeats of the British Forces in the early part of the Second World War. Sean, Brendan's half-brother, was a member of the I.R.A. and an active Communist while other I.R.A. men of the left—George Gilmore, Neal Gould Verschoyle, Luke Madden,

Jimmy Boyce and others—were frequent visitors to the Behan household and the Behan boys around the fireside heard discussions on Lenin and Marx, as well as on Lalor and Tone, and other Irish revolutionaries.

Brendan was a rebel almost as soon as he could read. Eva Traynor, wife of the Assistant Adjutant-General of the I.R.A., remembers a little boy marching into a meeting of the separatist women's republican organization in Marlborough Street, in 1937, and giving them a lecture on republicanism which lasted half-an-hour before walking out, leaving them all breathless. The Chairman that night was Sean MacBride, a former Chief of Staff of the I.R.A. and later Minister for External Affairs in a coalition government. The child, whom they thought at first was a street urchin, turned out to be Brendan Behan. Desmond MacNamara, the Irish sculptor, remembers Brendan a little later at a left-wing club demonstration, looking rather like 'a miniature Stewart Granger, carrying one end of a banner which read "Release Frank Ryan and Jim Larkin".' Later on in the evening, there was a tussle with the police and MacNamara could see Brendan holding on with one hand to the banner and with the other to the toothbrush which he always kept in his jacket pocket like a pen so that he could clean his teeth, at any time, night or day.

This tiny revolutionary, with the phenomenal memory and store of knowledge, would have seemed merely precocious had it not been for the sincerity with which he spoke. Bob Bradshaw, a member of the I.R.A. in the 'thirties, who was staying with Brendan's Granny at 13 Mountjoy Square, remembers that Mrs Furlong was constantly talking about her clever little grandson. One day, a little boy about eight years old, with coal-black curls, clear white skin and blue eyes, was ushered into the room and proceeded immediately to launch forth on Shaw, Yeats, Synge and O'Casey, in a most knowledgeable fashion for twenty minutes without stopping. When he finished, he became covered in confusion and rushed from the room, but not before those who had heard him had recognized that they had witnessed an unusual performance.

He joined the Fianna at eight years of age. This was the youth organization of the I.R.A. On Sundays, he would put on a green shirt with epaulettes, a lanyard and a shoulder cord which would one day hold a gun, and an Australian-style army hat, and set out for the Hardwicke Hall where Fianna meetings were held.

The object of the Fianna was to train boys in the revolutionary tradition so that they would be imbued with this spirit when they became old enough to join the I.R.A. proper. Instead of the usual scout tests, Fianna boys were required to have a thorough knowledge of Irish republican history from Wolfe Tone to the present day, and to learn close order marching, foot drill, semaphore and Morse code. Fianna scout leaders had military titles— Quartermaster, Adjutant, O.C., and wore Sam Browne belts and riding breeches. Brendan, writing in the *Wolfe Tone Weekly* in October 1937, quoted with pride what Captain H. B. C. Pollard of the British Secret Service had said of the Fianna, that it had 'a para-military aim and proved, as might be expected, an excellent incubator for young assassins'.

By the time he was twelve, Brendan was writing regularly for the Fianna magazine and contributing to adult republican journals such as the *Wolfe Tone Weekly* and *The United Irishman*. He wrote well-constructed articles which avoided most of the clichés and were composed in a terse, economic style. Usually they were biographical pieces on Irish historical figures, like Roger Casement, but occasionally he wrote short stories or verse. One of his poems appeared in *The United Irishman* in May 1938, described as 'the answer of a young Fianna boy' to an imperialist poem which had recently appeared in an Irish newspaper.

> O God! why do they mock me
> With paper 'Freedom' under England's Crown,
> Even while they forge another link to bind me
> Another traitor's chain to drag me down?
> But God be praised! My lovers are not vanquished,
> Their arms are strong as steel, their hearts are true;
> Another day will see my armies marching
> To strike another blow for Roisin Dhu.[2]

[2] Roisin Dhu is a traditional name for Ireland.

Through the Fianna he came in contact first with the culture of rural Ireland. In the republican clubs around Parnell Square, Irish music and dancing were available, almost as if it was in a parish hall in the countryside. Pipers, fiddlers, tin whistlers, traditional singers, gathered there in the evenings to play and sing. There Brendan first heard Irish sung and spoken as a natural means of expression, and listened to native music played on whistle or pipes. From his mother he absorbed the ballad culture. Now he was to come in contact with a more sophisticated tradition, preserved among the country people, the ancient music of pipers and harpers, part of a courtly culture that had disintegrated centuries before.

One of the privileges conferred on members of the Fianna was that they could join the I.R.A. without undergoing a probation period. When Brendan was fifteen, he made an attempt to join but was rejected as he was a year under age. He did, however, work for the I.R.A. as a courier. Though he claimed later that he was expelled from the I.R.A. because he took part in an episode which concerned the seizing of a film on Queen Victoria at the Astor Cinema, Dublin, this is doubly untrue as he was not in the organization at that time nor did he take part in the seizing of the film which was done by Brendan's brother, Sean, and an I.R.A. colleague, Tom Langan.[1]

By becoming a courier of the Republican Army, however, Brendan entered the twilight world of the revolutionary. It meant being associated with a para-military organization organized along military lines. It meant acquiring a knowledge of the paraphernalia of military life, a knowledge of drill, firearms, marching, of submitting to a form of military discipline, which included court martial and the death sentence among the penalties. It meant entering a world where you met a companion for a few seconds at street corners for a whispered word or to pass messages in code, where you lived in an atmosphere of doubt and suspicion which often made you suspect your best

[1] Brendan's uncle, Seamus de Burca, maintains that Brendan was expelled from the Fianna for being drunk in uniform at a Wolfe Tone Commemoration in Bodenstown.

friend. It meant, if you were to be a reliable revolutionary, cultivating a relentless hatred of those that opposed you—even your own countrymen—so that in the end you preferred to shoot at them to kill rather than be captured by them.

By 1938, the I.R.A. had lost a good deal of support in the country. It had been split asunder by internal factions. The Spanish Civil War had syphoned off a portion of its membership. About 200 volunteers under Frank Ryan, a former G.H.Q. staff officer, had gone out to fight in the International Brigade in the Spanish Civil War; an action which was opposed by right-wing members of the I.R.A.[1] Mr de Valera, the Prime Minister, whom the I.R.A. had regarded as friendly to their cause and whom they had helped to bring to power, had established intern-ment camps meanwhile, in which members of the organization had been imprisoned.

In 1938, Sean Russell, the newly-elected chief of staff, returned from America with a plan of operation which was to be the first attempt at organized action by the I.R.A. since it took its new form after the Treaty in 1922. Briefly the plan was to bomb civilian installations in England with a view to paralysing communications there. It was hoped that this would have the effect of inducing the British to withdraw from the six counties of Ulster and thus lead to the unification of Northern and Southern Ireland.[2]

The campaign began on January 12, 1939, with a formal warning sent to the English Prime Minister, the Governor of Northern Ireland, the German Führer, the Italian Duce and others, that, unless within four days a statement was made signify-ing the intention of the British government to withdraw from

[1] Brendan volunteered for the Republicans in the Spanish Civil War when he was fifteen, disguising his age. His mother kept on intercepting the papers accepting him, so that he never discovered why he had not received a reply to his application.

[2] This bombing campaign was probably a throwback to the grass roots of the physical force movement. In the last decades of the nineteenth century Fenian dynamitards had terrorized Britain with a series of attacks. That organization was directed from the United States where the Fenian Brotherhood had ample opportunity to absorb classical revolutionary techniques from anarchists and socialist groups in exile there.

Northern Ireland, the I.R.A. would be compelled to intervene in the military and commercial life of Britain.

On January 16, the first explosions began. There were three at an electrical plant in London, and gas and electrical plants were destroyed in the North and Midlands. From January to July, 127 incidents were to occur, some of them resulting in the death of innocent civilians.

The excitement generated by the first few months of the campaign gave a new lease of life to the I.R.A. in Ireland. Young men, affected by the chronic unemployment and low standard of living, seized the chance for adventure and an opportunity to work against the traditional enemy. The year before, Brendan had been making a house-to-house collection for the I.R.A. with his best friend Cathal Goulding (the present Chief of Staff of the Official I.R.A.). They were told by one woman at whose house they knocked 'You ought to have more sense. You weren't born at the time of the Troubles. All that has been finished for years.' But none the less, at Easter 1939, after the annual celebrations of the 1916 Insurrection at the G.P.O., recruits poured into the movement. Brendan and a friend acting as stewards at the Easter parade in 1939, noticed people in a tram taking photographs; the two of them went upstairs and took the rolls out of the camera at the point of a gun—it turned out, however, that they were only harmless English visitors. Nevertheless, photographs of men marching in the parade might have been dangerous to the I.R.A. should they have got into the hands of the Special Branch police in Dublin.

After Easter, Brendan was sent as a courier to London. He was given an envelope with instructions to contact a man carrying a copy of *Picture Post*, standing beside the entrance to Goodge Street Tube Station, near Tottenham Court Road. He was to ask the man, 'Can I have a look at your magazine?' After some adventures, he reached Goodge Street Station. He couldn't find the man he was looking for. Finally, after a quarter-of-an-hour's frustration, he saw a middle-aged woman reading *Picture Post*. This was his chance. He went over to her and repeated the question he had been told. Her face contracted in a paroxysm of

34

indignation: 'You will see the inside of Cannon Row Police Station, young man', and started to shout out loudly, 'Pick-up, pick-up.' Brendan moved away, scarlet with confusion. A few minutes later, he felt a hand on his shoulder. He thought it was the police. But it was his I.R.A. contact carrying a copy of *Picture Post*, who laughed when Brendan told him of his experience with the middle-aged lady.

Shortly after Brendan got back to Dublin, he received a message that he was to be at Rathgar Church at eight o'clock one evening. He stood there until a black Austin car drove up with Myles Heffernan and an I.R.A. brigade officer in it. They drove out towards Killiney on the south Dublin coast, and on the way out, they had a bottle of beer. The I.R.A. officer said to Brendan: Drink up. It will be the last you'll have.' When they reached Killiney, the car climbed up the hill towards Killiney Castle. Heffernan put his hand in the ivy at the gate and pushed a hidden bell. The door swung open. There were two men on guard inside. One had a Thomson machine gun and the other had a Webley revolver. The camp commandant was Mick Conway, who later became a monk in Mellifont Abbey. (Conway had been tried and acquitted a few years before for the shooting of John Egan, a Waterford man.)

Forty I.R.A. recruits were in the camp for special training. There was, in addition to Killiney, another house in Harcourt Street, in the centre of Dublin, where the men lived and then came out to train at the Castle. Brendan's group lived in the groom's quarters in the back. From time to time, they noticed important people admitted to the central part of the Castle. These were presumed to be members of the Clann na Gaedheal,[1] from New York.

Most of the men who attended this training camp believed that its purpose was to prepare them for guerilla war in England and Northern Ireland. In fact with Sean Russell back in America and the outbreak of war in England, there appears to have been a reorganization of strategy among the G.H.Q. of the I.R.A. The emphasis now was to be on attacks launched from Southern

[1] Clann na Gaedheal was an Irish-American revolutionary organization.

Ireland against British troops and installations in the North. From now on, the bombing campaign was to be subsidiary and only a preliminary to fighting in the North. The men in Killiney were taking both courses, guerilla and bombing; Brendan was only required to take the bombing course. He soon became the favourite of the camp. Most of the volunteers were from Northern Ireland or from the country. These were somewhat shocked by Brendan's Dublin swearing. Because he was the youngest, he became a pet. They called him 'Kimmage'. The men in charge of this 'Training College' were Lanty Hanagan from Limerick, Harry White from Belfast, and Sean Fuller, the only man to survive the massacre at Ballyseedy in 1923. The volunteers worked very hard. They were up at seven each morning for a half-hour's physical training and after that they recited the rosary. Then they had breakfast. No drinking or smoking was allowed. After breakfast, the intricacies of bomb construction were explained to them.

Brendan later described the training methods as he remembered them:

> We had to learn about both explosive and incendiary bombs. Most explosive bombs were worked by clocks. Ordinary clocks were used, but French clocks were supposed to be the best because their ticking wasn't too loud. They had a lighter and a main lead. The main lead was 'Paxo', a mixture of chlorate of potash and paraffin.
>
> We put a wooden switch on the clock. Two wires, one with a piece of copper on it, the other with a farthing on it connected with the lighter and with a bicycle lamp battery were connected to that. When the clock struck it would bring the copper and the farthing together and induce an electrical circuit. There was a special low-powered wire which could not take much electricity. It would become red hot and that would explode the pulminate of live silver; that in turn would explode the 'Paxo'.

Nick Lynch, an older volunteer at the camp, remembers how advanced for his age Brendan seemed to the others in the camp. He would say in ironic tones to some of the older men who were reading the papers: 'How are Guinness Ordinary today?'

On July 25, a major tragedy occurred in England. An attempt was made to blow up the electrical generating station in Coventry. Through carelessness, five civilians were killed and sixty wounded.

Feeling ran high against the I.R.A. as a result. A few days later, Nick Lynch was walking through Liverpool when an incendiary bomb exploded in his pocket. He was nearly torn apart by the crowd before the police came and arrested him. One reason for the failure of this bombing campaign was inefficiency. Sean Russell had gone to America to raise funds shortly after it had started and his deputy had not been capable of conducting a dynamitard campaign, requiring precision and organization. Dick Timmins, O.C. of London, recalls that he regarded the whole business as 'madness' because of the lack of preparation. He only heard about it in November, two months before it was due to commence. A number of the I.R.A. in London had training in arms and drilling but few of them had any training as dynamitards. A typical result of this was the attempt to blow up Hammersmith Bridge with an amount of gelignite which would have barely blown up a canal lock. Recruitment after the first heavy intake was sluggish, often dependent on contacts made in the bars of emigrant boats with builders' labourers on their way over to work in England. The result of all this poor planning was that ten British civilians were killed and 250 wounded in the course of the campaign. Public opinion reacted violently against the I.R.A., not only in England but in Ireland as well. Nevertheless, the original plan as outlined in the carefully prepared 'S plan' (later captured by the police) was not entirely impractical. Properly organized, the campaign might have achieved some of its objects. Had communications been paralysed with consequent loss to English commerce, pressure would almost certainly have been brought to bear on the British Government to take some action on the position of Northern Ireland. There was also the hope that, with the arrest and perhaps execution of some of their members, the I.R.A. could touch on the traditional martyr complex of the Irish masses and thus consolidate the position at home.

In the meantime Granny Furlong was determined to do her bit. One day in 1939, Rory Furlong and Brendan called at her home in Clontarf to find her in the process of closing up her house and moving to England. This would be a blow to Rory, Sean and Brendan since they had always been sure of a good meal and plenty of song and music there. But Granny Furlong had been so disheartened by the timidity of the annual Republican parade in Bodenstown that year, that she had decided to go to England and start the ball rolling herself. She wanted action, and she was bringing her two daughters, Evelyn and Emily, with her to help. When Rory suggested that she might put a bomb under Buckingham Palace and blow up the Houses of Parliament, Granny Furlong looked darkly at him and replied that there was many a true word spoken in jest. Her son was a groundsman with Aston Villa Football team and she intended to go and live in Birmingham with him. She was seventy-seven.

Shortly after she arrived in Perry Barr, Birmingham, there was an explosion at her house. The police arrived and arrested an I.R.A. man, Martin Clarke, who was living there at that time. Granny Furlong hid some gelignite in her bosom and was most indignant when the police refused to accept her explanation that she thought it was a 'Peggy's leg', the Irish name for a stick of peppermint rock. Some weeks later she, her daughters Emily and Evelyn and Martin Clarke were tried at Birmingham Assizes in front of Mr Justice Singleton. Emily (38) got five years penal servitude, Evelyn (28) got two, and Granny Furlong (77) got three. She was mumbling to herself when Judge Singleton called on her to stand up for him to sentence her.

'Stand up for My Lord', said the Clerk of the Court.

'Patience', she said, 'I'm saying me Angelus, if you ever heard of what that is. Now,' she said when she was finished, 'what do you want to say to me?'

The judge gave her three years' penal servitude, and said that she was as bad as the men.

'That's what they always say', she said, turning from him without paying any attention to him. 'Up the Republic!' Martin was saying, struggling with the guard. 'Again and again after that', said the old lady, walking proudly down the stairs.

Meanwhile Brendan was at work in the same line of country. Kathleen had noticed smoke coming from his room upstairs. She knew that he was fiddling with some form of explosives and was afraid he might injure himself and wished he would spend more time in his den downstairs writing away like he used to. His father, too, heard the rumours and spoke to him, ordering him on no account to use 70 Kildare Road as a jumping-off ground for the campaign in England which he, Stephen, strongly disapproved of. Brendan replied coldly, suggesting that Stephen's spirit had ebbed since he had left the I.R.A. in 1923. Stephen, who had lost his job and spent a term in prison for his political beliefs, was understandably hurt, and he and Brendan were not on speaking terms for some time afterwards.

About this time, Brendan's step-uncle, Paddy English, decided to make a visit to Kildare Road. Essentially a one-street man who never strayed far from his mother's tenement room, it took a lot of inducement to get him out of Russell Street up to the purlieus of Kimmage at all. The general impression in Russell Street was that this new suburb was a place where they 'ate their young'. Family courtesy, however, demanded some show of interest from him. So he made the journey out and knocked at the door of No. 70, only to be met, as he said later, 'by the bathroom coming down the stairs', the result of a miscalculation with the nitro-glycerine by Brendan. Paddy English went back to Russell Street and did not return.

One night shortly afterwards, Bob Bradshaw, his I.R.A. friend, saw Brendan standing in the doorway of a shop in O'Connell Street:

'I'm going to England tomorrow', Brendan said, with a truculent air.

'You eejit. You know everybody's being tagged these days from Dublin.' Brendan looked sullen and stubborn. 'I'm going anyway', was all he said.

Stephen was reading *Pickwick Papers* in 70 Kildare Road on the evening that Brendan set off for England, ostensibly to visit Granny Furlong in Liverpool; in fact to do a bit of bombing on his own for the cause.

" 'Dismay and anguish were depicted on every countenance. The males turned pale and the females fainted. Mrs Snodgrass and Mrs Winkle grasped each other by the hand and . . .' "
'. . . danced the Walls of Limerick', interjected Brendan.

Stephen turned on him fiercely: 'You keep your witty remarks to yourself and carry on with whatever you're doing.'

Brendan ignored his father and asked Dominic to get him a piece of string. He wanted to tie up his parcel of bomb material. Dominic wanted to listen to *Pickwick* and the night was cold. He hesitated. Brendan went out in a huff with an oath to his father, who replied: 'And you too.'

Brendan never forgot that Dominic had refused to get him the piece of string. When he came back from England two years later and out of prison, he ignored the hand which Dominic held out when he came to the house: 'You little bastard!' he said 'You wouldn't get me a piece of string in 1939.'

CHAPTER THREE

BRENDAN was tailed on the boat over from Dublin and the day he landed in Liverpool the C.I.D. got him in his digs. Bob Bradshaw's prophecy had turned out to be true.

The police had been watching the boats for I.R.A. men. No doubt they hoped Brendan would lead them to an arms dump or hide-out. But all they got was a sixteen-and-a-half year old, with his private bombing set—not even instructions from H.Q. to slot in their filing system.

Later at his trial in Liverpool, on a charge of being in possession of explosives, evidence was given that he had made a statement to the detectives who questioned him, in the course of which he said:

> I have been sent over to take the places of Chris Connelly, Nicky Lynch and the others who have been arrested. I was to reorganize further operations in Liverpool. I intended to put bombs in big stores, 'Lewis and Hughes' I think they call it. I was making up some to put in letter-boxes tonight. I would have put one in Cammell Lairds shipyard if I had the chance.

This is typical of the type of moonshine Brendan used to indulge in when he discoursed on his revolutionary activities. In fact Brendan had no instruction or mandate from the I.R.A. G.H.Q. to undertake any bombing operations at all. The Assistant Adjutant-General of the I.R.A. at that time, who sent Brendan over, recalls exactly what happened:

> Brendan was always mad to get to England. At home he was full of high spirits, he was always chatting and laughing. Some of the boys thought that because of this he might be a security risk, so I decided to send him on a reconnoitring expedition to England. It was really to get him away so he wouldn't get into trouble at home. He certainly had no instructions to bomb anywhere from anybody at G.H.Q.

An indication that Brendan was on a solo job is the fact that he brought what he calls his own 'conjuring box' with him. It was never the custom of the dynamitards to bring the 'stuff' with them from Ireland to England, since this would mean eluding the Customs, both at Dublin and at Liverpool or Holyhead. The material for the bombs was always supplied in England and assembled there. It is more than possible that Brendan was seen with the bombing material boarding the ship at the North Wall in Dublin and was followed as soon as he reached the other side.

Brendan had described his arrest in an article written in *Points* (Winter, 1952) a magazine edited by Peggy Guggenheim's son, Sindbad Vail, in Paris. (This was a draft for the first chapters of *Borstal Boy*:)

> Friday, the landlady, an Irishwoman, shouted up the stairs: 'Jehsus, oh, Jehsus, boy there's two gentlemen to see you.' I knew by the screeches of her; they were not calling to enquire after my health, or to see if I'd had a good trip. I grabbed my suitcase containing: Pot. Chlor., Sulph. Ac., gelignite, detonators, electrical and ignition, my Sinn Fein conjuror's outfit and carried it to the open window. Then the gentlemen arrived.
>
> A young one, with a blond Herrenvolk head and a B.B.C. accent, shouted, 'I say, greb him, the behstud.'
>
> All the Liverpool C.I.D. didn't speak like this. He was something special. A gentleman copper from Hendon College.
>
> When I was safely grabbed, the blond one gave me several punches in the face. An older man, with a heavy Jewish face, told him to leave me alone and give over making a fool of himself. Then the old one, a sergeant in charge of the others, took some Pot. Chlor. and sugar out of the suitcase, put it in the empty fireplace and lit it with a match. It roared into flame and filled the room with smoke. He nodded to me and I nodded back.
>
> Saxon-head and a third man, a quiet one, had me gripped by the arms.
>
> 'Got a gun, Paddy?' asked the sergeant.
>
> 'If I'd had, you wouldn't have got past that door so f—ing easy.'
>
> He looked at me and sighed. Obviously a boreable man.
>
> 'Turn him over', he said to the other quiet one.
>
> Blondie began to search me with violence.
>
> 'No, not you,' said the sergeant, 'Vereker'.

They found money, a letter in Gaelic and a forged travel permit in his pockets.

Nordic-nuts, grim, studied the Gaelic characters over Vereker's shoulder. Disgusted, he turned to me and shouted: 'You f—ing behstud, how would you like to see a woman cut in two?'

This, I understood, did not refer to a music-hall entertainment, but to an I.R.A. bomb which, being conveyed through the streets of Coventry, exploded prematurely and killed people. The British arrested two Irishmen, not the right ones, and hanged them for it.

I answered Blondi-bollocks on the same level, mentioning the R.A.F. bombing of Indian villages, Amritsar, the burning of Cork, and Croke Park, where the British attacked, with aerial support, some thousands of people watching a hurling match. By Jesus, I overwhelmed him. Only a deaf mute could be reared by my mother and be unable to catalogue England's misdemeanours from Africa backwards. Blondie, short of an answer, gave my arms a bit of a twist.

A hostile crowd had gathered round the house, as it was in the Orange quarter of Liverpool. Brendan was pushed through them by the police and taken to the C.I.D. headquarters in Lime Street. There he made a statement, taking care to insert a reference to the Irish Workers and Small Farmers Republic which would please the left-wing of the I.R.A. at home, and annoy the pious ones.

My name is Brendan Behan. I came over here to fight for the Irish Workers and Small Farmers Republic, for a full and free life for my fellow countrymen north and south and for the removal of the baneful influence of British imperialism from Irish affairs. God save Ireland.

Even at that early age, Brendan was not unaware of what the public reaction might be. He could hear them saying at home:

'Ah, sure, God help poor Brendan. Wasn't I only talking to him a week ago?'
'By God he was a great lad, and him only sixteen and all.'
'Sure it was in him. All belonging to him was out in Easter Week.'

On Monday he was taken to the Juvenile Court. He demanded that his case be heard in public. The magistrate assured him he would get all the publicity he wanted when the case came up on remand in a week's time. Brendan was then transferred to Walton Jail, where he was to remain two months and five days, until his trial on February 8.

Walton was a remand prison and while he was there he came in contact with criminals of every description. He was shocked and horrified by his first few days there. However, he soon slipped into the prison routine. He learned how to sew mail-bags without piercing his finger with the needle. He used to look forward to the exercise periods, when he could chat out of the corner of his mouth with his mates as they walked round the jail-yard. Being shut up was no problem for Brendan with his passion for reading. In his cell, he had undisturbed quiet for his favourite pursuit the material, in this case, consisting of the Bible and *News of the World*.

But he was sixteen-and-a-half and very lonely.

He looked forward eagerly to Mass on Sunday. This would be his link with home. The language of the universal church would be invariable even in alien England. He would answer the responses and sing the Latin hymns as he had done at home. They would be the same ones sung by his people through the generations when the Saxon had tried to make them change their religion. Catholicism had become a symbol of resistance to the foreign oppressor, so that the fuse that drove the Irish patriot was often a blend of both religious and republican ingredients. Brendan writes in *Borstal Boy*:

> At least in Walton I had the Faith to fall back on. Every Sunday and holiday I would be at one with hundreds of millions of Catholics, at the sacrifice of the Mass, to worship the God of our ancestors, and pray to Our Lady, the delight of the Gael, the consolation of mankind, the Mother of God and of man, the pride of poets and artists, Dante, Villon, Eoghan Ruadh O Sullivan, in warmer, more numerous parts of the world than this nineteenth-century English lavatory, in Florence, in France, in Kerry, where the arbutus grows and the fuchsia glows on the dusty hedges in the soft light of the summer evening. 'Deorini De'—'The Tears of God'— they called the fuchsia in Kerry, where it ran wild as a weed. 'Lachryma Christi'—'The Tears of Christ'—was a Latin phrase, but in future I would give Him less reason for tears, and maybe out of being here I would get back into a state of grace and stop in it—well, not stop out of it for long intervals—and out of evil, being here, good would come.

As a little boy, Brendan had prayed after his First Communion, as Napoleon had prayed after his, that God would take him and

44

he would go straight to heaven. 'Brendan was most religious', his mother remembers, 'he would . . . get up early to go to daily Communion. He was always reading religious books, Lives of the Saints.' Throughout his life, although his ardour waned, he never lost this religious bent. It was an obsession with him that he must have a priest if he was dying, and as his illness increased in the last months he used to make his wife and friends promise that they would see he was annointed by a priest if he fell down in the street, or became otherwise unconscious.

> But I wanted to be, and I would, and maybe here I could get closer to God, and I was sorry that it was only in a place like this you appreciated Him, but that's the way with human beings, and He'd know our weakness, and I'd make it up to Him, when I got outside, just to show that it wasn't only as a friend in need I wanted Him.

Shortly after his arrival in Walton Jail he was taken to see the prison chaplain. It was an unfortunate interview. The priest, an Englishman, bluntly told him that he would have to promise to give up his I.R.A. activities, or else be refused the Sacraments of the Church. In other words, he would be excommunicated unless he denied his political beliefs. Now this was nothing new to the Irish Republican Army or the earlier Irish revolutionary movements. The Irish bishops, as a conservative body, had always been in opposition to revolutionary activity in Ireland. But at home the Church was part of the people. Its struggle had been Ireland's. The priests had lived like wolves in the hills during the Penal Days (in the eighteenth century) and celebrated Mass under rocks in the mountains for congregations who were forbidden to meet in public to hear Mass. They had risked their lives to land, like smugglers, on the coast after having trained in seminaries on the Continent, to keep the faith alive among their people. When the Catholic nobility had fled to the Continent, it was the priests who came back to bring comfort to a leaderless peasantry. If the priests in Ireland condemned physical force (and not all of them did), they didn't do it because of absence of patriotism but because, in the eyes of the I.R.A. and the Fenians, they confused theology with politics.

45

What happened to Brendan in Walton was that a fat little English padre had given him a lecture on Catholicism, a faith which the padre's own countrymen had abjured, and denied Brendan the right to partake in a ritual which was as important to him as his national beliefs. Brendan lost his temper. He read the horrified man the riot act, cataloguing the mistakes of the Church in Irish politics from 1172 down to the Famine, and the Black and Tans in 1921, with all the bitter accuracy of an I.R.A. excommunicate. As he went on, the unfairness of his situation struck him and he lashed out in abuse of the priest:

To hell with you, you fat bastard, and to hell with England and to hell with Rome, up the Republic.

The two warders grabbed him and took him out screaming, leaving the priest purple with rage. They dragged him up some iron steps outside, pulling him so that he fell on the way and split his head. In his cell they gave him a beating on the chest and kidneys and hit him with keys in the face. He was to keep the mark of the steel stairs on his forehead for the rest of his life. At least one doctor later on was to wonder if the nervous condition which was precipitating his drinking was not due to the beating up he got from the warders after his meeting with the chaplain in Walton Jail.

But it wasn't just his head that was gashed. Something entered Brendan's soul that day that made him bitter for a long time after. He had been deprived of a support that had been bred into him; something which was part of his upbringing, part of his country, part of his city, his home, his instinct. He was a religious animal, and to take it from him was in a way to pervert his nature. In the back of his mind he had always felt that he could slip from the confines of Walton and England into a ritual that was part of something known to millions of other worshippers. Now this solace had been taken away from him by an Englishman.

He had another nasty experience before he left Walton. Two Irishmen, William Barnes and James McCormick, were due to be hanged on February 8 for their part in the Coventry bomb explosion. A bicycle with a bomb placed on the carrier had been abandoned in a shopping centre in Coventry, and the subsequent explosion had killed six people. It now seems certain that both men were nowhere near the crime, and that the bomb was intended for an electrical installation, but was abandoned hurriedly in the crowded shopping centre by another terrorist, who believed that it was about to explode prematurely. The sentence on the two men had aroused a good deal of protest and Mr de Valera, as Minister for External Affairs in Ireland, had intervened with the British government unsuccessfully on their behalf. As Brendan had come over to do precisely the same sort of operation that Barnes and McCormick, it was alleged, had done, his involvement with their fate was all the more complete. Had he succeeded in planting his bombs and been a few years older, his punishment, if he were caught, would have been the same as theirs.

A few days before the executions were to take place, Brendan encountered another Irishman in Walton. He attempted to enlist Brendan's sympathy over the Barnes and McCormick executions. But, though Brendan had plenty of sympathy with them, as he said himself after his recent beating, 'he was anxious for a truce with the British'. He knew well that the executions would arouse resentment in Irish circles in the U.S.A. and at home. 'But it didn't inspire me. I thought it better to survive my sentence and come out and strike a blow in vengeance for them, than to be kicked to death or insanity here.'

When Brendan heard that Lawlor, his fellow-prisoner, had tried to start a riot in the carpentry shop over the executions he was terrified that it would involve him, too. The night of the executions Lawlor started a caterwauling protest from his cell.

'Up the Republic, up the Republic, up the Republic.' He shouted to Brendan to join in. Brendan was afraid not to and let a timid 'To hell with the British Empire' down the ventilator, hoping the screws wouldn't hear him. All he got from Lawlor was, 'I can't hear you. Do it louder.'

At the time the row started, Brendan was reading Mrs Gaskell's *Cranford*—'I often feel tipsy from eating damson jam'. Then all hell was let loose on either side of him as Lawlor was done over by the warders. Curiously Brendan gives quite a different account of the incident in an article published in *The Bell* magazine in June 1942. In this he describes himself as the leader of the riot:

> A whispered conversation ensued. 'Brendan', Gerry whispered, 'they died two minutes ago'. Down along the rows of brown-clad remands and in the convicted pews where the blue uniform of the Borstal Boys contrasted with the grey slops of the penal servitudes, one could see on every Irish face the imprint of the tragedy that had been enacted that morning in another prison and that was to every Irishman present a personal sorrow. Ned and Gerry nodded to me. 'O.K., Brendan, say the word!'
>
> I stood in my pew and raised my hand in the signal we had decided upon the previous Sunday.
>
> 'Irishmen attention!'
>
> A rigid silence gripped the chapel. The warders stood bewildered. No doubt many of them thought it was a special ceremony of the church in which the congregation took part. One young warden fingered his baton nervously.
>
> 'Irishmen attention!'
>
> Ned and Gerry were already on their feet.
>
> 'We will recite the *De Profundis* for the repose of the souls of our countrymen who gave their lives for Ireland this morning in Birmingham Jail.'
>
> Gerry, who knew it, began 'Out of the depths have I cried to thee, O Lord . . .' Back down the serried rows came the response, 'Lord, hear my voice.' An old Cork man, serving seven years for manslaughter, was standing in the rows reserved for elderly preventive detentions. In front of him was a big Mayo lad . . . awaiting transfer to Parkhurst or Dartmoor. 'And let my cry come unto thee. . . .'
>
> Suddenly the Principal Officer appeared to regain his composure. He shouted orders:
>
> 'Remove Lawlor and Behan to their cells. Sit down the rest of you. Damn you! Silence.'
>
> Soon I was struggling as two warders grabbed me. Ned, the big Carlow soldier, was fighting madly. Gerry's head went down amid the impact of batons. The old Cork man I last saw as they were removing him, a scarlet gash showing vividly against his white hair. Raising my head I saw a baton raised ready to strike. I crouched tensing myself for the blow, but it never came. The P.O.'s voice cut in clear above the din:
>
> 'Don't strike Behan! He's for Court today.'

But, when Brendan wrote this in 1942, in *The Bell*, he was in prison with the I.R.A. It didn't do then to joke at their tradition. By 1957 when he published *Borstal Boy*, the writer in him had taken over.

On Ash Wednesday, February 8, 1940, he was tried at Liverpool Assizes in front of Mr Justice Hallett. He was driven to Court in a van with a man accused of murdering his wife, who was confident of being acquitted. They wished each other luck. The *Irish Times* on February 8, 1940, reported:

A 16 years' old boy, who was said by the police to have stated that he had been sent over by an illegal organisation to 'reorganise further operations in Liverpool', was sentenced at Liverpool Assizes today to three years' Borstal detention. He was Brendan Behan, a painter, of Kildare Road, Dublin, who smiled as he stood in the dock accused of being in possession of explosives, and declared that he had no interest in the proceedings of the court. His 'No Interest' remark was construed as a plea of not guilty.

While Detective-Sergeant Earps was giving evidence, the boy shouted: 'That's a lot of damned lies', and was warned by Mr Justice Hallett that if he did not remain quiet he would be removed from court and the case conducted in his absence.

The detective gave evidence that the boy made a statement in which he said: 'I have been sent over to take the places of Chris Kenneally, Nick Lynch and the others who have been arrested. I was to reorganise further operations in Liverpool. I intended to put bombs in big stores—Lewis's and Hughes's I think they call it. I was making up some to put in letter-boxes tonight. I would have put one in Cammell Lairds if I had the chance. I am only 16 and they can't do much with me.'

Judge's Threat

Behan interposed that he did not make such 'ridiculous assertions'. The Judge asked if there was any truth that Behan was only 16. The maximum penalty for an adult in his position would be 14 years' penal servitude.

Behan—'It is my proud privilege and honour to stand in an English court to testify to the unyielding determination of the Irish people to regain every inch of our national territory, and to give expression to the noble aspirations for which so much Irish blood has been shed and so many hearts have been broken, and for which so many friends and comrades are languishing in English jails.'

Sentencing Behan to three years' Borstal detention, the Judge said that Parliament in recent years had taken an extremely lenient view of what ought to be done with young persons found guilty of offences.

As Behan went below he shouted: 'God save Ireland.'

Potash and Acid

Mr Eric Errington, M.P., prosecuting, said that the boy was found in a house in Aubrey Street, Liverpool, standing by an open suitcase, which contained a bottle of acid. He had a fountain pen filler in his hand. In his possession were also found 20 ounces of potassium chlorate and sugar and 16 rubber balloons. Later he made a statement to the effect that he was a member of an organisation, and that he would blow up places if he got the chance.

According to the version Brendan gives in *Borstal Boy* (page 132) of his trial, he succeeded in saying considerably more than was reported in the newspaper. In the book he describes having prepared his speech for some days beforehand, and as he fancied himself in the tradition of the Irish dock-patriot—he knew Robert Emmet's famous speech when he was six—he was unlikely to lose this opportunity of practising his patriotic oratory and perhaps of entering the pages of Irish dock literature. In *Borstal Boy* Brendan grandiosely acquits himself in this speech:

> You have done this to a proud and intelligent people who had a language, a literature, when the barbarian woad-painted Briton was first learning to walk upright.
>
> By plantation, famine, and massacre you have striven to drive the people of Ireland from off the soil of Ireland, but in seven centuries you have not succeeded.
>
> Many times have you announced that you had stamped out the rebels, that 'you had terrorism by the throat', that you had settled the 'Irish Question'.
>
> But there is but the one settlement to the Irish Question, and until the thirty-two-county Republic of Ireland is once more functioning, Ireland unfree shall never be at peace.
>
> God save Ireland. No Surrender

CHAPTER FOUR

AFTER sentence, Brendan was kept in Feltham prison for a month before being allotted a place in a Borstal Institution. Feltham had had a Borstal section of its own but was also used for boys with Revoked Sentences and judges' permits. At Feltham Brendan heard that a new Borstal Institution had been started up in Hollesley Bay near Woodbridge in Suffolk. It was run on advanced lines by an enterprising Governor, C. A. Joyce. It was the second open Borstal in England. Joyce had introduced to it public school methods such as houses, housemasters and matrons, instead of the usual machinery of prison administration and as a result there was much competition among junior offenders to secure a place there. It was necessary to volunteer first. Then, having been inspected by a committee they were selected or rejected. After a short interview with the Commissioner of Prisons, the Governor of Feltham and C. A. Joyce— whom Brendan noted parted his hair down the centre, like the Everton soccer player Dixie Dean—Brendan found himself accepted for Borstal training in Hollesley Bay. It was to be the start of a new life for him.

C. A. Joyce was a remarkable man. After serving in the First World War, he had decided to devote himself to prison service, and had previously been in charge of Camp Hill on the Isle of Wight, where his methods had been so successful that a number of the boys had elected to go with him to Hollesley even though it meant an extension of their prison sentences if they went with him.

One of Joyce's beliefs was that prison itself never reformed anyone; it merely made it possible for a man to reform himself.

He was an equally firm believer in dialogue. It was a rule with him that if he met one of the boys under his control by chance they must stop and talk with him. If the boy did not want to speak, Joyce knew there was something wrong and would make a point of going up and having a conversation with him. He had, too, made a study of violence and the motives behind it. It was, he felt, a sign of failure. He believed, nevertheless, in corporal punishment properly administered, but it was not to be delivered in anger. He was capable of intense self-criticism. Once he found a boy ill-treating a dog; Joyce was extremely fond of animals and in temper he struck the boy. Later he reported himself to the Prison Inspector on his annual visit. The Inspector said he regretted it but if it happened again Joyce would have to go. The boy, who was present, burst out involuntarily, 'Oh, no Sir, please don't ever do it again. We don't want to lose you.'

Joyce had incorporated many of what he believed were the best aspects of public school life into the routine of Borstal. Hollesley Bay was divided into four houses, St Andrew's, St George's, St Patrick's and St David's. Each had a housemaster. There were inter-house football matches, both rugby and soccer. There was a school debating society and a drama society, and an excellent library as well as numerous sport's clubs. The boys often went on thirty-mile rambles, during which it was possible for them to escape if they wanted to. They were, however, on their honour not to do so and only one boy absconded in Joyce's time at Hollesley Bay.

The most important moment of the day for the Governor was evening prayer at eight o'clock. This lasted fifteen minutes. It was short and to the point. Joyce regarded himself as a flying buttress of the Church, rather than an orthodox churchman, but his unorthodox approach made an impression on the boys. Once at an eight o'clock talk, Joyce took out a cigarette case. 'If I open it twice you see, it works well,' he said, pressing the button and letting it spring and showing the cigarettes inside, 'but if I do it too often it weakens the spring. It's the same with sex.' His trust in God and lack of prudery made an impression on boys to whom religion had hitherto been a meaningless mumbo-jumbo for the upper classes.

C. A. Joyce remembers very well his first proper meeting with Brendan, in an interview at his office on his first day at Hollesley.

> He was a very good-looking young boy. He looked decent, clean-cut, fit. He had black hair, very clean skin and I remember he had a lovely smile always. He came in and I asked him would he like a cigarette. He seemed surprised at this. His first question was, 'Am I to be treated fairly?' I said, as carelessly as I could, 'Why, certainly'. 'Well, Sir', he said with a grin, 'I have been examined by the doctor and I want to tell you that I have no inhibitions and my complexes are all in order.' I roared with laughter at this. After that we got on very well indeed.

It was Joyce who succeeded in softening Brendan's attitude towards the Church. Since his experience at Walton, Brendan had grown bitter and resentful of religion, more so because what had happened prevented him from exercising what was in him a spiritual appetite. One day the Governor asked him why he wasn't attending church. Brendan told him that he was not able to receive the Sacraments because he had been excommunicated and therefore saw no reason to go. Joyce thought for a minute and said to Brendan:

'What would you do if you went into the Catholic church here?'

'I'd say a prayer.'

'So would I.'

'That's right.'

'We'd both be talking to the same bloke.'

'Sure.'

'We'd both be refused communion.'

'I suppose you're right.'

'Let's go on Sunday.'

'O.K.'

Next Sunday the Governor and Brendan went to Mass together. Joyce played the hymn in the organ loft while Brendan sang it in his sweet tenor voice. Down below the priest, who was an Italian, went on with the Mass.

Later Brendan used to say that his period at Borstal had been one of the happiest in his life. Again, he had ample opportunity to indulge his appetite for reading in the excellent library there. The librarian, a languid former public school boy, lent him books by Frank Harris, Somerset Maugham, C. E. Montague, D. H. Lawrence, Thomas Hardy, James Joyce, as well as poetry and criticism. The Governor's wife was an artist and wanted to sculpt his head. The assistant-matron read the *New Statesman* each week, and when she had finished it, gave her copy to Brendan. The matron was delighted with his stories of Dublin, of Yeats and Maud Gonne, and James Stephens, for she had grown up in an era when, as Brendan noted, 'the educated English liked the Irish for a while'. When he criticized Hollesley Bay for its lack of literary associations she reminded him that Dickens had Steerforth drowned just up the beach and Edward Fitzgerald translated *Omar Khayyam* only a few miles away.

Brendan was the star figure at debates. His two main rivals were Neville Heath, who had a posh public school accent, and John Smith, a Cardiff negro. Once, when Brendan appealed to Smith to give Heath a chance and not heckle so much, Smith turned round and said sarcastically, 'That's right, Paddy, stick up for the bloody gentry against the working-class'. (Heath was hanged for the sadistic murder of two women in 1950. His last letter was to Governor Joyce saying he would be with him every night, for as long as he wished, at eight o'clock for prayers.)

In the nativity play at Christmas, Brendan played the part of one of the Wise Kings. As he backed away from the manger after delivering the frankincense, he tripped on the rug and Governor Joyce remembers hearing very clearly, 'Oh that effing rug' coming out of the whiskered features of the third king. He won the essay competition at the summer Eisteddfod, with an essay on Dublin. He wrote of the city of Shaw, Wilde, Sheridan, Yeats, O'Casey, Joyce, with an erudition that must have startled the judges when they read it.

Brendan played hooker in the rugby team. This was an upper-class game in England and Ireland at that time, and it is indicative of Joyce's outlook that it flourished in the school side by side with soccer, the usual working-class game. Up to this Brendan had only seen rugby played by the boys at Belvedere College in Dublin, who passed in their green caps and black blazers to their grounds at John's Road, a few hundred yards from his home in Russell Street. He was influenced in his enthusiasm for rugby by reading a book by an Irish international, Dr Robert Collis, called *The Silver Fleece*. Collis inspired him so much with his descriptions of the Irish pack thundering for the line, that Brendan, with his vivid imagination, was not above seeing himself as a member of the same pack at some stage of his life. In a small way this helped to give an identification with a class which he would have otherwise felt cut off from in his own city.

It is inherent in Brendan's style of recounting autobiographical episodes that he slips easily into the story-teller's device of exaggeration for the sake of the effect on the listener. Thus, throughout his account of Borstal days, whenever he can startle the reader by a casual reference to shocking crimes committed by fellow Borstalians, he is always prepared to do. For instance, if the St Joseph in the nativity play can be played by an 'H.M.P. bloke' in for slicing his mum, so much the better for the tale, even though in fact the part had been played by a boy in for non-attendance at school: if the front row of the rugby scrum had a murderer as one prop, Brendan would invent a ponce for the other, so that as hooker he could hang between the two, for the delectation of his reader.

Thus, a somewhat false atmosphere of Hollesley Bay is conveyed in his autobiographical writing about it. There were boys there, of course, who had committed serious crimes. But each boy at Hollesley had been selected specially for his character and potential for reform. As well, there were many boys there who had been imprisoned for 'crimes' that in today's permissive age would merit little more than a mild warning from the magistrate.

Nor was the working-class atmosphere as thorough as Brendan liked to make out. There were ex-public school boys at Hollesley Bay, including the head of Brendan's own dormitory. One day, when Brendan was saying that he had as much right to ordain priests as a cardinal, this boy passed and said, 'Marlowe said he

55

had as good a right to mint money as the Queen of England. Did you know that?' And Brendan replied, 'I did, and I'm glad to see someone else knows it'.

Brendan identified himself with the working-class boys at Hollesley Bay:

> I had the same rearing as most of them—Dublin, Liverpool, Manchester, Glasgow, London. All our mothers had all done the pawn, pledging on Monday, releasing on Saturday. We knew the chip-shop and the picture house and the fourpenny rush of a Saturday afternoon, and the summer swimming in the canal and being chased along the railway by the cops.

But this is not an entirely true picture. Brendan really had as much in common with the public-school boys there as he had with the working-class boys. The fact is that, as a Dubliner, Brendan was classless, and impossible to fit properly into any English category of social distinction. It was part of the illusion that he liked to cultivate which made him identify so much with the working-class; an illusion too that he should have chosen to think, despite the chip-shop and the pawn-shop, that his parents and relatives, with their background of general culture, had much in common with the average Borstal boy's parents. Of course he spoke the same language as the other boys and had a natural gift of adaptability. This combined to give an illusion of similarity with them which did not in fact exist. His family background, had he revealed it to them, would have seemed as exotic as that of a South Sea Islander.

In England the Industrial Revolution had cut the people off from what folk-culture had remained among them, while Brendan had had contact with a culture that had remained unchanged among the people for a thousand years. Through the Irish-Ireland movement he had made contact with a folk tradition of Gaelic poetry and song.

At Feltham, he had sung a song in Gaelic about Bonnie Prince Charlie to keep him in mind of home. It was about the Irish longing for deliverance and the hope that the Stuart would return and bring with him their freedom.

> Wide was your heart, and mild was your eye,
> My sorrow without you, for ever I'll cry,

> . . . Is go dtéighidh tú a mhúirnín, slán,
> Walk my love, walk surely.
> White as new lime, your thighs and hips,
> Your clustering hair, and your sweet-bitten lips,
> My last blaze of strength would die in their kiss . .
> Is go dtéighidh tú a mhúirnín, slán,
> Walk my love, walk surely. . . .

In Walton, when he had nothing else to do, he had set a hymn by Thomas Hardy to an Irish air. When he was asked to sing at a concert in Hollesley Bay, he sang the 'Coolin' in Gaelic, one of the two or three loveliest of Irish airs, full of love and defiance, that brought a hushed silence down on an audience who knew neither the language nor the music he was singing. In the fields, while other boys cursed, swore or made jokes, while he raked the ground he was thinking of a poem by the bard of the Connacht countryside, Raftery:

> . . . Now in the springtime, the day's getting longer,
> On the feastday of Bridget, up my sail will go,
> Since my journey's decided, my step will get stronger,
> Till once more I stand in the plains of Mayo . . .

Even the seasons had a meaning for him that they had not for the other boys: 'The first of February is St Brigid's Day', he wrote in *Borstal Boy*. 'She was from the County Kildare, and is called Mary of the Gael, being very beautiful and a great friend to the poor.'

At Hollesley Bay, when he thought of Joyce's kindness and the genial attitude of the Italian padre towards his political leanings, Brendan told himself that his religion was not the religion of Newman—'a soft easy theological swap'—but that of the Gaelic poet Tuige O'Sullivan kneeling out on the wet grass at a mountain altar in West Cork fifty years before.

> Brightness of my heart your Heart O Saviour,
> Richness of my heart the gaining of yours,
> If I have filled Your Heart with my love,
> Inside my heart leave yours for ever.

The quality that Brendan most admired in both Governor and boys at Borstal was that of fair play. Good-humoured English banter or 'taking the Mick', was common in all circles in Borstal. Joyce, in fact, had deliberately set out to apply English rules of common sense and fair play in his dealings with delinquent boys, believing that concepts of honour and decency, by which the upper-class professed to govern themselves, could be equally applied to people of other backgrounds if they were presented in terms they could identify with. All this had an effect on Brendan. After Borstal he found it impossible to hate Englishmen any more. He had grown up with a picture in his mind of the very worst type of Englishman, the Black and Tans who had murdered men, women and children, and wounded others only a few yards away from his own house on November 21, 1920, at Croke Park. Now, in the person of Joyce, he came in contact with a type of Englishman that was completely new to him. He found he could disagree with the Governor on politics and still be his friend. Here was a man from the ruling classes acting in a way that was wholly admirable—from the class that Brendan had been taught were the traditional oppressors of his country.

One day Governor Joyce and his wife were driving Brendan back from hospital. They left him alone in their car while they went to do some shopping. He could have driven away. Brendan never forgot this appeal to his honour. He was as keen to show Joyce in later years that he had lived up to the standards that he had taught him. Before Brendan's release, the question of his parole came up. Joyce put his cards on the table and said that he would like to advise the Home Secretary favourably in the matter but could not do so unless Brendan would promise not to renew his I.R.A. activities after his release. Brendan hung his head. In all sincerity he could not give the promise. Suddenly, Joyce had a brainwave. 'I tell you what', he said, 'Give me your word that you won't injure any of my countrymen.' A grin came on Brendan's face. 'O.K. Sir, that's a deal, I won't fire at an Englishman until we've beaten this bastard, Hitler.'

Six months later, Brendan was to receive fourteen years for shooting a policeman in Dublin. He wrote to Joyce immediately to say that he had not broken his promise, that he 'had snatched the gun from a fellow who was going to use it'. Though the reverse was true (Brendan had actually snatched the gun and fired it himself, because his companion would not use it), his letter shows that he was trying to keep faith with his former headmaster, and probably justified the deceit to himself on the grounds that he had not fired at an *English* policeman.

Brendan's whole life had been conditioned by a hatred of England. His period in Borstal and his acquaintanceship with both Joyce and the boys with whom he became friends there, gave him a new image to grapple with, that of the decent Englishman, which he gradually began to blend with his political beliefs. At Borstal, in fact, he learned to play up to the English. In the British Isles, none of the four nationalities is more popular with the English than the Irish. The Irishman seems to embody all that the Englishman seems to have exorcised from his life in the pursuit of duty. He is the anti-self of the Saxon. With his wealth of colourful phrases, his songs, and wit, his quaint proverbs, his laughing, joyful personality, Brendan was the most popular boy at Hollesley Bay.

'He's a comical bastard, ain't he?' his mates used to boast when a new prisoner met Brendan. Phrases like 'He'd say Mass if he knew Latin', or 'He'd mind mice at a cross-roads', had a sharpness which appealed to the working-class ear, and an imagery which at the same time they found impossible to duplicate. He learned quickly what the English demanded of the Irish in order to enjoy them. He found the formula and played up to it. He wanted to please, to be liked. All his life this was to plague him— the desire to shine: the fatal formula he found in Borstal of how to play Paddy to the Saxon was to contribute to his downfall when he set out to conquer the world of letters and drama in London twenty years later.

As with English boarding schools of all kinds, public and grammar, Borstal boys lived together in the monastic seclusion demanded by the English system, and did not meet with, nor were encouraged to meet with, members of the opposite sex: and as a natural consequence sexual practices were common among a section of the boys. With the majority, no doubt, it was a passing phase, but on others it left its mark. One of them was

Brendan. For the rest of his life he was to be bi-sexual. The type of boy or man he admired sexually was the type he had met at Borstal—clear-skinned, athletic and fair—'the typical English boy you'd see in an advertisement'. Later on Brendan would refer to his experiences at Borstal as having given him the first opportunity to recognize that he could enjoy sexual congress with either sex.

CHAPTER FIVE

WHEN Brendan Behan returned to Dublin in December 1941, he was to find that the public's attitude towards the I.R.A. had undergone a considerable change in his absence. The country was insecure, in a state of uneasy neutrality, uncertain as to whether it would be invaded by either the Allies or the Axis forces.

A section of the I.R.A. were known to be in favour of collaboration with the Germans and this for a start made them unpopular. But between Brendan's departure and return, the conflict between the I.R.A. and the Government had widened. A raid on the Magazine Fort where army ammunition and guns were stored, the killing of two detectives in a Chicago-like gun battle in Rathgar, a Dublin suburb, and the wounding of three more at Holles Street in an attack on the escort bringing the diplomatic bag to the British Embassy, provoked the Government into stern measures.

After the Holles Street attack in October 1940, over a thousand I.R.A. men were interned in jail and a Military Court set up to try political offences. This Court was empowered to pass only one penalty, the death sentence. Sixteen defendants were to be tried in front of it, four of them were to be acquitted. The sentences of six were commuted and the remaining six were executed. In the summer of 1940, the first two I.R.A. men were executed, Paddy McGrath, (a veteran of the 1919–21 Anglo-Irish war) and Patrick Harte, as a result of their part in the Rathgar shooting.

The leadership of the I.R.A. at this period was still inept. Sean Russell had not returned from America. From there he had gone to Berlin and died of a perforated ulcer on his way back to Ireland in a German submarine in July 1941. Stephen Hayes, who had been temporary chief of staff, had been arrested by the I.R.A. and tried as a spy. He escaped and handed himself over to the police. His place as Chief of Staff was taken by Sean McCaughey, a man of fanatical disposition from Belfast. Under his leadership, with the majority of seasoned I.R.A. men in prison, the movement was largely composed of very young men under orders from McCaughey to resist arrest if necessary rather than surrender to the police.

It seems clear from those who knew him at this period that Brendan was disheartened by the reception he got on his return from Borstal. He had expected that the glamour of an English prison sentence would endow him with the sort of patriotic splendour that shone round the returned heroes he had heard of in histories of the Fenians and the Irish Republican Brotherhood and the Volunteers in 1917.

Those of the I.R.A. who were left outside jail at this time were desperate. They had their backs to the wall. Two detectives, Walsh and O'Brien, had been killed in gun battles in the autumn of 1942 and the Special Branch police were hot on the trail of the organization. The I.R.A. now had little time for heroics and Brendan (who claimed to Ultan O'Neill, an I.R.A. friend, that he was both Marxist and pro-German) was not taken as seriously as he would have wished as a veteran of the bombing campaign. He was hurt by this and known to have a grudge and be anxious to prove himself.

He was to display this at the Easter commemoration at Glasnevin Cemetery on April 5, 1942, in an episode which was to have disastrous consequences for him. This was the day of the annual Easter Sunday celebrations of the Rising of 1916, in which national organizations took part.

The parade began outside the University Church in St Stephen's Green. The I.R.A., or what remained of them, were to join in the parade with the National Graves' Association, the Fianna, Cumann na gCailíní, Mná na Poblachta and others. Only about thirty or forty I.R.A. men turned up, much less than expected, A rumour had got round that something was in the air, and at least one of the men, Martin Quearney, an intelligence officer in the Dublin Battalion, believed that a major demonstration of some kind, involving shooting, was to take place.

> We were most of us armed. Behan and I were standing outside University Church. We called him 'Mickey' then, and Lazarian Mangan 'Glycerine', because we could never remember his proper name. We were all cheesed off because so few had turned up. Someone said, 'Call it off', and Brendan said, 'You little bollix', and I said, 'I'll form the march'. Behan said then, 'If we're going at all, we're going at the top'. So the I.R.A. marched in front. When we got to the Cross Guns Bridge, some of them lost their nerve as the police were very much in evidence, and dropped out to give Andy Nathan their guns. This was observed by the police and gave the game away to some extent.
>
> At Glasnevin we listened to the speech. A few left before the oration was over. You could understand this if you had listened to as many Republican orations as we had to. Brendan, Mangan, Buckley and Nathan moved off towards de Courcey Square.

Nathan, without knowing it, was tailed by Special Branch police officers. They had seen him receiving a gun at the grave-side, as rebels and police knelt side by side reciting the rosary, and had followed him as he left. On the road outside the cemetery Detective Officers Doran and Donegan moved in on him and grabbed him by the arms. Nathan was wearing a Burberry coat and was difficult to keep a grip on. Lazarian Mangan meanwhile sprang away, pulling out a revolver as he did so. He stood there for a second or two unable to make up his mind what to do with it. Brendan came running down the road, 'frothing with excitement' at this stage. He threw his overcoat, jacket and waistcoat all off in one throw and was standing in his shirt sleeves in the middle of the road shouting 'Shoot the bastards' to Mangan. Then he grabbed the revolver and fired wildly at another Detective, Martin Hanrahan, who had come on the scene with a Detective Kirwan. Hysterical with excitement, Brendan fired three shots at them, one of which pierced Hanrahan's overcoat under the arm, who was then about ten yards away. Brendan then ran off, followed by an I.R.A. colleague, Dick Flaherty. Hanrahan fired back as Brendan disappeared and then he and Donegan set out in pursuit. He took aim to fire again but lowered his revolver when he saw women and children scattering across the road as

Brendan ran through them. It was lucky for Brendan that Hanrahan did not fire again at this stage as he was a crack shot and had taken first place in the Irish Police Championships. Brendan and Flaherty succeeded in losing the two detectives along a side road which ran off from the cemetery. Meanwhile, Nathan, Mangan and Buckley had been apprehended. They were taken to the Bridewell Prison where Nathan is alleged to have said: 'I would have used my revolver only I did not get a chance. You were too smart for me.'

Brendan and Dick Flaherty had jumped over the wall of a small suburban house in the street they had escaped into. They hid there, trembling and out of breath. Brendan, who had nothing on but his pullover, slipped on Flaherty's overcoat, Flaherty having a suit on underneath. After a few minutes they decided to make a move, slipping in through the back door of the house whose garden they had been hiding in. The man of the house though, who was small but plucky, confronted them, and when Brendan tried to push him upstairs at gun-point, he refused, saying: 'I won't be ordered around by a pup like you.' Behan was nonplussed for a second. He was beginning to feel the reactions from the events of a few minutes ago and was having difficulty in keeping his teeth from chattering. He almost fired the gun when the door opened and a pretty young girl came in. She was the daughter of the house and appears to have some sympathy with the I.R.A. for she showed the grateful Brendan and his friend Flaherty out through a side gate of Glasnevin into the main road towards Santry. They thanked her and set off as fast as they discreetly could in the direction of Brendan's Aunt Maggie's house in the outer suburbs of Santry, their nearest bolt hole.

On their way, they passed a pitch-and-toss school. The fugitives had only fourpence between them. They decided to chance it in the toss school. After a few minutes, Brendan was ten shillings up. More money was needed, however, to keep them supplied while they were on the run. Not having time to push his luck, Brendan put himself in funds by producing his gun and holding up the toss school and collecting the pool. He and Flaherty cleared off admidst imprecations from the infuriated gamblers: To clear their minds, the two men went into Belton's pub in Santry for a drink, and in a few minutes, their escape money had been converted into liquid assets. They then proceeded to the house of Maggie Bourke, one of Brendan's numerous aunts. Dick Flaherty recalls that Mrs Bourke received them kindly. They had to leave shortly after, however,. as Brendan refused to put away his gun which frightened Mrs Bourke's young daughter.

After leaving Bourke's, they headed towards the city where Brendan and Dick Flaherty decided it would be better to part. Flaherty left Brendan at Capel Street Bridge. After wandering about for some time, Brendan spent the night in a slum where a friend of his mother's made him a bed on the floor with rugs and cushions. Meanwhile, the names of the two fugitives had been broadcast on the radio. They had been identified shortly after the shooting occurred. In the atmosphere of the times, any attack on the police was bound to be taken seriously and a very large detachment of Special Branch police was searching the city for Brendan Behan and Dick Flaherty.

Brendan's mother and father heard the news at 70 Kildare Road. Their rebel son was in trouble again—though this time it was the Irish police, not the English, who were after him. As Brendan had discovered on the eve of his leaving for England and the bombing expedition, his father no longer approved of the aims of the I.R.A. But a crisis like this brought out all the innate affection that Stephen had for his son. Brendan was in trouble and something had to be done. Rumours were flying round everywhere. Detective Superintendent Gantly of the Special Branch was reported to have said: 'Brendan Behan will be shot before night.' As soon as he heard this alleged statement of Gantly's, Stephen put on his hat and coat and got into a taxi: 'I'm not having my son shot like that', he said, as he set out for the house of the Minister for Local Government, Sean T. O'Kelly, 'Sean T,' who had been a friend of his in the early days of Sinn Fein, before the First World War and in 1946 was to be elected the second President of Ireland. When Stephen found him in his house, Mr O'Kelly listened carefully to what he had to say.

According to Stephen, 'Sean T.' immediately contacted another influential member of the Cabinet and succeeded in having an order issued that Brendan Behan was to be taken alive.

On the Monday night, Brendan was nearly caught at an I.R.A. sympathizer's house, the Parnells' in North Great George's Street. 'I'll shoot my effing way out', he told Georgie Parnell as he slid out of the back door down the garden to the wall there, which he succeeded in getting over before he was caught. Martin Quearney came into town that night and met George Tancred and Harry Jacobs, I.R.A. friends of Brendan's, and told them that there had been a raid on Parnells'. They went up to Findlater's Church and found two police trucks there. The place was swarming with uniformed men.

Next day a detachment of Special Branch police officers caught sight of Brendan near Parnell Square. When he saw them, Brendan ran into an alley, pulling out his revolver as he did so. The police followed him with their revolvers cocked. However, some school children ran between the police and their quarry again and, by the time they had cleared off, Brendan was gone.

There is no doubt at this time that Brendan meant to shoot it out with the police. He made this clear to Beatrice, his wife, many years later. It is also borne out by his actions during the three days he was at liberty. He was in hiding at one period at Hollybank Road, Drumcondra, on the outskirts of Dublin. He had told the people there that he intended using his gun and this was reported to one of the I.R.A. officers at G.H.Q. The result was that a deputation was sent to get his gun off him. This consisted of George Dempsey and Ultan O'Neill. O'Neill recalls:

> I heard that Behan was acting the cowboy with his gun in front of the children at Hollybank Road. 'You're the only one that can handle him', they said. I picked up Dempsey and said to Brendan when I reached Hollybank Road, 'What the effing hell are you doing? Give me that revolver.' Brendan said, 'You're getting no revolver'. I said, 'I want it back.' He said he'd fire it at me. I said, 'Go ahead'. Then he handed it over.

On April 10, at 7.00 p.m., Detective Officer Doran was waiting for his colleague, Officer Donegan, at Blessington Street. To his surprise, he saw Brendan coming towards him instead.

He hid in a doorway and, as Brendan passed, jumped on him. Brendan had no gun and surrendered quietly enough. Doran waited until Donegan arrived when they both escorted the prisoner to the Bridewell Police Station.[1]

[1] When it came to describing his own rebel activities, Brendan was not a reliable source. If we compare the events related here with the version Brendan later set out in *Confessions of an Irish Rebel*, it can be seen there are many discrepancies in the two accounts. On page 31 of *Confessions* he writes:

> 'The hungry-faced police jumped out of their cars and went to arrest Andrew, Lazarian and Joseph.'
>
> Everyone was shouting and saying things, and one big ugly-faced policeman going mad with the temper, and shouting himself to tell them to shut up, when all of a sudden somebody screamed, 'That man has a gun,' and I looked round and saw the steel glint of a revolver in one of the I.R.A. officers' hand and he was altogether hysterical.
>
> 'I'll use it, I'll use it,' he screamed.
>
> As I snatched the revolver out of the officer's hand, the police opened fire. I didn't and not until they opened fire did I fire back at them, and, still firing, Flaherty and I made a desperate run for it.

If this version is compared with the events related above, it will be seen that the two accounts are in conflict. As the present narrative has been compiled from information from a number of people who witnessed the episode, including I.R.A. men and the two policemen involved—Detectives Hanrahan and Donegan—it is probable that Brendan was at his old trick of polishing up the facts to make a good story.

Brendan also states in *Confessions of an Irish Rebel* that while he was on the run, he and Dick Flaherty robbed pawnshops. Flaherty indignantly denies this, and points out that in March and April of 1942 the pawnshops in Ireland were on strike.

Another ploy of Brendan's was to suggest that he was drunk on this occasion. 'I saw three Hanrahans' he used to tell groups in the Bailey 'and I didn't know which one to shoot.'

But a careful survey of many of his actions from the time that he left Kildare Road at ten o'clock that morning till the incident occurred about mid-day, shows that Brendan had taken no drink before he seized the gun from Mangan.

Brendan's account of the arrest also appears to be a fictitious one. On page 47 of *Confessions of an Irish Rebel* he describes how he was captured in bed in Blessington Street by Superintendent Gantly:

> They searched me, putting their hands along the seams of my trousers where they found the gun.
>
> 'You wouldn't have come in here so shagging easy', I said, 'if I had the time to use it. You'll never drive the Irish out of Ireland, and that's for fughing sure.'

But as has been seen the gun had been taken off him two days before by Ultan O'Neill. Brendan was not in a house in Blessington Street when he was arrested, but walking along the street, when Detective Doran grabbed him from behind.

The day after his arrest, he was charged with the attempted murder of Detective Officer Kirwan. The trial took place on April 25 before a Special Criminal Court presided over by Colonel John Joyce. Brendan remembered afterwards how surprised he was that the police gave evidence without venom. He reflected, as he heard them speak, on the sadness of Irishmen fighting Irishmen. Never a man to waste a good line, when asked by Colonel Joyce had he anything to say before sentence was passed upon him, Brendan delivered the same speech he had given when on trial before the Assizes Judge in Liverpool. After the oration was over, Colonel Joyce, the President of the Court, delivered the sentence. In a matter-of-fact voice he sentenced Brendan Behan to fourteen years' penal servitude. Deceived by the Judge's bland attitude, Behan had not expected this. 'My stomach twisted up inside me with fear' he recalled in *Borstal Boy*. He was nineteen years of age. Even with remission, he would be thirty when he came out of jail. Unlike the other I.R.A. men who were tried with him on lesser charges, Brendan knew what it was like to be in prison. His six months of freedom had given him a taste of what life outside was like compared with the restrictions of prison existence.

Yet he should have considered himself lucky. In the summer of the same year, Maurice O'Neill had been executed for an incident in which shots had been fired which killed a detective, and it was not alleged by the State that O'Neill had fired them. George Plant, another I.R.A. man was executed the February before Brendan went in, having been discharged by the Special Criminal Court for lack of evidence and re-arrested for trial by the same Military Court which had sentenced Brendan. With penalties of this kind in vogue, fourteen years for attempted murder was not, in retrospect, a harsh sentence.

Later when he arrived in Mountjoy Prison, Governor Kavanagh, who was expecting a hardened young desperado, was surprised to find in Brendan, 'a mild-mannered boy who gave one a feeling of anti-climax. Surely this was no trigger-happy gunman. The better one got to know him, the more the impression grew that basically he was a very gentle person who in his senses would not hurt a fly.' Governor Joyce in Hollesley Jail has also had the same impression of Brendan. But there was no doubt that Brendan was on a killing mission in April 1942. In fact, Dempsey and O'Neill were afterwards reproved by the I.R.A. for taking the gun off Brendan and therefore preventing him shooting it out with the police. Martin Quearney recently described the position:

> If Brendan had to die he might as well have brought some of the police with him. This is part of being a republican after all, to shoot your way out. He could take three or more. After all, as far as we were concerned then, there had been no truce in 1923. There had been a declaration of war on the whole lot, Free State and all of them who accepted the truce with England, including that old — de Valera.

Why should young men of sensitive, idealistic and often religious temperament have nourished the killer instinct with such intensity?

They were victims of a tradition that had become irrelevant as the new State evolved. Michael Collins had demonstrated the scope of terrorism as a revolutionary tactic. Without his genius to guide it, the organization which claimed descent from the original I.R.A. at times degenerated into one which merely dispensed licences for acts of individual terror. But the system of planned killing created by Collins had received official benediction with the establishment of the Irish Free State. The new State was the child of terror as well as of Arthur Griffith's democracy, no matter how much the young cabinet ministers in their silk hats and striped trousers might try to forget it.

Ingenious logic and subtle theology had been necessary to justify terror as a means of attaining freedom; these were quickly found and many who held office later in Irish governments were among those who had carried out the most terrible of Michael Collins's commands. The Easter revolution of 1916 itself had been brought about through the dream of one man, Patrick Pearse, who thought it was necessary to wash the soul of Ireland clean with the blood of martyrs, and another, James Connolly, who held that only through bloodshed could the Socialist state he believed in come into being. It is not, therefore, surprising to find, less than three decades later, young men who felt it was their duty to continue policies of political assassination in pursuit of a united Ireland, even if it was against their own fellow-countrymen. A conditioned reflex is not so easily eliminated from the national being.

CHAPTER SIX

AFTER his conviction, Brendan was brought in a crowded prison van to Mountjoy Prison. This was the largest jail in Dublin and housed criminals of all sorts as well as political prisoners. It was to have one advantage at least for Brendan in later life. Mingling with the 'lags' there, he was able to get material which he used in his first successful play, *The Quare Fellow*.

Political prisoners had certain privileges in Mountjoy; they were allowed to wear their own clothes and they moved in and out of one another's cells a great deal more freely than prisoners in on criminal charges. In fact, there was a certain club atmosphere among the I.R.A. inmates when Brendan arrived there.

Governor Kavanagh has a clear recollection of him.

He arrived in April 1942. He was a slim, good-looking youth of nineteen, five feet eight inches, and 130 pounds. He had been released from Borstal only a very short time before so he was in very good physical condition. I remember particularly his beautiful, shining teeth. One could not avoid noticing his presence around the place, for he was a character, a complete extrovert. Gay, witty, amusing, always in good humour and his strong voice with a slight stammer could often be heard above all others in the exercise yard or from one of the D Wing landings.

Sean O'Briain, a Kerry schoolteacher, who was to become one one of Brendan's closest friends, remembers the first day he met Brendan in prison. O'Briain had been interned some months previously.

On that morning of our first meeting in jail, Brendan, then in his teens, appeared wearing a black heavy overcoat several sizes too big for him. He was slim and well-built and marched along cocky and light-hearted with the tail of his unbuttoned coat trailing on the ground. He looked as if he would fit in the pocket of the coat.

'Barr na maidhne, a Sheain', he said, 'and how are the balls of your feet?—What sort of an ould station is this?' (All in one breath.) 'Not bad', I said, 'better nor the Glasshouse anyway.' ''Tis not the station that matters', said he, ''tis the station master.'

He was soon very popular with the other prisoners and became a sort of pet. He was constantly singing and, as he walked up and down the corridors between the cells, either a song or a stream of witticisms would issue from his lips. Yet he was sharp enough. Michael Traynor, who as Adjutant General in the I.R.A. had sent Brendan on his mission to England, remembers being struck by Brendan's ability 'to pin-point anybody's character in a sentence. He could strip them bare of pretence in a few words'. Traynor used to lend Behan books, mostly the Russian novelists, Dostoevsky, Turgenev, Chekhov or Gorki. When he had finished with them, usually in a day or two, because he read with great rapidity, Brendan would come along and, standing in front of Traynor in his cell, proceed to act out sections of the book which he had read the night before. 'They were marvellous impersonations, very life-like; the fact that I knew the passages well made no difference, he brought them to life again.'

Sean O'Briain remembers another example of Brendan's ability to improvise a one-man-show for the prisoners. One day, lying in the prison recreation yard in the sun, they were discussing 'The Invincibles'. This was a Dublin anarchist group who had assassinated Lord Frederick Cavendish and Secretary Burke in the Phoenix Park in 1882. Three of them, including a Dublin man, Joe Brady, were hanged, and the cabman, Skin-the-Goat, who drove them to the scene of the assassination, was sentenced to fifteen years in prison as an accomplice.

On a fine summer day in Arbour Hill, a group of us were lying down or sitting with our backs to the prison wall—well inside the outside wall, of course. Brendan came along and stood there. Somebody asked him, 'Brendan, do you know anything about "The Invincibles"?' 'You mean Joe Brady and Skin-the-Goat? Wasn't my grandmother and poor oul' Joe Brady's oul' one great buddies, before and after. And sure my grandmother—she had it from the inside, of course—she often told us the whole story.'

There he stood, in his pants in the sunshine, no shirt or shoes on, his tangled uncombed hair falling down over his forehead and a grand smile on that youthful face. He started off. Whatever story he got from his grandmother was the basis of a drama that must have lasted over the next half-hour. The dramatist, the author, the poet with the wonderful imagination, and the actor himself were playing the Phoenix Park executions—an original play if ever there was one. He was never stuck for dialogue. He spoke and acted Joe Brady and Skin-the-Goat. He made up the play as he went along. Then he came to 'the job' itself. There he did Skin-the-Goat, the jarvey—standing by the horse's head. In Brendan's improvised play, Joe Brady comes back to where Skin the-Goat is waiting: 'Joe Brady,' says he, 'I think I seen that man moving.' Joe goes back and finishes the job. 'That's right,' says Skin-the-Goat, 'A dead cock doesn't crow.'

It was not at the gruesome details of that part of the story that we laughed next day. It was his telling of the story—never hesitating for a sentence—sometimes inventing very serious conversational passages—plenty of witty cracks and Dublin humour all mixed together. He was very good at portraying real live characters—putting them in a play or in a story. But then he added a bit of Brendan himself for good measure.

Brendan started to write almost immediately he came into Mountjoy jail. The Governor supplied him with material—paper, books, pen, ink and anything else he wanted. To encourage him, he invited in the Irish novelist and short-story writer, Sean O'Faolain, who was then editing *The Bell*, an Irish literary monthly of some importance. O'Faolain visited Brendan a number of times and eventually published his first serious article, *The Experiences of a Borstal Boy*, in *The Bell* for April, 1942.

Mick Traynor remembers that Brendan wrote as he spoke. He never corrected a line. 'He just liked the act of writing. I was always at him to re-write but he never would.' He would write in his cell with the blankets thrown over him. Sean O'Briain remembers him peeling the pages off and flinging them in the air as he finished them. Only occasionally did he collect them together. But O'Briain recalls that there 'seems to have been an awful lot of writing done'.

It was in Mountjoy that Brendan wrote his first play, *The Landlady*. It was based on his memories of his Granny English and her cronies and the atmosphere surrounding Russell Street.

There is a scene in it where a girl cuts her throat which was a re-enactment of an event in Brendan's own life, when his step-uncle, Paddy English, had got a girl into trouble, and Brendan's mother had found the unfortunate creature in the lavatory in a dying condition.

The play was impressive enough for Michael Traynor to persuade some of the prisoners to give it a production. Traynor remembers it as an interesting work. 'But there was a good deal of swearing in it and references to whores and the brothel area which Brendan placed his own home in.' (His home, of course, was on the outskirts of this area and not in it). The production succeeded in provoking a riot among the political prisoners. Some of the more pious among them thought the play blasphemous and obscene, and objected to it. There were fights between them and members of the cast. So, though the production on it was well advanced, Brendan's first play was dropped before it reached performance.

Three years later Brendan was to rewrite this play, translate it into Gaelic and send it to the Abbey Theatre. It is not certain that he sent the whole of it, for only one act survives in the Abbey archives, though in a covering letter to the Managing Director of the Abbey Theatre, Brendan stated that he had sent the other two acts.

The surviving first act gives an idea of the nature of the rest of the play. It has an interesting cast; Mrs Cleary, an astute, grasping landlady who conducts her business in bed because of the 'pains' in her legs; a hypocritical neighbour whose daughter has an illegitimate child; Mrs Cleary's son Jacko, clearly modelled on Brendan's step-uncle Paddy English, a 39-year old bachelor tied to his mother's apron strings and Norah Creedon, the handsome country girl he wants to marry.

Mrs Cleary is determined to retain her son's company and there is a suggestion in the first part of the play that the relation between them is more than that of mother and son.

Without the rest of the play, it is difficult to assess *The Landlady*. But in a relatively short first act Brendan has contrived an interesting situation and has presented his characters with skill.

Mrs Cleary has the news relayed to her by a talkative neighbour, Mrs Kane, that her son is going out with Norah Creedon. She discusses the matter with one of her toadies, Mrs McCann. Later she sends for the offending girl, Norah Creedon. When Mrs Creedon finds out that Mrs Kane has been speaking about her daughter, there is a fight between them which is broken up by Nellie, Mrs Kane's daughter, who has become a prostitute as a result of having an illegitimate child. Norah Creedon is forced to leave Jacko, who is obviously under his mother's thumb. That Norah is pregnant and will subsequently cut her throat we know from Michael Traynor's recollections of the play as he produced it in Mountjoy.

The Landlady has some of the qualities of O'Casey's dramas; the savage sarcasm of the dialogue, the humorous delight in the hypocrisy and change of mood of the characters as they suit their words to different occasions; the poetry underlying their everyday speech. This was not because Brendan was copying O'Casey, but because he was reproducing the same world that O'Casey did.

When Mrs Cleary remarks to Mrs Kane that her daughter's 'trouble' was a hard blow, Mrs Kane replies

> That's what I said to the priest too, and he said that Job, the lad in the Bible went through great difficulties too and came through them, with his flag flying. 'Well, Father,' says I, 'but was Job's daughter left with a bellyful of disgrace by a dirty animal like Mickser Moran, was she Father.' 'Oh' sez he, 'These little crosses are a sign of God's favour.' 'Well, Father', sez I, 'even if they are signs of favour, I'd sooner have no more of the same signs.'
> MRS CLEARY: Wasn't it a wonder the priest didn't make him marry her, even if you didn't want her tied up to the like.
> MRS KANE: Married to Mickser Moran, is it. I'd sooner to see her in the Liffey. I cursed him—and 'twas a great curse—that he mightn't have luck the longest day he lived—that he'd die galloping like O'Mara's ass, calling out for mercy and the priest deaf—that he'd be sent for the time his sins were blackest. I know, Mrs Cleary, it's not right to give anyone the cross word, and I wouldn't wish too much harm, only that he'd fall down the stairs some night he'd drink taken and break his dirty neck.

Though Mrs Cleary is shocked to learn that her son Jacko is going round with a girl, she sees the situation as a device to get rid of 'troublesome' lodgers whom she resents because their rents are regulated by Law.

> Well, I did hear there was music and dancin' but (*sadly*) I think they're entitled to that under the Act, you know, ma'am—that blackguard Lloyd George. Well, it wasn't enough for him to send in the Black and Tans and all, he passed an Act during the last war lettin' the tenants bate ye, almost, and he stopped you risin' the rent if they were there before the war, and there's many a tenant near enough to know all about it, and quote you this clause and that paragraph out of it.

She abuses her son for letting people know his age:

> Thirty-nine! In the name of God keep your big mouth shut—it's a wonder ye didn't stop the Insurance man in the street to tell him that— thirty-nine! My God, I'm hardly that age myself on the policy. And if ye are anxious to get married, God knows I wouldn't stand in yer way, but in the name of the Lord, get yerself a nice clean dacent girl—and don't be looking for—(*here apparently she is stifled by emotion.*)

There are vivid phrases in the dialogue.

> A slut of a woman who is as squeezed out as a melodeon at a wake.
> She'd sing High Mass for me if I'd give a stick to hit the bell with.
> My Jacko will marry your daughter when an Irishman cries at an Englishman's grave.

While there are elements in this section of *The Landlady* which belong more to the short story form than to drama, in production the whole work could have been considerably tightened, and the less effective episodes omitted.

Though he was now plunged into a revolutionary hotbed in Mountjoy and the bitterness between the Government and the I.R.A. was at its height, Brendan seems to have decided at this time to adopt a literary rather than a revolutionary career. A number of his companions in jail had literary interests. Some were intellectual. Some, like Traynor, actually wrote stories and drafts for novels, but none of them afterwards continued to write seriously. Brendan on the other hand had conceived a set purpose. After this, he would be a writer first and his duty as a revolutionary would have to take second place, though he later never ceased to feel guilty about this.

A letter he wrote to his friend Bob Bradshaw from Arbour

Hill jail, where he had been moved, makes it clear what direction his mind was taking. He had sent Bradshaw a copy of *The Landlady*.

Arbour Hill Jail,
Dublin.
Saturday, December 4, '43.

Dear Bob,

You are the elect of God. In that you are the first person I ever wrote to by return of post. Of course this won't be posted till Wednesday, but still, considering that there are people who wrote to me twelve months ago and I haven't had time to answer them yet, you should be 'ighly h-onoured. Well, I thoroly enjoyed your letter for a start and was in general agreement with your sentiments expressed regarding the landlady. You note the lack of inverted commas. The L'lady is, or was, a very genuine person to me (I'm getting literary and so am attempting to be legible). She was to every one that knew her, in just the same way as you are to your fellow-inhabitants of Bray or Enniskerry or whatever outlandish place you've pitched your tent, or I am to the bloke in the next cell to me (that's not a very good comparison. Tom Boule, ex-Civil Servant chap lives next door and tho' we sometimes earnestly discuss religion, he seeks my salvation, we know very little of each other.) Because the landlady, like you guessed when you gave me that much pull over Synge, really lived. Ask our Sean, he knew her well and all the rest of the tribe, too. I don't mean to say that any of them are exactly and in every detail as I described them (and I painted them, didn't photograph them). But I do claim to have taken nine real Dublin slummies and stuck them on paper. I even go so far as to claim that they are as genuine as any of O'Casey's battalion—maybe more so, because O'Casey was born a Protestant and that seems a big lot. But them that says they're not true-to-life, are illiterate. They definitely are, and I hope you'll tell them so. You might also add that they have their excrement—in bucketfuls. No, I don't think the faults of the piece lie there. I've a good idea of them and the principal one is that altho' one section of my family were then and are, immersed in the theatre, I myself never went to a play except to be entertained and sometimes even left the theatre then before the third act had got under way in the pursuit of drink. Therefore I know little of the art of stagecraft and, until I had the idea of writing plays, cared less. And I can safely say that the plays of which I've seen two thirds left me with the idea that any literate person could do that sort of thing, which is, I discovered, a bad way to approach anything. Then of course since I was 16 (all but a few months) I've been in jails and Borstal institutions. I don't regret my time in England. (I.R.A. prisoners in Ireland I've discovered are an uninteresting and boring lot.) It provided me with material for a book on Borstal which I'll get fixed up after the war and with material for numberless short stories, one of which *Borstal Day* you may borrow from Sean, you know the address, don't you? 70 Kildare Road. You can see an improvement in the caligraphy, can't you? The first lot was written at great speed as we, in here, were in the throes of an election. By the way, tell Sean that Jim Griffith took *Borstal Day* with him after the visit. I had some other stuff I'd like you to have seen. Some short stories about the '39 campaign and the beginning of a long novel I'm doing on it, title *The Green Invaders*. Traynor, Adams, etc., have apparently accepted me as a sort of official historian of it and it's with their assistance I'm doing it. (I mean in the line of verifying facts, etc.— the impressions noted and conclusions drawn will of course be mine.) Mickey (Traynor) himself has taken to short stories and I'm damned sure they'd be publishable if he were outside. He has the rather rugged style that seems to be expectable (Joyce couldn't do better!) from the North. Anything he writes is well worth reading. His stories are rather sparse and economical, but this I consider a great advantage more than anything else. Of course, you are a rather sparse and economical people up there, except yourself Bob, who was born a naturalised Dubliner. Excuse the incoherency of this and the Ogham style handwriting. I'll write you a decent letter when I've time. Get the story from Sean. I believe your friend Sheehy has read the play. Ask him if he would give me an idea of it, I'm sure it would be helpful. Please post the enclosed to Miss Maureen Mooney, Bolton Parade, Dublin.

See you in Church,
Brendan.

P.S. I think the Nazis are finished and if I'm to be shot for the admission I can't say I'm sorry.

P.P.S. If you can get me the loan of books of any sort or degree I'll make novenas for you.

P.P.P.S. You and I'd better curb our Social Consciences. I'm very sorry that you are out of Solus Teo.[1] I thought you'd a good berth there. Stand up to your conscience like a man. Don't let it ride you altogether. I intend to put a curb on my own when I get out.

Years later, when he gave a copy of his play *The Quare Fellow* to Sean O'Briain, he was to write on it:

I bpriosun teann niorbh annamh duinn sport agus greann.
(Held fast in prison had we not laughter and sport.)

[1] Solus Teo is an Irish electrical manufacturing company.

Another most important thing from Brendan's point of view was that this prison interim gave him the opportunity to learn Irish well. Sean O'Briain was a schoolteacher and a native speaker and, under his tuition, Brendan very quickly became a good and then a fluent Gaelic speaker. O'Briain was a walking repository of the Munster Gaelic poetic tradition, O'Bruadair, Merriman, O'Suilleabhain and others. He had a copy of Merriman's *Midnight Court* with him in prison: 'We needed something to fall back on.' *The Midnight Court*, an eighteenth-century Rabelaisian satire on the hypocrisy of Church and State, became a sort of bible among the prisoners, who would quote bits of it to each other as they passed in the exercise yard: 'It was a sort of gospel of defiance.'

O'Briain knew these poems as an educated Scot would know Burns or an Englishman Shakespeare. They were part of a tradition he had grown up with and he communicated his familiarity and enthusiasm to Brendan. No doubt there were Gaelic enthusiasts in prison who liked Irish poetry simply because it was in Irish and not in English, but there were others who had grown up in the tradition and who loved it because it was fine poetry and liked to recite it and discuss it among themselves with the excitement that lovers of high language everywhere enjoy.

'Brendan truly loved the language and the literature', recalls Sean O'Briain. 'He had a great *gradh* (love) for the *Cuirt* (*The Midnight Court*), and also for *An tOileannach* (*The Island Man*) and the stories of Sean-Phadraig O Conaire. He went far deeper into the subject than his gaiety would suggest, and he loved to talk and learn about life in the Blaskets, Dun Chaoin and Ballyferriter.'

In prison too, Brendan encountered men of iron endurance who had undergone long hunger-strikes. Some of them, like Mick Traynor, were survivors of the December 1940 hunger-strike which lasted forty-one days and during which two I.R.A. men, Darcy and McNeela, had died. No weapon was more calculated to terrify an Irish government. They remembered the effect of hunger-strike on their own campaign for freedom between 1916 and 1921. Waves of spiritual strength had been unleashed in the people as a result of the deaths of Terence MacSwiney, Lord Mayor of Cork, and Thomas Ashe.

On more than one occasion during World War II, the Government's fate trembled in the balance as the sap of life oozed out of stubborn republicans, dying for an ideal which, if it was confused at first, became as the strike continued more and more indentified in the public mind with recognizable religious parallels. It was the perfect expression of the nihilist doctrine, a destruction of self that bred converts to the creed which the sufferer had put himself upon the rack for. There is about their sacrifice the superb purity of classical Russian nihilism, nourished by the Christ-image and the mystical element in the religion of both peoples.

Brendan grew to admire the fortitude and stoicism of these men who had suffered such privations and never forgot it in later years. Their asceticism was to be his ideal, however much he failed to live up to it himself. He would hear the I.R.A. men discuss their strikes in technical terms like boxing or bull-ring afficionados:

Sean did thirty days' hunger strike but he wasn't a patch on Liam. Liam did forty days' hunger and thirst—that was a record. Did you know that MacSwiney took water every third day?

While Brendan was in Mountjoy prison, two prisoners were in the condemned cells awaiting execution. One of them, Bernard Kirwan, was in for the gruesome crime of killing his brother. With some training as a butcher, he had dissected him so skilfully that not even the State pathologist was able to identify the sex of the torso found in the bog. But circumstantial evidence trapped him in the end. He was a strange outsider of a man, dark-featured, extremely good-looking, a creature baffled by society, who, in better circumstances, might have made his mark on life. He and Brendan met occasionally. The night before he was hanged, he said to Brendan: 'I'll be praying for you in Heaven tonight.' The warder said Kirwan balanced a glass of water on his hand to show how cool he was before he went to be hanged. Later, when Brendan came to write *The Quare Fellow*, he based it on the reaction throughout the prison to Kirwan's hanging. The other prisoner was Timothy Flynn who was due to be topped for shoving his wife down a well. He was later found insane and committed to a criminal lunatic asylum.

'I always said', said Paddy Kelly, who was in prison with Brendan at the time, 'that he saved Timmy Flynn's life. Brendan used to prance around the prison in trousers and bare feet without a jersey or vest on in summer. Flynn was waiting execution for the murder of his wife, Hannah. Brendan used to come up behind him and suddenly shout, 'Ding dong dell, Hannah's in the well, who threw her in, little Timmy Flynn.' This used to make Flynn so angry that he had to be held down. Subsequently his sentence was commuted and he was sent to Dundrum Asylum. I think Brendan put him in there with his antics.'

In June 1943, the political prisoners in Mountjoy were moved to Arbour Hill Prison and three months after that they were transferred to an internment camp in the Curragh. The Curragh is a military encampment on a stark, flat plain in County Kildare, about thirty miles south-west of Dublin. The famous racecourse is nearby. It is in fact an Irish Aldershot and in British days it was a centre for military training for the whole of Ireland. Here the I.R.A. prisoners found themselves in the same camp with German, British and Canadian prisoners of war, most of them pilots and other air crew interned after forced-landings in Eire. As Brendan put it: 'The I.R.A. didn't take sides. We were neutral, in favour of one side only, our own.'

A few days after he had arrived at Arbour Hill, as he sat up at a party in the Military Hospital drinking Guinness and eating chicken, he turned round to a friend and said: 'Make no mistake about it, this is a good kip.' One of the military police, that night supplied music and sang arias from 'Lucia di Lammermor' and 'Faust'. The Irish army, during the periods they were required to look after political prisoners, on the whole managed to do so with the maximum of efficiency and the minimum of severity.

Brendan always kept his memories of the Curragh as pleasant ones. After all, he had time there to do what he wanted to his heart's content. He liked to read; he wanted to learn Irish and read Irish poetry. He was among native speakers and men to whom a turn of phrase or a quotation in Gaelic was second nature.

He always kept a sort of narcissistic memory of himself at this period as having 'nice teeth, good hair, good complexion, no stomach, clean skin and as light on my feet as a feather'. Drink was limited, the air was healthy and the food was good. He was so fit he ran round the entire compound one night stark naked for a bet although snow was on the ground. There were classes every day in the Irish and French languages, European history and literature. Some of these were given by university professors and Brendan joined in those which suited him. His Irish progressed so well that before he left he was almost indistinguishable from a native speaker; and he had learnt a great deal of seventeenth and eighteenth century Gaelic poetry by heart, including the whole of Brian Merriman's epic *The Midnight Court*.

When he left prison, Brendan was to pay many visits to the Blasket Islands, Dingle, Connemara and other Irish-speaking parts of Ireland. He found himself accepted there and at home as he was nowhere else except among his own people in Dublin. Here the two elements in his background fused into one, the indigenous culture of Dublin and the folk culture of the countryside which he had first come in contact with in the Gaelic clubs in Parnell Square.

For six years after he left prison the Irish language was to obsess him. He wrote his poetry only in Gaelic; the first versions of two of his three plays were in Gaelic: *The Hostage* in 1958 and *A Fine Day in the Graveyard* in 1962. Through Irish he was seeking to touch that hidden spring that might unlock the ancestral memory in the back of his mind and bring it to full fruition in the tongue of O'Casey, Wilde and Joyce, the English of his native Dublin.

At the Curragh he translated his first play *The Landlady* into Gaelic and sent it by instalments to Ernest Blythe the Managing Director of the Abbey Theatre. He explains in a letter written on May 18 how he had been rewriting the play as well as putting it into Gaelic.

Dear Sir,

I enclose the first Act of my play—*The Landlady*—you might, perhaps, also be interested in the bilingual sketch '*L' o Loin*. If I don't get word from you that it is not worth continuing with, I will go on with rewriting the other two Acts, and I will send them to you next week. As regards *The Landlady*—I had two Acts written of a play in English and one of a play in Irish—they both had a fault—the characters of the two plays should be in one play, for they came from the same period of my life and from the same house—I decided to bring them together—that's what I did in *The Landlady*.

I have written one Act of another play. *The Twisting of Another Rope* I call it, because everything is shown in the *black cell* in some prison. Two men are condemned to death and waiting for the Rope—I would send it with this but better not scare the Department of Justice before we have anything done. There is nothing political in it, of course. I'll send it to you, if you like.

Every thanks to yourself, Ernest Blythe for your kindness to,

Brendan Behan

P.S. You know I have no chance of typing the M.S.

It is clear from this letter that he had begun in 1946 the first draft for the play that he was later to make his name with in London *The Quare Fellow*. It's original name was *The Twisting of Another Rope*.

A few weeks later he wrote to Ernest Blythe again telling him of his plans for a novel.

Cell 8, The Glass House,
The Curragh of the Liffey Plain.
Friday, 6–VI–46.

Dear Ernest Blythe,

I hope you will excuse me writing this letter to you personally, instead of sending it to the Manager under the official title, but I should like, first of all, to thank you for your kindness to me. There is another reason. I should like to enter the competition which the Oireachtas has for a novel. Could you give me permission to go in for the competition? I have no novel written, but for a hundred pounds, I could translate *Finnegans Wake* into Irish. Here is the third Act of *The Landlady*, and again, I thank you sincerely.

Brendan Behan

The I.R.A. had split into groups by this time in the Curragh: those who supported the official I.R.A., those who supported the unofficial I.R.A., and those who formed a group of their own. Brendan belonged to none of these but sympathized with all of them. Occasionally events outside helped to unify them. In October 1944, Charles Kerins was sentenced to be hanged for the killing of Detective Sergeant O'Brien in the autumn of 1942. There were protests all over the country, and in the Dáil (the Irish Parliament) violent scenes took place. Deputy Finucane, of Kerry, said the night before the execution: 'His name will live until Fianna Fail (the Government party) is blasted into oblivion.' (the Government party) is blasted into oblivion.'

Two years later, in May 1946, Sean McCaughey died on hunger strike in Portlaoise prison. He had refused to wear prison clothes. This was a traditional form of protest among political prisoners in Ireland beginning with the Parliamentarian, William O'Brien, who had remained naked for three months in 1896 before being allowed the privilege he demanded.

Twelve years previously, the I.R.A. had helped Mr de Valera to power, believing that he would support their objectives.

'We did all the usual things for Mr de Valera's party in the 1932 election,' Sean MacBride, former Chief of Staff of the I.R.A. and later Secretary of the International Organisation of Jurists, recalls. 'We canvassed from door-to-door. We ferried people to vote. We organized groups. We even spoke at meetings and, of course, we heckled.'

Now, under the same Government, a little more than a decade later, internees at the Curragh saw companions taken out and shot, and others allowed to die on hunger-strike. The very methods which the first Free State government had used against the de Valera Republicans in the Civil War of 1923, de Valera himself was now using against the I.R.A.; executions, imprisonments, arrest without warrant, trial by court martial. But those who seek equity should do so with clean hands. The I.R.A. knew, many people in the country knew, that as regards the shooting of Irish soldiers and police twenty years before, the hands of some members of the Government were far from clean.

Perhaps, with Ireland treading the tight-rope of neutrality in World War II, a violent conflict between the Government and the I.R.A. was inevitable. Certainly it is not hard to understand the bitterness and disillusion of the internees.

Brendan, though, does not seem to have been affected by it, perhaps because he was already half way out of the revolutionary mould. Besides, unless you took life very seriously, there was much gaiety, roguery and laughter in the camp—as there is likely to be whenever Irishmen get together anywhere.

In the summer of 1946, most of the prisoners were released, but Brendan was among those selected to remain behind. There were only twenty-two of them and these last internees were fed like fighting cocks. But he was longing to get out. Five years of his manhood had been spent in prison of some sort.

On Christmas Day, these last few in the camp made illegal poteen (Irish whiskey) between them. First of all, keeping strictly to the tradition, they gave the first three drops from the 'worm' to the fairies. Then all got plastered, together with the Military Police who sang rebel songs with loud ferocity in company with their prisoners.

A few days later, Brendan was released under a general amnesty.

CHAPTER SEVEN

IMMEDIATELY after the war ended, Dublin was deluged with visitors. Ireland had been neutral for five years and possessed in abundance what the war-starved countries hungered after. There was no food or clothes rationing. The English and American servicemen stationed in England flowed in to sample what seemed to them riches beyond measure—steaks in Jammet's Restaurant or the Dolphin, butter and cream in abundance, your tweed suit cut to measure in a week. The Dublin clubs were full of stories of unfortunate Englishmen who had eaten too much too quickly and had to return to their own rationed land before their stomachs could recover.

For a while, in fact, the city became a sort of Atlantic Havana. An illegal casino flourished in Mount Merrion. 'Scotty', a retired army captain who ran it, claimed to have six Daimlers, four Rolls Royces and a brace of Jaguars in his yard, the property of clients who had gambled not only their money but their means of transport as well.

Drug-peddlers, touts, chancers, con-men, blackmailers, flitted in and out of the bars and race-tracks. It was typical of the euphoria of the time that the two most notorious operators in the city should have been the son of a Baronet and an Alderman's son educated at the Jesuit College of Belvedere. Their speciality was to lure American priests into bed with their mutual girl-friend: then either would enter the room with a revolver and claim compensation from the terrified padre for seducing their wife.

Down Grafton Street like a figure out of a Greek myth strode Jack Doyle, film star, lover, boxer and singer, six feet three inches in height and of astonishing good looks. In America, he had been discouraged by more than one family to prevent their daughters marrying him. As he strode down the most fashionable street of the city with his Irish wolf hound and his film-star wife, Movita (she later married Marlon Brando), he seemed to epitomize something of the spirit of those Dublin years.

Life in the city was geared to the needs of the pleasure-seeker. The pace was still fluid in a place where gentry and professional men had not yet to compete with commercial pressures on a large scale. Within an hour of Grafton Street there were ten race-courses, twenty-seven golf courses and six yacht clubs, all regularly patronized and not just at week-ends. Fashionable Dublin wore an air of affluence. Michael Farmer, Gloria Swanson's former husband, who lived in Pembroke Road, once hired a pilot to fly him round the Spa Hotel in Lucan for a bet. When he came back to the hotel to collect his wager, he gave the hundred pounds he had won to the barmaid to buy nylons.

Two things had altered the literary scene—the war and the death of Yeats in 1939. Drama had benefited from enforced isolation. With no outside competition, the theatres were crowded. Literature on the other hand was subject to a severe censorship by a board which had succeeded in banning practically every living Irish writer of note, except, inexplicably, James Joyce.

The isolation of the war had given impetus to a reactionary element who favoured censorship of a lunatic kind. Writers like Sean O'Faolain, who edited *The Bell*, were forced to syphon off energy, which they would have better spent at writing, in combating the pietistic and philistine elements who were gaining power in the community.

Salon life was gone. Yeats's Monday, Æ's Wednesday and George Moore's Friday had been occasions when writers and poets had gathered in the high period of the Irish literary revival. Now the younger writers tended to meet in pubs and, in reaction perhaps against the mild dandyism of the drawing-room scene of the decades before, they tended to pay less attention to their personal appearances. The London literary pubs of Soho and Fitzrovia had their counterparts in Dublin in the 'forties. The sawdust floor and unpainted walls, the slight smell of unwashed bodies in McDaid's in Harry Street—this was the new Bohemia's answer to the Salon.

This tendency towards a Chelsea atmosphere was accelerated to some extent by the presence of a group called the 'White Stags'. These were mostly English writers, artists and poets who had come over to avoid the war, and included T. H. White (*The Once and Future King*), Basil Rakosi and Phyllis Teal. Remnants of the old literary set met in the Bodega in Dame Street, presided over by Seamus O'Sullivan, one of the last of the poets of the renaissance, and editor of the *Dublin Magazine*.

In the 'twenties upper-class Protestant Dublin, following in the footsteps of the landed gentry, had discovered the 'literary thing'. From tennis club and croquet lawn, with a background of public school and good form, came Samuel Beckett, Denis Johnston, Ralph Cusack, Patrick Campbell and actresses like Geraldine Fitzgerald, Sheila H. Richards and Betty Chancellor. Their parents' class had tended to reject the Celtic Twilight as a landed gentry hallucination, and maintained an ambivalent attitude towards the new state whose formation had deprived them of much of the social position inherited from the old regime. They preferred the Gate Theatre of MacLiammóir and Edwards with its avant-garde European atmosphere to Yeats's and Lady Gregory's Abbey with its emphasis on cottage and tenement life. The late Lord Glenavy, who earlier had connections with the Bloomsbury group, kept a weekly evening going at which this set largely predominated. Lord Glenavy, who had thrown in his lot with the Free State by becoming a higher Civil Servant, frequently at these evenings took issue with her Ladyship, a painter of distinction who, despite her husband's political outlook, regarded the leaders of the Rising as irresponsible and lacking in manners 'who had set Ireland back fifty years with silly notions about a blood bath'.

Yeats's death had had a tremendous effect on the Irish literary scene. He had been the Arch-priest, the father figure of the renaissance. He had shaped it, moulded it, encouraged Joyce and Synge, helped O'Casey and watched over the birth of countless other writers. Now he was gone and younger artists had set out to shake themselves free of his influence. Later they would return to him as the source of the modern Irish imagination. Presently they were in revolt.

'I no longer need Yeats. I have outgrown him', Patrick Kavanagh, the leader of the new poets, declared at a public meeting: it became fashionable to denigrate Lady Gregory, Hyde and Synge, as gentry unable to interpret the true peasant spirit for modern Ireland.

Though Brendan did not decry Yeats, as a good Socialist he could not bear to admit that the landed gentry had had anything to do with the Irish literary renaissance. He was constantly inveighing against what he called the 'Horse Protestants'. (His definition of an Anglo-Irishman was 'a Protestant on a horse'.) Ingeniously he separated Yeats, Wolfe Tone, Robert Emmet and Sheridan and others whom he admired, from the 'Horse Protestants' by pointing out that they were from the Protestant middle-class and not the gentry. He conveniently ignored the fact that the renaissance had come out of three great country houses within an hour's distance of one another—Lady Gregory's Coole, Edward Martyn's Tulira and George Moore's Moore Hall—and that Douglas Hyde, the John the Baptist of the movement, came also from this despised gentry or 'Horse Protestant' class. As he was to write to Sindbad Vail in June, 1942:

Not that the aforesaid Horse-Protestants were any better. They've been longer at it. They are just as ignorant except that their ill manners are sharpened by time: the myth of the Anglo-Irish (Brinsley Sheridan, a peasant's grandson; Yeats, artist's son; Wilde, a doctor's son; Wolfe Tone, a coach-painter's son; Parnell, the grandson of an American sea-captain; Robert Emmet, a doctor's son; Bernard Shaw, a clerk) and the present attempt to drag Irish writers who happened to be Protestant after the fox-hunt and the Royalist inanity, would have us believe that the most rapacious rack-renting class in Europe were really lamps of culture in a bog of darkness, doing good by stealth and shoving copies of *Horizon* under the half-doors of the peasantry after dark and making wedding presents to the cottagers of Ganymed Press reproductions of Gaugin.

There is, of course, no such thing as an Anglo-Irishman, as Shaw pointed out in the preface to *John Bull's Other Island*; except as a class distinction. All Protestant genius, even, is not nobbled for the stable boys and girls.

It must at least wear a collar and tie. Sean O'Casey is not claimed as an would hold on the sill of a Northside tenement: the Belfast industrial workers who are the thickest concentration of Royalism and pro-Britishism in Ireland are never claimed as Anglo-Irish, and Lady —— would feel herself a brood sister to a Shankhill Road Orangeman only at such times as the Mick niggers were getting out of hand and he could shoulder a gun for her, like Scarlett O'Hara and the poor white.

As often with Brendan, his opinions were probably influenced by his current activities. Shortly after he left prison, he began to mingle with the bohemian set and had got into the habit of attending parties given by a well-meaning lady in her country house near Dublin. To her home, in the hope of creating a literary ambience, were invited younger members of what passed for the London literary set and any local gentry who liked to come and gawk. The object of most who hurried from London at the news was to pick up convenient colleens and free beer. Dublin Bohemia, who crowded in once they heard what was going on, had much the same idea.

But this was not Lady Gregory's salon or Sarah Purser's, and Brendan should have known better than to confuse it with them.

CHAPTER EIGHT

THE first contact in the literary world that Brendan made after he left prison was with John Ryan. Ryan was an attractive young man of some wealth which he derived from a family chain of creameries. A year or two later, he was to found and edit an excellent literary magazine *Envoy*. Ryan had I.R.A. sympathies and had first encountered Brendan as a released internee. He was surprised to find that he had literary aspirations. Brendan came up one day to borrow his typewriter. When Ryan saw the sort of stuff Brendan was producing, he recognized his talent immediately and was later to publish him in *Envoy*.

> He was rather good looking when I first met him. He'd classical features, a mane of black hair and extraordinarily small hands and feet. His feet at the same time were extremely neat.

At six o'clock, young writers and artists used to meet in Desmond MacNamara's studio. He had his rooms above one of Ryan's Monument Creameries in Grafton Street, the main Dublin street. MacNamara was a sculptor and papier mâché worker who had known Brendan slightly when he had been a boy in the Irish Worker's League before the war. Among regular visitors to the studio were J. P. Donleavy, Phyllis Teal, Ernie Gebler (later to marry Edna O'Brien), Dan O'Herlihy, H. A. L. Craig, Patrick Kavanagh and Anthony Cronin. Former I.R.A. internees, Peter Walsh and Eddie Connell, their intellect sharpened by the austerities of prison life, were others who turned up from time to time. Erwin Schroedinger, who had provided the equation for Einstein's theory of relativity, was a shy but clever talker at these gatherings. He would say, at the end of a particularly brilliant exposition of some point: 'I'm only a naïve physicist.'

The remarks were not always in such a mild key. Once, an aggressive young woman, enraged that the poet Kavanagh had not offered her a drink, said 'Did you not see I had a mouth on me?'

'How could I miss it,' said Kavanagh, 'and it swinging between your two ears like a skipping-rope'.

Across the road in Harry Street, Tom Nisbet, the water-colour painter, had a studio beneath his gallery. Brendan was a frequent visitor, bursting noisily down the iron stairs into the studio at all hours. Next door to Nisbet's was McDaid's pub, where the group gathered for their drinking and where the publican was known as 'Mr Er', because of his inability to re-member any customer's name.

In this milieu, Brendan first appeared publicly as a brilliant raconteur, singer and mime. Often it took time for him to grip his audience. But after a while he would get on the beam and keep them entertained for hours. He was an inspired harlequin who could act all other parts in the *commedia*. Bob Bradshaw, to whom Brendan had sent his play, *The Landlady*, from prison, remembers how Brendan could continue all night with an in-exhaustible repertoire of songs, stories, imitations and parodies at a party.

> The parties would often begin in daylight and end in it, but Brendan would never stop. He had a beautiful tenor voice and of course he knew every ballad there was. People who only met Brendan in later days can have no idea what he was like. Singing, mimicry, everything; he would do Toulouse-Lautrec the painter and D. H. Lawrence, interspersed with songs and ballads. The impersonations had a high intellectual quality.

Benedict Kiely, the novelist, remembers this same ability:

> He was the most entertaining companion I've ever known. One night in Michael O'Connell's 'White Horse', he had us sick with laughter at his antics. One minute he was Toulouse-Lautrec, walking up and down the floor on his knees; the next he was The Poor Old Woman, Mother Ireland, with the tail of his coat over his head for a shawl; then an inspiring Irish politician mouthing every platitude ever heard from an Irish platform and borrowing a few from the pulpit; and then sex in the Abbey Theatre, for which there were no words but only a very personal mime. I remember thinking then if he only got a wider audience, he'd make a fortune.

Anthony Cronin, the novelist and poet, in whose room Brendan occasionally slept at this time, remembers how he would roll up in the early hours of the morning to give his impression of famous figures in literature whom he would place against grotesque and ludicrous backgrounds. After a while Cronin discovered that these were based on Frank Swinnerton's *The Georgian Scene* which Brendan was currently reading. This, however, made them no less funny since Brendan changed their mood completely in the way he presented and acted them.

One of them was Ruskin counting the stones of Venice with his mother; another was D. H. Lawrence and his mother at a football match. Then there was Rupert Brooke down a coal mine. Brendan's real gift should have been as a cabaret entertainer.

John Ryan has been able to recall the details of one or two of Brendan's charades. One of his most memorable was a send up of the late Paul Vincent Carroll's plays. Carroll had had a Broadway success with *Shadow and Substance*, a play about the conflict between an out-of-date parish priest and a new-thinking young curate.

In a pub or in a drawing-room, anywhere, he would suddenly leap up and go into this act. He used to imitate the Canon by getting into a chair and pretending it was a wheelchair.

He would do all the movements of turning the wheels with his hands as he moved the chair across the room. He would then call on the house-keeper. The housekeeper would come in and Brendan would put his coat over his head to resemble a shawl. There would be a lot of stuff about 'hot toddy', 'not enough whiskey', and the housekeeper would grumble, 'You'll have to get out of the wheelchair to get it'. Then the young curate would enter, full of bright ideas, raffles and trips to the country. Brendan would be the young curate. Then he would mention a dance on Friday night and he would jump back into the Canon's part.

CANON: 'What are you torturing me about? Didn't I tell you you could have lemonade at the dance?'

CURATE (nervously): 'But, Canon, I was wondering about the men and the women.'

The Canon would turn round irritatedly, using his hands to swing the wheels of the chair round all the time, and say:

'What about the men and women? Didn't I tell you you could have men and women at the dance?'

CURATE (this time very nervous): 'Yes, Canon, but I was wondering if you would allow the men and the women to dance with each other.'

CANON: 'How dare you! I might as well have a Protestant for a curate as you.'

Brendan would also do a version of Dame Clara Butt singing the Lord's Prayer in Welsh on a pre-1914 gramophone record. It came out with an extraordinary cacophony of sounds. As in the old records, the voice of Thomas Edison, full of crackles and scratches, would announce 'This is an Edison-Bell recording'. Then he had another one on Hugh MacDiarmid, the Scottish poet: he would pull up his trousers and put his coat round his waist for a kilt and then say, in a Scotch accent, 'I will now sing you a Scottish border ballad—scarcely more than eighty verses'. The ballad would usually begin with something like:

> You can squiggle your giggle,
> You can toggle your noggle.

I remember another act of Brendan's. One day I was in McDaid's pub. Suddenly the door opened and there was no one behind it. It was quite uncanny. Then I looked down and I saw a hand on the floor. It was Brendan's. A voice said 'Enter an Irish peasant disguised as a Scullabogue'. Slowly the hand came forward and behind it came his nibs, with an agonised face on him. He was up in a second, of course, roaring, laughing and ready for a drink.

Tom Nisbet remembers an impersonation of Brendan's when he would lay himself out as an I.R.A. hero in death, with an accompanying commentary which included Gaelic, English and Latin responses for the dead. 'With the candles which he had placed around him lighting his face it seemed in an uncanny way to become pallid as in death; only a Rembrandt or Daumier could have done justice to him.' The extraordinary thing was that he could embark on these long hours of performance with the remains of a stutter still in his speech. The slight stoppage which he retained from his childhood was much more noticeable on tapes and records: it is probable that his magnetic personality and the mobility of his face diminished the deficiency once he was face to face with his listeners.

Singing played an important part in his repertoire. He had a splendid voice, a high tenor. As he sang, the tension and violence would disappear from his face and the sensitive human being came to the surface, especially when he was singing the slow Gaelic airs which he had a feeling for, like 'Róisín Dhu' and 'The Coolin'.

Once he sang 'The Coolin' after coming out of Davy Byrne's public house in Duke Street at closing time. Eamonn Martin, a writer and I.R.A. friend, who asked him to sing it that evening recalls:

> I was never so proud of anything in my life as having asked Brendan to sing that night. There was a usual noise of people coming out of pubs, doors slamming, chatter, cars starting up. But his voice rose over it all. Suddenly there was silence. There we stood in the street, people of different types and background, while Brendan with his head thrown back, lost in a dream of his own, sang in a full-throated tenor a song of a girl in the fields 400 years before. It was the beauty and passion of the way he sang it that held the crowd. Windows were opened in flats, and when he finished there was a sudden hush and then a burst of clapping. Magic!

(In 'The Coolin' a girl sings of her lover and his 'golden head of hair'. It is a sixteenth century air referring to an English law which forbade the Irish to wear their hair Gaelic fashion, straight back, and with no parting).

Brendan had a flair for practical jokes of an elaborate kind. Once, he and Desmond Macnamara planned to erect a statue of Brendan overnight in Stephen's Green in the centre of Dublin. It was to be called Monsieur Rabelais, and would appear suddenly one morning in the park, green with age, as if it had been there for years. They even planned to manufacture artificial bird-droppings to give the statue an authentically venerable appearance. Macnamara spent some time modelling the head—a splendid, jowlish Rabelais-Brendan. But Brendan had gone to prison again before the rest of the job could be finished.

On another occasion in County Down in Ulster, Brendan landed himself a job painting lighthouses. A tweedy Presbyterian lady of Loyalist background became suspicious of his Dublin accent and began to spy on him. To raise her blood pressure, he painted on the door of the lighthouse 'Permission to use this building must be obtained from Eamonn de Valera, Dail Eireann,

Dublin'. The apoplectic Loyalist ran to the Police Station to report the outrage. By the time she came back Brendan had painted it over again and was cheeky enough to suggest that the lady should see a psychiatrist, preferably a Catholic one.

It was known at this time that Brendan was writing poems and short stories. When he was at the Curragh he had written to Valentine Iremonger, the most notable of the younger Irish poets at the time, to ask if he could translate some of his poems into Gaelic. But Brendan had never succeeded in having anything published, apart from newspaper articles and his Borstal account in *The Bell*, so he was not taken seriously as a writer at this time.

He was also known to have bi-sexual tastes.

John Ryan remembers he was quite open about this, even defining the type he liked best: 'clean-skinned fresh lads'. And Desmond MacNamara remembers he would usually add to this statement: 'Preferably working-class.'

Brendan used to boast about it almost as if it was a new discovery he had made at Borstal. He would refer to it half-mockingly as his 'Hellenism'. It did not worry him particularly, perhaps because he was equally attracted to girls.

'Brendan would get up on anything in those years', an I.R.A. man put it to me. Another I.R.A. officer remembers the shock he got when he was walking down Fleet Street after an I.R.A. meeting in Jury's Hotel in the centre of Dublin and came on Brendan in an alley kissing a man they both knew well, a composer with left-wing sympathies, though he was not a member of the I.R.A. What puzzled Brendan's I.R.A. friend was that, a few days previously, he had been involved in trying to get Brendan out of trouble he had got into with a girl whom he had made pregnant.

He had rung up the girl's mother and she had shouted down the phone, thinking it was Brendan who was speaking: 'Brendan Behan, you have destroyed my daughter.'[1]

A few years later, Brendan published a story in *Points* magazine,

[1] Brendan was deeply disturbed over this affair, and had consulted his uncle, Jimmy Bourke, about it. In the end, the woman concerned went to North America, where the child was brought up.

which was published in Paris by Peggy Guggenheim's son, Sindbad Vail. This clearly sets out his interests in men. The story, *After the Wake*, is told in the first person:

> He was tall and blond, with a sort of English blondness. He had, as I said, pretensions to culture and was genuinely intelligent, but that was not the height of his attraction for me.
>
> Once we went out to swim to a weir below the Dublin Mountains. It was evening time and the last crowd of kids—too shrimpish, small, neutral, cold to take my interest—just finishing their bathe.
>
> When they went off, we stripped and watching him I thought of Marlowe's lines—which I can't remember properly:
>
> > Youth with gold wet head, thru'
> > water gleaming, gliding, and
> > crowns of pearlets on his naked arms.
>
> When we came out we sat on his towel, our bare thighs touching, smoking and talking.

But 'He' is married and the writer of the story is cast in the role of the admirer of the wife:

> My jealousy of him sweetened by my friendship for them both.

The writer is fond of the wife, but in a different way. When he learns that she has to go into hospital for an operation, his campaign begins in earnest.

> The first step—to make him think it manly—ordinary to manly men— the British Navy—'Porthole Duff', 'Navy Cake', stories of the Hitler Youth in captivity, told me by Irish soldiers on leave from guarding them.
>
> To remove the taint of 'cississess', effeminacy, how the German Army had encouraged it in Cadet Schools, to harden the boy-officers, making their love a muscular clasp of friendship, independent of women—the British Public Schools, young Boxers I'd known, (most of it about the Boxers was true), that Lord Alfred Douglas was son to the Marquess of Queensberry and a good man to use his dukes himself. Oscar Wilde throwing old 'Q' down the stairs and after him his bally boy attendant.
>
> On the other front, appealing to that hope of culture—Socrates, Shakespeare, Marlowe—lies, truth and half-truth.
>
> I worked cautiously but steadily. Sometimes (on the head of a local scandal) in conversation with them both.

The night before she goes into hospital, the schemer sings 'My Mary of the Curling Hair'.

> When we came to the Gaelic chorus—'walk my love'—she broke down in sobbing and said how he knew as well as she that it was to her I was singing, but that he didn't mind. He said that indeed he did not, and she said how fearful she was of this operation, and that maybe she'd never come out of it.

Next day, she is dead. After the wake the plan is followed to its completion, when the husband gets very drunk.

> I had almost to carry him to the big double bed in the inner room.
> I first loosened his collar to relieve the flush on his smooth cheeks, took off his shoes and socks and pants and shirt, from the supple muscled thighs, the stomach flat as an altar boy's and noted the golden smoothness of the blond hair on every part of his firm white flesh.
> I went to the front room and sat by the fire till he called me.
> 'You must be nearly gone yourself', he said, 'you might as well come in and get a bit of rest.'. .
> I sat on the bed, undressing myself by the faint flickering of the candles from the front room.
> I fancied her face looking up from the open coffin, on the Americans who, having imported wakes from us, invented morticians themselves.

This summary hardly does justice to the story which is beautifully worked out with not a word to spare. But that Brendan should have published it as early as 1950 shows that, within limits, he was not averse to showing where his tastes lay.

The extraordinary thing is that he was not generally known in Dublin or elsewhere to have these leanings. This was to some extent due to his being bi-sexual which deflected a good deal of the suspicion which otherwise might have attached to him. But it is also due, no doubt, to his superb sense of public relations. Later on, it would have been disastrous to his image as the 'broth of a boy', soldier of the Republic and 'laughing garsoon', if it became known that he had bi-sexual tastes. With the genius he had for manipulating his image in the public eye, he was able to conceal this side of his nature from the newshounds and present himself in an altogether different light.

Later, when his life was falling apart, he clung desperately to the mask he had created for himself. It terrified him that some rash sexual approach might destroy in a minute the image which it had taken him years to build up and which he recognized was the basis for much of his success.

CHAPTER NINE

CONDITIONS were difficult in the Behan household in the middle 'forties. Brian Behan remembers that his mother used to have a regular 'Goebbels hour' every day, encouraging them to look more industriously for work. But work was not easy to come by in post-war Dublin. The war-time factories in England had closed down. A number of the emigrants had returned. The Irish army, which during the war had absorbed a quarter of the unemployed at its full strength of 80,000, went back once the war was over to its normal strength, and the country returned to its pre-war state of chronic unemployment, eased by the daily flow to the Liverpool and Holyhead boats. Without this safety valve serious unrest could have developed in the country.

Brian remembers that at 70 Kildare Road they had to split a loaf between six at times and even maintains that they once ate the sawdust out of a pincushion, though none of the others can remember this extremity being resorted to. In Granny English's days in Russell Street, the Behans had never known want. They had been persons of substance there, with memories of their former gentility lingering in the neighbourhood. Now they were swallowed up in an anonymous working-class council estate. They were hungry and frustrated by lack of recognition.

We can visualize the scene. Brian, Sean, Brendan and Dominic, all voracious readers, sitting round the fire discussing Marx, Dickens, Joyce, Hemingway, the I.R.A., football—setting off each other's personal and considerable store of information against one another: Kathleen interested in it all as she busies herself about the house and yet, as a practical housewife, wondering how they were going to get the money for the next meal. Stephen, their only regular breadwinner, would arrive in the evening after his day's work, regarding them with a somewhat resigned tolerance and then becoming as worked up as any of them in the argument, discussion and chat that might well end in an evening of singing and drinking they could ill afford to indulge in. None of the boys was completely without work. They were all tradesmen or had been apprenticed to a trade. There was casual labour going but a very small proportion of regular work.

Shortly after he came out of prison, Brendan was offered a job restoring the house of Daniel O'Connell, the nineteenth century Irish leader, in Caherdaniel in County Kerry. A member of the restoration committee had suggested that ex-I.R.A. prisoners released from England be employed in this project. The idea was taken up and another incongruous touch was provided to Irish life: I.R.A. men restoring a house which had been lived in by an Irish nineteenth century leader completely opposed to physical force.

Brendan, to his surprise, found himself appointed foreman. His only exercise of this duty was to fire someone who had reported a fellow worker for drinking on the job. Brendan had been too long in the nick to like squealers. When the job was finished, Brendan returned to Dublin and after Christmas he secured work at Government Buildings which were being re-painted at the time.

He was not exactly a foreman's dream of the ideal painter. He was always singing, arguing, chatting on the job, though he could be first-class at his trade when he applied himself. If the foremen joined issue with him, Brendan was likely to come out with a brilliant display of knowledge of trade union bye-laws to show he was in the right and the foreman wrong. Actually Brendan was only a fourth-year apprentice and was not really a qualified painter at all. But as he said himself, he was almost born in a paint pot, his father being the best sign-painter in Dublin and his grandfather a contractor in the trade. Brendan's reputation for argument and back-chat spread and after only a few months he had become a legend in the trade. A foreman complained to their father about Brendan and Dominic:

The greatest bastards I've ever come across. One wants the men to strike

for an incentive bonus so that the other one can bring them down to the
pub to drink it. And now they told me this morning they want a five-day
week. The only difference being that they want Monday off and double
time for Saturday and Sunday.

Brendan wrote an anthem for the trade which was sung with
gusto by the other workers when the foreman was not present.

Hand me down me paper knife, and me stirring stick,
Hand me down me overalls we've a big job in the nick,
The boss is a quare one, fall di do yeh gow a that
A quare and a rare one I'll tell you.
In the cold hard wintertime they have us on a cross
Stuck up like Christ between two thieves, the foreman and the boss
Who is it that we're workin' for? It isn't he called 'sir',
He has a whore in Monto Town and ye chokin' yer balls for her.
The autumn leaves are falling, the nights are getting dim
There's not a stroke to be done till March, so hand your brushes in.

One day, as he intoned this, he noticed the others were not
joining in with him as heartily as usual and he turned round to
discover the foreman behind him with his cards ready and
instructions to get the hell out of it as quickly as he could.
'Don't sack me, Sir', said Brendan in a mock humble voice,
grovelling at the man's feet, 'I'm a publican and five little barmen
depend on me'.
But he was out of a job again and back at number 70 with his
mother giving him dark looks. He maintained later he was
getting a small monthly allowance at the time from Clan na
Gael (an Irish-American revolutionary group) in America
which he got as an ex-I.R.A. man, but it has not been possible to
check this. One way or another he had very little money to buy
drinks in McDaid's of Harry Street.
Conditions were reverting to those of pre-war days when the
curate in the Behans parish in Kimmage had prepared a survey
which showed that one-third of the people in the area were
unemployed and living on State assistance of one pound a week.
Bound for the Midlands and London each evening, thousands
set off in emigrant boats, most of them to lead troglodytic

existences in British slums relieved by week-end frenzies of drinking till ill-health or alcoholism brought them down in a foreign land far from the friendly laughter of the Gael.

As the unemployment situation got worse, there were marches and demonstrations in the street, after which some of the leaders were prosecuted. Ireland was young and poor. The people had rejected extremes of left and right, a decision which encumbered legislation with the checks imposed by parliamentary democracy. It was to take a few more years before emigration, education and health benefits came under scrutiny from Irish governments. With the I.R.A. in a disorganized condition, the only outlet for the unemployed were strikes, protests and acts of individual defiance.

The Behan household, during this period, became a meeting place for dissatisfied workers. Sean and Brian were Stalinists. For a while they allied themselves with a group which considered employing terrorists' methods against individuals in the community whom they considered were hindering the cause of the workers.

During a farm labourers' strike in 1947, this group planned to assassinate such a man—a rich and influential County Dublin farmer whom they considered was obstructing settlement in the dispute. The plan misfired but it is an indication of the frustration and sense of impotency affecting the under-privileged at the time that such a group should have existed and attempted to carry out such a plan at all.

In a fit of temper one day, Brendan himself actually grabbed a Parabellum revolver and went out to shoot the owner of a dairy in Rathfarnham, who was involved in a strike with his workers. Having reached the house, Brendan was informed that the man was sick upstairs and made the ambiguous rejoiner: 'Well he won't be ill much longer'.

In the family's worst periods, there was Kathleen with her fierce optimism to fall back on. She retained her passionate sense of justice and fair play for the poor, even to the extent of prosecuting a local butcher in 1947 for serving meat underweight in contravention of the current food laws: her less civic-minded neighbours called her a Communist for her troubles. No calamity, however fearful, seemed to daunt her. She had a witticism, a proverb or a song to divert it, and was always on the lookout to convert a day of disaster into an evening of music and song with her talented family.

She regarded her children as a brood in need of constant protection, even when they had become adult with families living outside Ireland. There was an occassion she was being interviewed in a programme on British television. At the time, her son Brian was involved in a massive building strike on the South Bank of the Thames.

In the warm-up for the programme during the afternoon, the interviewer had asked her casually had she had trouble with Brian as a child, intending presumably to imply during the programme that Brian's trade union activities were connected with his early delinquency. Kathleen said yes, Brian did give her trouble. On the programme that night, the interviewer asked her with a smirk: 'And now, Mrs Behan, your son Brian, didn't you have a lot of trouble with him as a boy?'

'Not at all', she replied, 'he was one of the best boys I ever reared. I hear he's causing a lot of strikes over here and more power to his elbow.' She turned to the interviewer: 'Sure the working man never got anything without fighting for it, did he?'

As Brian says, 'What could the man do, but smile wanly and say what a wonderful woman she was.'

After Christmas, in January 1947, Jim Larkin died. Nearly forty years before, he had arrived as a Messiah to the stricken Dublin proletariat. He had pulled them off their knees and promulgated the message that they were no longer slaves but human beings with rights. A passionate orator with great poetic flair, he had a Trotskyesque gift of igniting words into phrases that spread like a flame through the mob mind. He was betrayed at home in his last years by the unions he had created, and forgotten in America where he had organized the Syndicalists and spent five years in Sing Sing.

'Jem' Larkin was for Brendan the spirit of defiant Dublin and after his funeral he wrote a poem in Gaelic in the March issue of *Comhair.*

He was me—he was every mother's son of us,
Ourselves—strong as we would wish to be
    As we knew we could be.
And he bellowing battle and promising redemption
Following his coffin through the mouth of the empty city,
    In great roars of fury.
Following his coffin through the mouth of the city last night.
Is it we who are in the coffin?
Certainly not! We are in the street marching
Alive—and thankful to the dead.[1]

Later in the same month, January 1947, the Reverend Hewlett Johnson, Dean of Canterbury, came to Dublin to give an address under the auspices of the Irish-Soviet Friendship Society. Dr Johnson, known popularly as the Red Dean, was to talk on 'Religion in Soviet Russia'. This was a period at the beginning of the cold war and the Soviets were still regarded, even in fairly liberal circles (to say nothing of neutral and Catholic Ireland), with suspicion. It was anticipated that there would be trouble in the form of interruptions and heckling at the meeting. Consequently the group organizing it sought help in controlling it from left-wing members of the I.R.A. and Communist organizations in the city.

On the night of the meeting, the street outside the Mansion House in the centre of the city was packed with police and members of the public. Brendan had been hired as a chucker-out and he shouted cheerily to members of the Special Branch as he marched into the meeting: 'It's good to see you here protecting us instead of attacking us for a change.' The Round Room of the Mansion House where the meeting was held was packed as the Red Dean, a distinguished and venerable figure, came on the stage. In a beautiful, deep speaking voice, he spoke of the 'complete religious freedom' he had found everywhere in Soviet Russia. Occasionally there were heckles which were promptly silenced. Presently a rocket whizzed past the Dean's head. 'Must be a leprechaun, what?' he said, genially, and continued to describe how the churches were packed and Russian priests

[1] Translated from the Gaelic by Ulick O'Connor.

allowed full permission to educate and to propagate the faith under Soviet rule.

About half way through, a group of students rose in the balcony and, walking down the stairs, announced they were leaving as a protest against the meeting. The bodyguards sprang to action and, in the mêlée which took place as the students left, some of them were taken to an ante-room and beaten up. Blunt instruments were used and one of the students had his glasses smashed into his eye, which was badly injured. As a result of the disturbance the police came into the hall and stopped the meeting.

Various people have since wrongly described this student group as a reactionary organization. Although there is no doubt that there were right-wing groups present who came with the object of breaking up the meeting, as well as representatives of religious organizations, the group in the balcony was not one of them. It was simply a casual collection of students who had decided over coffee that morning to go along and protest at the meeting. The only thing they had in common was that they had been at the same school together and had played in the same rugby teams. They were led by the youngest member of the group, aged seventeen, who was the biographer. Our only purpose in going was to make a protest and leave and it was to our horror that, shortly after the meeting started, we saw right-wing republicans raising Nazi flags. It was noticeable that neither the Nazi group nor the religious caucuses dotted through the audience were anxious to engage in any form of active protest.

They knew of the tough group of stewards at the door; we did not.

There were six of us and I was the only one who emerged unscathed.

Later two of the stewards were prosecuted for assault and received prison sentences. Afterwards, Brendan used to say that he was in the crowd that attacked the students. But Paddy Kelly, an I.R.A. man who was in prison with Brendan assures me that Brendan was up on the stage, protecting Dr Johnson. When the mêlée started, Brendan made off for it but Kelly pulled him back saying that if they left the stage, the others might leap on to it and attack Dr Johnson.

As Brendan was leaving the hall though, he found himself grabbed from behind by a Detective Officer of the Special Branch whom he happened to know. As he was marched to the door, Brendan suggested to the man that they have a drink together. Nothing loath, the officer took him by the arm and they slipped across to the Dawson Lounge, for a few double brandies. When they eventually got back, the hall was deserted. Even the police had gone home.

On the following Saturday, a large meeting was held in University College, Dublin, to protest at the treatment of the students. Standing orders were suspended at the Literary and Historical Debating Society and a motion proposed supporting the student protest at the Mansion House, and threatening reprisals should there be any similar show of force at meetings of this kind in the future.

Brendan had heard about the meeting from his friend, Micky Gill, a law student at College and son of Mr Gill who owned the bar at the corner of Russell Street. He came along and decided to speak against the motion. This took a good deal of courage. The 'L. and H.' was a real forcing house of debate. Argument was something the Irish were good at and the audience made full use of their native gifts of repartee and heckling which could be silenced only by unrehearsed and genuine oratory from the speaker. Brendan asked permission to speak as an outsider, which was granted to him, a privilege extended on occasions by the Society. He rose to his feet and gave a defiant look around the hall. Then he turned his gaze on the injured students, some of whom had bandages on, and who occupied a prominent place in the front row. This was the first occasion I had the opportunity to observe Brendan Behan at close quarters. Slowly but surely, in a series of defiant asides accompanied by eloquent passages of indignation, he won the audience round to his side. It was a *tour de force* which lasted twenty minutes and ended by the audience cheering him loudly for five minutes after he sat down.

A few days later, I was walking past Government Buildings in

Merrion Square. I looked down in the basement and recognized Brendan, who was there with a brush in his hand painting the wall. As soon as he saw me, he snarled.

'Are you an effing student?'

'Certainly.'

'I put the students in their place in the Mansion House.'

'The police will put you in your place next week.'

'I spoke at the College and told them that they were a shower of bastards.'

'You're a great man at talking.'

'Come down here and I'll show you whether I'm a talker or not.'

'Come up and I'll break your face.'

'Come down.'

'O.K.'

As I put my foot over the parapet to jump down into the area, it struck Brendan that, if he was caught on the job with his props up, he would be looking for another one very soon. With several oaths, he intimated that we would fight some other time.

A year later, I was introduced to him in Davy Byrne's public house. As soon as he heard my name, he shouted: 'Effing informer.' (This was a reference to evidence I had given at the prosecution of the two men who had assaulted the students.) In a second we were at each other's throats. But Dublin, city of spontaneous factions, also fortunately possesses a large population of peacemakers coiled and ready to prevent them. We were grabbed almost instantly and pulled apart. I have a clear memory of one well-bred voice shouting persistently in the background: 'Don't fight him! Don't fight him! He's a Borstal bastard. He'll kick you in the privates.' I could see Brendan's face clearly in front of me. It was contorted into an animal snarl, a sudden eruption of naked hate. It is my last memory of him face to face and I was never actually to meet him again, though I saw him on many occasions afterwards about the city.

Was this an example of the vicious streak that his father had noticed in him as a young boy—the spoiled child who blew his top if he did not get his own way, who threw his little brother down the stairs for getting a penny from Brendan's Granny before he had?

Desmond MacNamara recalls that Brendan had a tendency at this time to quarrel over abstractions with people he did not know, taking a quick objection to them which he afterwards got over if he came to know them properly. Brian his brother remembers that 'underneath Brendan's ebullience he was a quivering mass of too much feeling. Feelings deep, raw and violent that were liable to explode at the slightest provocation. Then like a mad stallion he couldn't bear to be bridled by anyone.' Michael Traynor admits that Brendan at this time could be vicious: 'But it was a sudden viciousness. That's different from hate.' There is no doubt, however, that Brendan frequently horrified people with his eruptions of violence. Patrick Kavanagh, the poet, was one of these. He was a County Monaghan man who had come to live in Dublin and who had come to be considered by many the greatest living Irish poet after Yeats. Kavanagh had been on friendly terms with Behan to begin with and had even on one occasion had him paint his room for him. But some dark hatred developed between them. A few months before his death in 1967, Kavanagh described Behan to me as 'incarnate evil', and shuddered and shook himself in disgust when he spoke of him.

What inner anger was eating Brendan?

He was engaged in what the Goncourts called 'the hard, horrible struggle against anonymity'. He had a burning desire for recognition. He always wanted to be the centre of attention. He had been since he was a little boy, sitting in the midst of his Granny and her cronies at Russell Street, a preferred Benjamin. As he grew older, his talent as a singer and raconteur satisfied his exhibitionist desires. But now he wanted more: he wanted recognition as a writer, to be accepted in the world of intellectuals and artists.

In a city of literary cliques, recognition could only come slowly and Brendan had no intention of waiting. If he could not get accepted, he was going to bulldoze his way in. This involved playing the roaring extrovert, the wild working man, more often perhaps than he intended. With students, to some extent, he was hoist by his own petard. Among a group of them, especially from Trinity College, where there was a large number of ex-servicemen, British and American, he had a following who were entertained by his singing and talking and thought of and referred to him as 'a broth of a boy'. On the other hand, if he introduced himself and played the part of a rough slum lad to other students who did not know him—as he often did—he could not complain if they did not recognize quickly his cultural background. Yet any hints that he was not being treated as an equal and he would often become unpleasant and provoke a fight to release his pent-up frustration and confusion.

Brendan regarded himself as having status in Dublin. After all, his uncle Lorcan Bourke was deputy Lord Mayor; and every time people stood to attention for the National Anthem they were honouring the song composed by his other uncle, Peadar Kearney.

One of the meeting places for the new Dublin Bohemia in the middle 'forties was a complex of cellars under a Georgian house in Fitzwilliam Street. These were known as the Catacombs. With its deserted pantries, beflagged kitchens and pokey maids rooms, this underground habitat of Edwardian servantry became the scene of nightly revelry. The rooms upstairs were occupied by a respectable dentist, but as he hastened home to the suburbs each night, as Anthony Cronin points out, 'the extraction of teeth downstairs by other methods created no disturbance to the public whatever'. The contrast between the reputable profession of the owner and the licence permitted in the basement was summed up neatly in a notice hung up outside early one morning by a departing reveller.

Extractions upstairs.
Insertions down below.

Here, students, painters, actors, writers, revolutionaries, socialists and many others besides, met to drink and talk the night away after the pubs had closed. J. P. Donleavy, who could write while the unruly were shouting and singing around him, was an astute spectator at these gatherings, taking notes for *The Ginger Man*. Alan Simpson, who later directed the world première of *The Quare Fellow* and the English-speaking première of *Waiting for Godot*, his wife Carolyn Swift, John Ryan, the editor of *Envoy*, the actors Dan O'Herlihy and Godfrey Quigley, George Jeffares, secretary to the Irish Communist League, Irene Broe, the sculptress, Tony MacInerney and A. K. O'Donoghue, who figure in *The Ginger Man*, were among the regular customers. Gainor Crist, an American student at Trinity College, whom Donleavy used as his model for Sebastian Dangerfield—the Ginger Man himself—was another constant client.

The tenant of the establishment, and impresario of the ménage, was an English dandy, of upper-class background, who eked out an existence on a tiny allowance from home. He was a good-looking young man of style and humour, who, even as he minced along, managed to convey an air of natural superiority and indifference. The bizarre delighted him. To the door of his room was affixed a plate 'Matron', snitched from one of the Dublin hospitals. He made his own exquisite clothes and striking cravats, from the cheapest material. He bathed daily at the public bath in Tara Street for twopence and, when Brendan became too unwashed for pleasant propinquity, took him along, too, for a scrubbing. He made the money for the rent by collecting the empty bottles next morning, left behind by the revellers he had invited the night before. He would drive in a taxi to the nearest public house, with the bottles in the boot, and collect the refunds. Further sums were floated by making sweets for export (they were still rationed in England), and by selling his blood (by a fortunate chance it was of a rare group) to the transfusion centre in Leeson Street.

Entrance to the Catacombs was by invitation only. The owner, though slim in build, had a deceptive wiriness so gate-crashers did not usually try more than once. He had once hiked from Dublin to Caherdaniel in Kerry for a £10 bet and walked, during the course of the journey, about a hundred miles in what amounted to dancing pumps. As he had the razor-like repartee of the natural queen, not too many were anxious to take him on in verbal battles either.

'I bet you buy your underwear in Madam Nora's', a coal heaver had shouted at him once, to be met with 'Oh *that's* where I first met you, was it, at the knicker counter?'

The Catacombs had quite a number of rooms and while there were occasional permanent tenants who lived a mole-like existence in a windowless cell there, the other rooms were free for whatever diversions the guests wished to provide for themselves. Most of the rooms had mattresses on the floor.

'Here,' wrote Brendan, 'there were men having women, women having women, men having men—a fair field and no favour.' One night Brendan brought the brother of Teresa, his boyhood girl friend, along. After a while it became clear what Brendan's intentions were. The brother fled, terrified, down the labyrinthine corridors, 'Brendan laughing his head off at me.'

J. P. Donleavy in *The Ginger Man* has given a picture of how Brendan appeared to him one night when he arrived in on a spree to the Catacombs.

There suddenly was a crash at the door, the centre boards giving way and a huge head came through singing:

> Mary Maloney's beautiful arse
> Is a sweet apple of sin.
> Give me Mary's beautiful arse
> And a full bottle of gin.

A man, his hair congealed by stout and human grease, a red chest blazing from his black coat, stumpy fists rotating around his rocky skull, plunged into the room of tortured souls with a flood of song:

> Did your mother come from Jesus
> With her hair as white as snow
> And the greatest pair of titties
> The world did ever know.

Mary tugged at Sebastian.
'Who's that? It's a shocking song he's singing.'

'That's the son of the rightful Lord Mayor of Dublin. And his uncle wrote the national anthem.'

Mary appreciative, smiling.

This man swept across the red tiles wildly greeting people on all sides, telling the room:

'I loved the British prisons. And you lovely women. The fine builds of ye. I'd love to do you all and your young brothers.'

He saw Sebastian.

'For the love of our Holy Father, the Pope, may he get himself another gold typewriter. Give me your hand, Sebastian, before I beat you to death with bound copies of the *Catholic Herald*. How are you for Jesus' sake?'

'Barney, I want you to meet Mary. Mary, this is Barney Berry.'

'Pleased to know you, Barney.'

'Why, you lovely woman, Mary. How are you? I'd love to do you. Don't let this whore touch or pluck your flower. How are you again, Mary?'

'I'm fine.'

Barney leaped away and up on the table and did a quick goat dance.

Around the Catacombs and McDaid's pub grew a cult of squalor. The open-necked shirt revealing the navel clogged with fur, the unwashed body, the leaking shoes and the overcoat with its aroma of spilt Guinness was a standard outfit for many Dublin writers and artists at this time. In the Catacombs, there were no moral restraints. There was a total defiance of convention for its own sake. What were they seeking then? To discover an identity for themselves, by shaking themselves free from the environment of their upbringing? Many of them were refugees from the middle-classes. Life in the Catacombs in fact was a microcosm of what was to happen more widely elsewhere in the late 'fifties and 'sixties when many young people in Britain, America and elsewhere were to immerse themselves in squalor, and embark on a Baudelaire-like search for experience in an effort to break down the calcification of their middle-class breeding. Sebastian Dangerfield is literature's first hippie.

In essence, Brendan's background was not working-class, but decayed genteel. But in the Catacombs, it suited him better to play the part of the working man. J. P. Donleavy remembers once when somebody complimented Brendan on a new suit that he went out in the gutter and rolled in it until it was creased and filthy. Then he was cast more perfectly in the role he had chosen. It attracted the Catacombs set. For them, he was a living proof that out of the proletariat could come unspoiled genius, uninhibited by the restrictions of class; a true-to-life rebel who had taken up the gun against the established order and served a prison sentence for it.

Later, he would more consciously play the same part and attract the attention of the rebel generation in other countries. For the moment it was mostly his instinct for anticipating the mood of the public that led him to create in his first years out of prison, this image of the slum rebel with the O'Casey touch.

CHAPTER TEN

THE Catacombs were one side of Brendan's development as a writer at this time. He cultivated an entirely different side of himself when he went on visits to the Gaelic-speaking parts of Kerry, as soon as he could, after his release from prison. He had got the feeling for this distant western world through two books he had read in prison by Blasket Islanders, *Twenty years a-Growing* by Maurice O'Sullivan and *The Island Man* by Tomas O'Crohan, the first of which had a preface by E. M. Forster and both of which have since become classics. Brendan was also influenced by the writings of Robin Flower, the keeper of the British Museum, who had lived on and written about the Blaskets since the early 'twenties. Sean O'Briain, his cell mate, represented the ideal of Gaelic-speaking Ireland for Brendan, and he longed to live amongst such people, at least for a while.

He set out for the Blasket Islands in January 1947. This part of Kerry, as well as the middle island of Aran and the coast of Connemara, were for years to come to be places where he could replenish his imagination and feel as much at home as in his native Dublin. He came in contact there with a world that was beginning to pass away half-a-century before, just as it was discovered by a handful of English and Scandinavian scholars, who, astonished at the novelty and beauty of what they found, dedicated their lives to preserving it in scholarly form.

Yeats, Lady Gregory and Synge had come across it mainly through Douglas Hyde's translations from the Gaelic and had learned to look among the common people, among vagabonds and beggars, for the foundations of an art they sensed could be unique, as the material for it had perished elsewhere. The spoken culture of the people, the stories and poems preserved on their lips, was the source from which the Irish Literary Renaissance drew its strength.

The people held on to their culture as a thread which bound them to a society which had disintegrated when the native aristocracy left for the Continent after the Battle of the Boyne in 1690. Disinherited, disenchanted, despised, beauty was their bulwark against the desolation that surrounded them. Yeats marvelled how half-a-century after her death men could still talk, and women too, of a Galway beauty whom folk would tumble over to see at a fair or a hurling match. They talked of beauty as if it was the source of some primal power which could influence the elements, diminish the sun or turn the tide.

> And since he is stretched in the grave
> The cold is gaining power over the sun.

It was an earth force competing with the Perfect Presence for mastery of men.

> You have taken the east from me; you have taken the west from me,
> You have taken what is before me and what is behind me;
> You have taken the moon, you have taken the sun from me,
> And my fear is great that you have taken God from me![1]

'It seemed,' wrote Yeats at the time, 'as if the ancient world lay all about us with its freedom of imagination, its delight in good stories, in man, force and woman's beauty.'

Elated, with finding that this life which he had heard and read so much about still existed, Brendan was swallowed up for a while in this Gaelic other-world. He loved to spend the night in story-telling and singing with the local people, and his days walking on the long, deserted silver strands and swimming in the sea warmed by the Gulf Stream. They would sing for him unaccompanied, traditional airs, while he would reply with the songs of his native Russell Street, part of a city tradition but containing the note of rebelry and thrill of failure as a common link between them.

---

[1] Anonymous seventeenth century poem, *Domhnall Óg (Young Donal)*, translater by Patrick Pearse.

Their music entranced him. He had first heard it in the republican clubs in Dublin where the culture of the countryside flourished side by side with the indigenous culture of the city. It entered into him now and, to some extent, during his whole life, he was a prisoner of it. Through it runs the theme of unfulfilment and unattainment, a voluptuous dwelling on failure. Along the melodic line, phrase builds upon phrase, like one wave folding into the next, mounting towards a climax that is sensed but never reached. No breaker will ever thunder on the shore. When the end is reached the mind is still poised in high expectation, the subtle solution of a psyche which sensed that fulfilment was inferior to expectation and turned the discovery into a national formula. No Irish battle that was ever lost, no leader that was hung, no lover that failed, was without assistance from this powerful conceit.

Un-Romanized, God and nature, and the perfection of the human form seemed one for them, so that when they sang of their lost nationhood it was in the idealized form of a woman they did so:

> Soft, soft Little Rose of the round white breasts,
> 'Tis thou has left a thousand pains in the centre of my heart:
> Fly with me my thousand loves and leave the land,
> And if I could would I not make a queen of thee, my Little Dark Rose.[1]

Were it not that the rhythmic line is over-long, this could be from the court of Aquitaine, or that its sentiment a trifle extravagant, the address of a Cavalier. Least of all does one think of it as a poet's address to his country in one of the traditional names that were used for Ireland in the seventeenth century, and that this was perfectly understood by the people when it was sung for them round their firesides or in the fields. It aroused not merely hope, or promise of freedom, but an exaltation of mind and a momentary presence with that harmony which binds being like a thread.

[1] Anonymous, seventeenth century poem, *Roisin Dubh* (*The Little Dark Rose*), translated by Patrick Pearse.

Had I my horses yoked I would plough against the hills,
In mid-Mass I'd leave the gospel for My Little Dark Rose,
I'd give a kiss to the young girl that would give her youth to me
And behind the woods, would lie embracing My Little Dark Rose.

No phenomenon is so unique to the Irish make-up as this metamorphosis of the national being into a creature of breasts and lips and thighs, capable of sensuous excitement, a superb pantheism where the nation, the individual and the god are fused in a single miraculous image.

Later Brendan would deny he was a poet. In an interview with Eamonn Andrews years afterwards he said that the difference between him and Dylan Thomas was that Thomas was a poet and he was not.

> Dylan Thomas wrote a poem called 'To a child killed in an air-raid fire in London'[1] that I most certainly could not have written in a thousand years. Not if I was to sit up like the famous monkey in the British Museum. I think he was a great artist.

Yet between 1945 and 1950, Brendan's reputation in Ireland rested largely on some Gaelic poems he had written in Irish-language magazines. It was obvious to the few who had read his poetry in Gaelic that here was a true poet. When *Nuabhearshaiocht*, a collection of poetry written in Irish since the beginning of the century, was published in 1950, two poems by Brendan were included in it. He was the youngest poet to appear in the volume.

He realized that, by writing in Irish, he was concealing his gift from all but a few Gaelic enthusiasts. Why then did he continue to do so? To an extent, it was because he still believed in the separatist ideal of the Republican cause. But there was another reason. He seems to have sensed that in the Gaelic culture he might find a mode of expression that he could never discover through English.

[1] Actually *A Refusal to Mourn the Death, by Fire, of a Child in London.*

Encocooned in a dying tongue was a poetic tradition more than 2000 years old, which had its heroic and romantic periods before the Christian era began, and later became remarkable for a monastic and courtly literature.

When Brendan began to write poetry in Gaelic, he wrote it after different schools, as an English poet might experiment with an Elizabethan, Augustan or Georgian style before finally forming his own. He had an uncanny flair for reproducing the flavour of a particular period. His 'Coming of Winter' for instance could be the work of a ninth century scholar-poet in his cell—iron asceticism tempered by a sensual appreciation of nature:

> Wild wicked Winter,
> Your harsh face I hate
> The North wind blows in
> Trembling, tormented, tough,
> Without growth or goodness,
> Loveliness or love,
> Till the white feast of Brigid
> And the resurrection of joy.
>
> Then comes the South wind,
> Promise of heat for my limbs
> Life leaping in me,
> Awakening of the blood.
> Winter, you wastrel,
> Old age is your season.
> Welcome and a thousand more to you,
> O Spring of my youth.[1]

Professor James Carney of the Institute of Advanced Studies in Dublin has pointed out the resemblance between the original Gaelic of Behan's poem and a section of an eighth century poem, 'The Questing of Aitherne', collected by the German scholar, Kuno Meyer. Brendan's poem in Gaelic begins:

> Geimradh Garbh Gealach
> Is fuath Liom do ghnuis

[1] Translated by Ulick O'Connor.

while the first lines of 'The Questing of Aitherne' are:

> Fri fuair geimradh garbh.
> Garbh, dubh, dorcha, detaithe.

Apart from the fact that two of the words are the same there are striking resemblances of alliteration and assonance.

It is unlikely that Brendan could have read 'The Questing of Aitherne' as it was published in an obscure scholarly magazine. Much more probably he had absorbed the essence of Gaelic culture so thoroughly that he created Gaelic poetry in its original idiom without being conscious of it.

These early Gaelic poems often have a Japanese quality which is caught in Brendan's 'Loneliness'.

> The blackberries' taste
> After rainfall
> On the hilltop.
>
> In the silence of prison
> The train's cold whistle.
>
> The whisper of laughing lovers
> To the lonely.[1]

The poets who influenced Brendan most were the Munster ones, David O'Bruadair, Eoghan O'Sullivan and Brian Merriman, who wrote in the seventeenth, eighteenth and nineteenth centuries. They were the end of the bardic tradition. Their existence had been bound up with the Gaelic aristocratic order and, when it finally collapsed after the Treaty of Limerick and the Dutch King in 1693, the court poets were left homeless. The great houses were gone, the Catholic nobility fled to Europe and their places filled by Cromwellian adventurers 'whose cautiousness displaced hospitality and whose ostentation ousted sociability'. 'Spaganai', the Irish called them, 'people who walked awkwardly on the balls of their feet'.

The poets fumed at the downfall of the old order that had carried away with it centuries of tradition which now was of no use to them. For them English was 'gliogarna ghall'—'the

[1] Translated by Ulick O'Connor.

babbling of foreigners'. They were most of them more familiar with Latin or Greek. Driven down, in their last degradation among farming folk, they continued their trade, writing verse on barmaids, boobies and blacksmiths in sophisticated forms that would have been used half-a-century before to gain favour with a Lord or Lady. Alliteration, internal rhyme, assonance, strict rhythmic content, the severe discipline of the bardic code— they clung to these as the last thin thread binding them to the aristocratic tradition that had crumbled beneath them.

'Their memory', wrote the Cambridge scholar, Robin Flower, 'and their influence lived after them and if the spoken Irish of today is perhaps the liveliest and the most concise and the most literary in its turn of all the vernaculars of Europe, this is due in no small part to the passionate preoccupation of the poets, turning and re-turning their phrases in the darkness of their cubicles and restlessly seeking the last perfection of phrase and idiom.'

There is great fury and sadness in their poetry, bitterness most of all: for they who had imagined that to squander reck-lessly the wealth of the world constituted the very essence of nobility, found themselves under the thumb of carpet-baggers who lacked style and whose names sounded crude in their ears, so that they could compose whole quatrains of scorn based merely on the sound of them:

> Upton, Evans, Bevins, Basset, is Blair,
> Burton, Beecher, Wheeler, Farran is Fair,
> Turner, Fielding, Reeves, is Wallis is Dean,
> Cromwell is a bhuidhean sain scaoileadh is scaipeadh ar a dtread.[1]

In spirit perhaps the closest to Brendan was Eoghan O'Sullivan, a handsome Kerry schoolmaster turned labourer, whose poetry held Munster spellbound for generations and whose wit and repartee were still repeated round the firesides when Brendan came to Kerry and West Cork in the 'forties. Eoghan, who was killed at an early age in a drunken brawl, wrote one of his last poems to a blacksmith, begging him to make a new handle for

[1] May Cromwell's crew be loosened and scattered like a herd.

his spade so that he could earn with it what learning had never given him, the wherewithal to quench his thirst—a quest seldom absent from Brendan's mind. It could be a poem addressed by Brendan to one of his tradesmen drinking companions:

> And whenever I'm feeling low at the end of the day,
>   And the ganger comes round and assures me I'm dodging well,
> I'll drop a few words about Death's adventurous way
>   And the wars of the Greeks in Troy, and the kings that fell.
>
> They'll give me my pay in a lump when the harvest's done,
>   I'll tuck it away in a knot in my shirt to keep,
> And back to the village, singing and mad for fun—
>   And I promise I won't spend sixpence until we meet.
>
> For you're a man like myself with an antique thirst,
>   So need I say how we'll give the story an end?
> We'll shout and rattle our cans the livelong night
>   Till there isn't as much as the price of a pint to spend.[2]

In prison, Brendan had first heard Brian Merriman's great hymn of defiance, *The Midnight Court*, recited by the prisoners as they sat in their cells or walked round the jail yard. It is a long poem, almost 10,000 lines, telling how the women of Ireland bring the men to trial for lack of passion in their loving, and the punishments that subsequently are meted out to these reluctant swains. Merriman wrote it in 1796 and died in 1817 and it contains many of the ideas of the Enlightenment in its satire of Church and State, besides having something of Rabelais' joyous frenzy. Brendan seemed designed by nature to translate it, and appears in fact to have done so. At least, he recited a full version he had made, one night in McDaid's pub in Harry Street in 1952. Three days after, he lost the manuscript in a fight in the Conservative Club in York Street. No copy survives, only a fragment quoted in *Borstal Boy*.

> I used to walk the morning streams,
> The meadows fresh with the dew's wet gleam,
> Beside the woods, in the hillside's shade,
> No shadow or doubt on the lightsome day.
> It'd gladden the heart in a broken man,
> Spent without profit, vigour or plan.

[2] Translated by Frank O'Connor.

> Let a withered old ballocks, but rich, in gall,
> View the trees' arms, raised, like ladies' tall.
> The ducks smooth-swimming the shining bay,
> The swan all proud, to lead the way,
> The blue of the lake and lusty wave,
> Battering mad, in the gloomy cave.
> The fish for energy, leaping high,
> To take a bite from the spacious sky,
> The birds all singing, strong and easy,
> The bounding grace of the she-deer near me,
> The hunt with the horn loud sounding o'er them,
> Strong running dogs and the fox before them.
>
> I saw as I suddenly looked around
> Approach from the bay with a horrible sound
> A big-bellied bitch and her bottom gigantic,
> Fierce, furious, fearless, formidable, frantic.

No poet more than David O'Bruadair felt the insolence of the usurper more; and none, not even Merriman, could unleash in a verse syllables of spitting, snarling hate that seem to run in and out of the lines like a terrier after a rat, as O'Bruadair did when he directed his dislike against his enemies. O'Bruadair can rhyme like a crossword puzzle down vertically through a quatrain, so that four lines can contain as many as sixteen similar rhymes or assonances, while at the same time one word follows another in a dazzling chain of alliteration.

Brendan was writing after O'Bruadair in his poem 'The Story-teller's Prayer', when he attacked the phoney Gaels of the new order, the Civil Servants and job-hunters who came down to Irish-speaking parts of Ireland to learn Irish for government appointments that required a knowledge of the language: a race of milk-fed puritans aeons away from the earthy Gaelic tradition they pretended they were part of.

> If I saw a fine fellow with fluent Irish
> Civilly spouting on deeds and people
> In our own language, a marvellous earful,
> Cocky, comfortable, casual, cheerful,
> I'd be well pleased to pay attention;
> Passionate poet, proud productive,
> Brave bard, brisk bouncing buccaneer,
> Pleasant, pagan-penned, perceptive.

> Alas, alack, what is my story?
> Civil Servants from Corchaguiney,
> Other eejits from Donegal foreshore,
> Clodhoppers from Galway to make my head sore.
> Puerile pioneers,[1] pansified and punctured,
> Vacant virgins, vehement and vulgar,
> All dedicated to prudence and piety.
>
> If a poet came to stir these embers
> I'd leave for home my task accomplished.[2]

One can scarcely give more than the flavour in English. The consonantal correspondence and vowel assonance, the alliteration which binds together for the ear the sense of the words, the verbal unity of the poem, defy translation. The best scholarly translator, Robin Flower, found Gaelic verse 'essentially untranslatable':

> There was something unconquerably native and original in the Irish contributions, an inbred tone and quality that comes from another tradition than the Common European, and that gives the peculiar edge and accent to these poems.

But this flirtation with the old Gaelic forms would have had little meaning for Brendan had he not been able to adapt them to more contemporary themes, as he does, for example in 'Oscar Wilde'. In this poem written in 1949, he takes a wholly modern subject matter:

Oscar Wilde Poète et Dramaturge, né à Dublin le 15 Octobre, 1856, est mort dans cette maison le 30 Novembre, 1900.

> After all the wit
> In a sudden fit
> Of fear, he skipped it.
> Stretched in the twilight
> That body once lively
> Dumb in the darkness.
> Quiet, but for candles
> Blazing beside him,
> His elegant form
> And firm gaze exhausted.
> In a cold empty room

[1] A pioneer in Ireland is commonly taken to mean a member of an organization who takes a religious vow to abstain for life from liquor.
[2] Translated by Ulick O'Connor.

With a spiteful concièrge
Impatient at waiting
For a foreign waster
Who left without paying
The ten per cent service.
Exiled now from Flore
To sanctity's desert
The young prince of Sin
Broken and withered.
Lust left behind him
Gem without lustre
No Pernod for a stiffener
But cold holy water
Young king of Beauty
Narcissus broken.
But the pure star of Mary
As a gleam on the ocean.

Envoi

Sweet is the way of the sinner,
Sad, death without God's praise.
My life on you, Oscar boy,
Yourself had it both ways.[1]

'L'Existentialisme: An Echo of Saint-Germain-des-Prés' is a satirical piece on popular Parisian philosophy of the late 'forties.

Watchman on the wall patrolling
Your empty building
How is the hunt going?
The graveyard doing?
Is our voyage to hell?
Must be! Is your mind well?
What went before us, tell?
Don't know; I was not alive
I am not, yet
Is our fate stinking?
Too lazy
To answer that one
Good; there's not a bit
Of sense or pain, still less
Truth, in what I say
Or in the opposite way.[2]

[1] Oscar Wilde became a Catholic on his death bed. The poem is translated by Ulick O'Connor.

[2] Translated by Ulick O'Connor.

Was Brendan persuaded by his political beliefs into writing in Irish? Or did he believe that through Irish he could come closer to his ancestral self than through English? Did he make the superb gesture and disdain an audience in the pursuit of his craft, working in silence at his artefact, seeking only its completion before turning to its successor?

Was poetry in Irish a beginning for him or a cul-de-sac? We shan't know. He stopped writing poetry after 1950.[1]

But it is possible to speculate on what he might have done. He was the full turn of the wheel. Yeats, Lady Gregory and Synge had presented aspects of the Gaelic tradition during the first decades of the century. But they had done it secondhand, largely through the translations of Douglas Hyde, Standish O'Grady and others. As he grew older, Yeats, it is true, came closer and closer to the real tradition, through the translations of Frank O'Connor and James Stephens.

> We remembered the Gaelic poets of the seventeenth and early eighteenth centuries wandering, after the flight of the Catholic nobility, among the boorish and the ignorant, singing their loneliness and their rage; James Stephens and Frank O'Connor made them symbols of our pride.

This pride had so moved him that he took a line from one of O'Connor's translations and incorporated it wholesale into one of his own poems:

> I shall go after the heroes, aye into the clay,
> My fathers followed theirs before Christ was crucified.

Other Irish poets writing in the 'thirties had tried with some success to capture the characteristics of the Gaelic tradition. Even those who earlier on had reacted against it like Joyce and Gogarty, wrote unconsciously out of this tradition. Joyce's *Gas from a Burner* is in the tradition of O'Bruadair: and Gogarty's savagery against de Valera in verse and prose had behind it the brooding bardic belief that 'words alone are certain good', that a phrase as well as a deed can destroy the object of dislike. But none

---

[1] 'There's no money in poetry' he told Rae Jeffs later.

of them had Brendan's opportunity or dual gift of being English-speaking and coming in contact at an early age with the oral Gaelic tradition, so that it became second nature to him to grapple with either language in a new and muscular way.

He might have come out of his Gaelic period with an original voice to express himself as a poet in English, daring assonances and alliterations, a mastery of the long riding rhythm of the Gaelic line which he could transfer to his other language.

But he wrote no more poetry in Irish.

Was he unconsciously saying goodbye to it all in his poem on the Blasket Islands, 'A Jackeen[1] says goodbye to the Blaskets'? The last Irish-speaking inhabitants left the islands in 1946, where, thirty years before, a Yorkshire man, a Swede and a Dane had come to gather what was left of its culture, before it died on the edge of Ireland, Europe and the world.

The great sea under the setting sun gleams like a glass,
Not a sail in sight, no living person to see it pass
Save the last golden eagle, hung high on the edge of the world,
Over the lonely Blasket resting, his wings unfurled.

Yes, the sun's at rest now and shadows thicken the light,
A rising moon gleams coldly through the night,
Stretching thin fingers down the quivering air,
On desolate, deserted dwellings, pitifully bare.

Silent save for birds' wings clipping the foam,
Heads on breast, they rest content, grateful to be home.
The wind lifts lightly, setting the half-door aslope
On a famished hearth without heat, without protection, without hope.[2]

[1] The Irish countryman's name for a Dubliner.
[2] Translated by Ulick O'Connor.

CHAPTER ELEVEN

In March, 1947, an I.R.A. friend asked Brendan if he would help to organize the escape of an I.R.A. man from Wakefield Jail. The prisoner was Dick Timmons, who had been sentenced at Cardiff in 1939 to fourteen years penal servitude for the possession of explosives. Brendan agreed, although to go to England meant that he would risk imprisonment, as the deportation order made against him in 1942 was still in force. He has given an account of his part in the escape in *Confessions of an Irish Rebel*, a dictated volume of autobiography recorded shortly before he died. He describes how he and a rescue crew sprang Timmons from Wakefield Jail and there is a detailed account of how they and some others then went to Leeds, Bradford and Manchester, on the run from their pursuers.

According to Timmons, Brendan's account of what happened is not correct.

Brendan had nothing whatever to do with my escape. I got out of Leyhill Open Jail in a suit smuggled in for entertainment by David Springhall. Then I went to Liverpool. After that I moved to Bradford. I was four weeks on the run. At no time during this period did I meet Brendan Behan. Then when I was in Bradford I heard that an I.R.A. man called Liam Dowling wanted to contact me and that he had some money for me. I arranged for him to walk up and down outside a pub and I watched him carefully from the pub, unknown to him. 'Jesus', I said, 'you're not Brendan Behan, are you?' You see he was in short trousers the last time I saw him. We went in for a few drinks. He was very likeable company. But I was worried about his drinking. He boasted that he had drunk sixteen pints. It didn't seem the right atmosphere for a difficult job of getting out of England as an escaped prisoner. What really put me off was the R.A.F. paybook he used for identification. He hadn't bothered to change the photograph on it and the man in the photograph had a squint which, of course, Brendan hadn't. Brendan said he was going to St. Helen's where I was to meet him. Actually I never contacted him again. Some telegrams came from Dublin to me and because it seemed these might compromise me by revealing my address I wired back to Dublin, 'Break all contact.'

Later, Timmons sneaked into Liverpool and stowed away on a ship to Galway. After a series of legal actions he finally secured his freedom and was allowed to stay in Ireland.

Timmons's account is supported by others who participated in the escape and it would appear that Brendan invented the role described in such detail in his autobiography, in the same way as he coloured the account in *Borstal Boy* of his 'bombing mission' in Liverpool in 1940, and his shooting at the detectives at Glasnevin cemetery in subsequent descriptions.

Later, when he was projecting his image in Britain and the United States, he seems to have known exactly, with his special flair, what part of his personality and background would appeal to the public. These he blew up like an enlarged photograph, so that it would be easily discernable at a mass level. In the enlargement process he was not concerned if the details became distorted, provided the effect created was the one required. That was what mattered.

A few days after his meeting with Dick Timmons in Bradford, Brendan was arrested by detectives in Manchester. It was almost certainly due to his own carelessness. He had phoned Frank Lee, an I.R.A. contact in London, to inform him about Dick Timmons. Lee's line was probably being tapped by Scotland Yard. He was making a nuisance of himself and, in addition, probably giving the English Special Branch a bird's eye picture of the whole escape. Whatever the reason for it, as he stepped off the train in Manchester, he was grabbed by two detectives.

If the bastards had offered me the Victoria Cross along with the King of England's blessing, I could not have been more surprised.

He was for it again, this time to be tried under the Prevention of Violence Act, 1939, and for being in unlawful possession of a false passport in the name of Liam Dowling. He was remanded for a week to Manchester Assizes after the charges had been read by Inspector Pierpoint.

During the week, he was summoned by the Governor of Manchester Jail: 'Look here, Behan, do you know the Pope, or is this a put on?' Brendan took the telegram the Governor handed to him and read: 'I am flying to defend you. The Pope.' He had some trouble explaining that this was the late 'Pope' O'Mahony, a well-known and chivalrous Irish character who was a member of the English and Irish Bars. Though a lifelong supporter of parliamentary Home Rule, O'Mahony had devoted a lot of his private income to securing the release of I.R.A. prisoners who had been jailed in England as a result of the bombing campaign of the 'forties.

Eoin O'Mahony had become friendly with Brendan after he had come out of the Curragh a year before and had taken him on trips down the country, introducing him to an Ireland he could not otherwise have known, an upper-class world of afternoon tea and late dinner among the gentry and other well-to-do people with country residences. Owing perhaps to the 'Pope's' plea Brendan was given a light sentence of four months, but once more, he faced the journey in a prison van from court to jail. This time he was to spend his sentence in Strangeways Jail, Manchester. Among his fellow prisoners was a group of former Desert Rats awaiting trial for mutiny. But, apart from these, there were the usual run of rapists, burglars, confidence men, to be found in prison anywhere. One group which he could not help noticing looked particularly dejected. They were miners who had been sentenced for sodomy in the coal-pits. The location baffled Brendan. 'Having sex down a coal-mine seems to me about the most depressing situation where you could possibly find it.' He was depressed himself. He was only out of prison five months and now he was back again. It seemed as if he would never be free.

At Strangeways, he was not put to a trade and spent most of his time there in solitary confinement. He was to note later that here he felt more 'uaigneas gan cuineas' (loneliness without peace) than in any other prison he had been in before.

He had begun to go to Mass regularly again in prison in Ireland, and afterwards, in the short period he had been free, he had met a priest, Father Behan, in Kerry, who had made a deep impression on him. One day, the priest had called on Brendan to ask him to help cut down a poor girl who had hanged herself. As they buried her in a graveyard on the edge of the Atlantic, Brendan, knowing the Church's attitude to suicide, asked the priest how it was possible to bury her in consecrated ground. 'Who are we to judge, Brendan', said the priest, 'it may have been an accident'. Brendan was impressed by this.

> I was never so proud of the Catholic clergy before as I was when Father Behan said this to me. My early experiences in jail in England had given me the idea that religion was nothing to do with mercy or pity or love.

But despite this return to his faith, he had gone on sexual and alcoholic sprees during the five months he was free, sampling whatever appealed to his parched senses in the Catacombs and the public houses. Now this, and the depression of prison life in Strangeways, seems to have brought on feelings of guilt about the life he was leading. Alone in his cell, the problem of sin and thoughts of damnation began to occupy him. In a poem 'Repentance' which he wrote in Gaelic at this time, there is an obsession with death:

> In that awful hour when I'm on my deathbed
> Stretched below on the cold bare board
> My friends and neighbours around me standing
> And weak in my ears the whispered word;
> In that time of affliction, O Mother Mary,
> With no respite and my soul alone
> But the saving grasp of your hand in my hand
> On that trembling voyage to the Heavenly Throne;
>
> That will be the time when my mind's tormented
> With thoughts that crawl behind my eyes,
> Following exhausted the glow of memory
> Which lights the deeds of my life as they rise;
> Calling my sins like an army sergeant
> Mounting a guard against my prayer;
> Don't ever abandon me, Mother Mary,
> Without your grace as a shield to wear.

My sins will gather like greedy fox-hounds,
Memory a horn to summon the pack,
And death on a horse, my life's course over,
The years safely ditched at his back;
When I'm run to earth and my lungs are panting,
At the hunt's end and death in my face;
Trembling, red-eyed while the hounds are baying;
O Mother, don't ever deny your grace.[1]

The first stanza is a rough translation of a hymn he had learnt from his mother: but the other two are a cry from the heart, a deeply felt personal emotion. A year later in Paris, he would succeed, to some extent, in losing this sense of sin. But it was never far from the surface. Brendan was a religious animal. He was always terrified he would die without the Last Sacraments. Once, in an interview with Eamonn Andrews, when asked if he believed in God, he replied indignantly, 'I do, of course. I'm a bad Catholic. It is the religion of great artists, like Rabelais and Michelangelo'.

Brendan was released from Strangeways in the first week of July. Back in Dublin, he quickly slipped into his old habits—McDaid's, the Catacombs, bottle parties with Trinity students, playing the part of 'the character' he had assumed in the life of the city.

At Easter, he had a tiny one-act play, *Winston Green*, produced as part of an I.R.A. commemoration concert at the Queen's Theatre. The concert was organized in aid of the relatives of Barnes and McCormack who had been executed at Winston Jail for their part in the Coventry explosions in 1940. Brendan's piece depicted the scene outside the prison walls on the morning of the execution. It had a good reception from an admittedly partisan audience.

He occasionally took a job to get money for drink. He worked himself into a mood of dissatisfaction and, after a night's drinking, frequently found himself in court next morning. After one of these bouts in May 1948 he ended up in Mountjoy prison again. An English visitor had commented in the Pearl Bar with some

[1] Translated by Ulick O'Connor.

satisfaction on the killing of Jewish guerrillas in the Palestine War. This enraged Brendan. He stuck his thumbs in his ears and, wagging them at the Englishman, began to taunt him with:

The man in the moon was a Jew, was a Jew.

A punch-up started and Brendan and two friends headed for the streets. The police had been called by this time and a large posse was in pursuit. As Brendan passed Trinity College in some haste, it struck him that he might use it as a refuge. He knocked furiously on the massive gates as the thud of the constabulary grew nearer and nearer. Since it was after ten o'clock the porter asked him why he required admission and Brendan told him he wanted to see the Book of Kells, the eighth century illuminated manuscript kept there. As the door slammed in his face, he turned to face his pursuers. He climbed on the railings in front of Trinity and, hanging with his two arms spreadeagled, lashed out with his small feet at the police. As he did so, noticing his companion adopting a boxer's pose with his left hand forward in the classical style, Brendan shouted: 'Eff the Marquess of Queensberry, Sean. Remember Oscar. Kick them in the balls', a remark that showed that, even in extremes, Dubliners were expected to know their literary references.

Next day, the three were charged with being drunk and disorderly, and with assaulting a policeman. The loyal 'Pope' O'Mahony was at hand as usual to defend them, but despite his efforts, Brendan and his butty received a sentence of a month each.

The difference between this period of imprisonment and the previous ones for Brendan was that now he was a lag for the first time. He was dressed in prison clothes and could no longer feel any sense of distinction from the rest of the criminals in jail. He was one of them. Had an I.R.A. prisoner been put in amongst them, he would have looked on Brendan, as Brendan had looked on other prisoners in the same jail in 1943, with a feeling of superiority and indifference. None the less, according to Governor Kavanagh, Brendan was a model prisoner, and renovated a number of cells while he served his sentence, though there is no doubt that this period in prison had quite a different effect on him from any of his previous ones. It was all right to be in the nick for Kathleen Ni Houlihan. It was a different kettle of fish to be inside for acting the hooligan.

CHAPTER TWELVE

It was this last jail sentence that made Brendan decide to clear out of Dublin. He had had enough. He wanted to make a clean break and start again. London was denied to him because of his prison record. Paris seemed an obvious alternative. So in August, 1948, accompanied by Leicester Jeus, an ex-American ex-airforce man who had come to Trinity on a G.I. grant, Brendan went to live there. He sailed via Newhaven and Dieppe, a risky procedure in view of his recent imprisonment for breach of the Prevention of Violence Act. But all went well and for the next few years, apart from a few trips to Dublin or Belfast, Paris was to be his home. He went there with the intention of becoming a professional writer and it was in Paris, certainly, that he acquired a sense of application and persistence in his work that he would not have learnt in Dublin.

Sartre and Camus held the centre of the Paris literary scene in the late 'forties. They moved between the Deux Magots and the Café Flore which Brendan soon termed 'the twin cathedrals of existentialism'. But when he read the books of the current hero of the existentialists, Jean Genet, he decided he had nothing in common with Genet except that they had both been in prison. ('He made the hair stand on my head', said Brendan). Brendan made friends with Camus and was delighted to find that they had a mutual interest in soccer. Camus had played in goal for Algiers and later asked Brendan to go to London with him to watch Spurs play Arsenal. But Brendan had to refuse, explaining that if he landed on English soil he was liable to be arrested immediately. Samuel Beckett also met him at this time and was pleasant to him in a slightly sad, sardonic Dublin accent. Beckett, like Joyce, was always pleased to meet Dubliners in exile as they evoked the atmosphere of his native city which, no matter how international his writing seems (he was at that time writing *Waiting for Godot* in French), is always at the root of his work.

Coming from Joyce's city Brendan made no secret of the fact—as in this poem 'Thanks to James Joyce'—and won himself many a free drink and meal on the strength of it.

> Here in the rue St André des Arts,
> Plastered in an Arab Tavern,
> I explain you to an eager Frenchman,
> Ex-G.I.s and a drunken Russian.
> Of all you wrote I explain each part,
> Drinking Pernod in France because of your art.
> As a writer we're proud of you—
> And thanks for the Calvados we gain through you.
>
> If I were you
> And you were me,
> Coming from Les Halles
> Roaring, with a load of cognac,
> Belly full, on the tipple,
> A verse or two in my honour you'd scribble.[1]

He sought out places of Irish interest. In the rue des Irlandais he found the Irish College where in the eighteenth century young Irish seminarians had studied the craft of their faith before returning to live among their people with a price on their heads. He reminded himself too that he was now in the city where Irish revolutionaries traditionally spent their exile scheming for their return to their native land. Wolfe Tone, John O'Leary, James Stephens and many others had spent a lot of their lives in Paris cafés making common cause with exiles from other countries. One day passing the Bastille, Brendan mentioned that it was a man named Kavanagh who had led the assault on the prison in the French Revolution and drew the appropriate remark from an American friend who was with him: 'You think of everything in relation to yourselves.'

In Dublin, as a child, Brendan had picked up a little French from his father and with his flair for words he very soon became a

[1] Translated from the Gaelic by Ulick O'Connor.

fluent, if ungrammatical, French speaker, able to converse with the Les Halles whores in argot and saunter down the Boulevard St Michel in the morning talking with the various Parisian characters he had come to know since his arrival. There was Monsieur 'Tram-track', who had been injured in a tram accident forty years before and had remained in bed ever since for fear he would lose his chances of compensation, and the 'Bonapartist' who strode about in a Second Empire rig awaiting the return of the Emperor's descendants, and Raymond Duncan, brother of Isadora, who ran a Greek Akademia. Brendan became friendly with him but was unable to take seriously the garments of Duncan's students, which consisted of sandals and sheets.

After a short run back to Dublin and a visit to Belfast, he returned again to Paris and soon he made friends with a group of pleasant young Americans who were engaged in the same occupation as he was, learning their trade as writers. James Baldwin was one of these. Milton Machlin, Terry Southern, Herbert Gold, and a writer named Mel Saber, who afterwards committed suicide, were others with whom he drank and talked.

During most of this time Brendan had not a penny. Machlin and Saber, who were ex-G.I.s, had their army grants and Brendan would often sleep on the floor of Machlin's room while all of them would include him in their food and drink whenever he was short. Machlin, who is now the editor of *Argosy* magazine and the author of an authoritative work on the Chessman trial, first met Brendan in the Prince Paul bar. Machlin was the bouncer there. He impressed Brendan immediately by taking him on and beating him in a test of strength in which they placed their elbows on a table and tried to bend each other's fist back towards the surface. Machlin remembers that Brendan had very small and well-shaped hands: 'Actually he was fairly strong, but he couldn't fight for toffee.'

What impressed Machlin and his American friends about Brendan was that by their standards he seemed a working writer. He *had* had articles published, and poems, and they had not. He was writing for English magazines occasionally and he once showed Machlin a cheque for twenty pounds, which seemed an enormous amount for anyone to get at that time for an article. He had a letter too from *Lilliput*, a prominent English journal of the time, asking for an article, which he used to display occasionally to his admirers, as well as giving them his latest work to read; but he was not always so anxious to hear their criticisms. One story in particular Machlin remembers as having been among the funniest he ever read: a description of the funeral of the Queen of the Dublin homosexuals. Machlin maintains it was a masterpiece, though most probably libellous of the living, if not of the dead.

Most of the time in Paris Brendan was very poor. He claimed later that he worked as a ponce in Harry's Bar, procuring French girls for rich Americans on commission. Seated at the corner of the bar he would wait for likely customers to enter. As soon as he had spotted one and chatted him up, he would make an appointment to meet him later and then head for the Trois Quatre where he would make contact with the prostitutes. The one he brought most business to he christened Jenny Étoile. He favoured her because she gave him a larger commission than the other girls.

Brendan also claimed that at this time he wrote pornography for a living, which was translated into French and published by an American called George. He used to say later that this was one reason why he was disliked by the literary set in Dublin. But whether or not he did write pornography at this time, when he states that he did so for a magazine called *Points*, Brendan was talking blatherskite. This was an interesting avant-garde magazine, considerably less phoney than many of the other small magazines of the time and bearing the individual stamp of its editor, Sindbad Vail. Brendan made two contributions to it, neither of which, by the widest stretch of the imagination, could be described as pornography. His first was the short story, *After the Wake*, referred to in another chapter, and the second contribution was an extract from what later became his best-selling book *Borstal Boy*. Sindbad Vail recalls:

I met Brendan somewhere in the very late 'forties. Big and burly as you know, putting on the Irish to ridiculous extremes and fascinating. He had heard that I paid 30,000 francs for a story, which was not much, but it was a token and no other little magazine did that. He came to our little office with 30 manuscripts and demanded 90,000 francs on the spot. He was broke and living from hand to mouth. It never occurred to him that I wouldn't take all his manuscripts and pay him in advance. That sum just about covered the printing bill for an entire issue. Anyway I think I gave him 30,000, which went somewhere in those days. It's too late to regret that I did not keep all his manuscripts, but most of them were illegible and even boring. We saw each other frequently, he always dropped by when he wanted a small loan or drink or food. I don't recall talking much about writing, he used to ramble on, sing Irish songs, tell dirty jokes and try to get off with a very pretty American girl who was helping me.

Despite the excitement of Paris, his thoughts were never far from Dublin. Milton Machlin remembers that Brendan would sometimes slip away from his American friends and head for Montparnasse solely for the purpose of listening to Breton bagpipes.

Another day, coming out of the church in Saint Germain des Prés, he was muttering some Gaelic to himself when he heard a voice behind him correcting him in the same language. He jerked round in astonishment and found himself facing Kathleen Murphy, a young Irish sculptress, who was studying church sculpture in Paris and later went out to see some Celtic stonework on a church outside Paris. Together they looked and mused on the primitive carving in front of them hacked out in stone twelve centuries before by their roving ancestors:

> I noted lovingly the twisted features of each cantankerous countenance and heard the waves of the Atlantic beat on the Aran shore and the praising voice of the holy Irish long since dead, soft in the gathering bustle of the day.

In need of money, Brendan took up his trade of house-painting again. He got small commissions from cafés on the Left Bank which were often paid for by giving him as much food and drink as he wanted for the short periods he worked in the bars. It is still remembered in Paris how he succeeded in making one bar the most popular on the Left Bank by painting on the outside of it 'This is the best fucking bar in Paris'. Another time in Paris he painted the house of a M. Monti in the suburbs of Saint Cotier.

After the job was finished he asked M. Monti to let him enamel the doors and the man was so impressed that he asked Brendan to show his son how to do this. Soon Brendan in his own way had the house singing. Instead of finishing the job, they sat down to an evening's entertainment, provided by this unusual Dublin tradesman. 'From the simplest ingredients', Brendan wrote afterwards, 'we made a night of gaiety. It was ever thus in France'.

Machlin cannot remember that Brendan showed any open homosexual leanings when he was with him and his friends but he often noticed Brendan lagging behind to talk to young men. 'We would just vanish and leave him with them. I assumed this was an affliction from his Borstal days.'

One night Brendan, Milton Machlin and an American, Jake Wallis, were walking in the small hours of the morning through the market at Les Halles when they came on a gendarme bullying a young prostitute. Among other things, he was entertaining himself by stubbing out his cigarette on the bare arm of the girl. Brendan murmured to Machlin that they had better put a stop to this. When the gendarme saw them he let the girl go. He then started to chat to them and discovered that Brendan was an Irishman. To ingratiate himself with the trio, he began to abuse the English vigorously. Brendan encouraged him, though when the gendarme recalled that he had been a Nazi sympathizer he had difficulty in containing himself. But they waited their chance. The policeman flourished his hand-cuffs, explaining that they had gripped the wrist of several Englishmen during the war. Could he show them how they worked, Brendan asked. The gendarme fitted one handcuff on his own wrist and closed it with an expert click. Quick as lightning Brendan fastened the other handcuff to the railings. The three of them then proceeded to thumb their noses at the gendarme, who roared like a Provençal bull, purple in the face, his veins bursting over his high collar. In his fury he managed to get his revolver out of his belt but fortunately it was not loaded. The lads then sped off, waving him dainty goodbyes.

Though he had begun for the first time to acquire a writer's discipline in Paris, Brendan behaved from time to time just as if he were back in Dublin. The difference was that in between bouts of drinking in Paris he worked hard: before this in Dublin the only time he had found himself able to write consistently was when he was in prison. Even at this period of his life (he was twenty-five) there were signs of a tendency that was later to dominate his personality. Sindbad Vail remembers that he

> drifted all over Paris and in the end I fear he bored all the people he visited and who wanted to help him. As you know he frequently got terribly drunk, and I'm no puritan when it comes to booze or most things for that matter, but he was awfully boring and abusive, insulting his friends, smashing their furniture and destroying pictures on the walls. In the end most of us thought he was just a bloody drunken show-off Irishman, the sort that is caricatured, and I think now he must have wallowed in it.

None the less Paris was important to Brendan in that it cut him down to size. In Dublin it was too easy to acquire a reputation as a pregnant writer. There, promise was regarded more highly than fulfilment. Reputations were gained on work that never saw the light of day. In Paris they were interested in what you had done, not what you might do. It was a working writer's city, with an indifference to reputation, especially to those gained outside it, that bordered on the insular. Here Brendan formed habits of regular writing hours and became aware of the need for re-writing. He *worked* at writing—as a craft and not as a means of occupying himself when he wasn't house-painting or drinking. When he finally settled back in Dublin in 1950 he was no longer just an entertaining talker who intended to be a writer: he was a writer who liked to talk a lot.

CHAPTER THIRTEEN

AFTER he had been back in Dublin some time, Brendan wrote to Sindbad Vail in May, 1951:

> Some months ago, I wrote you that I had started a book. I am calling it *Borstal Boy*.
>
> Here is a bit of it.
>
> I might see you in the summer if you are still there. I was in Dieppe last month but only on a jump with an Irish boat. Got drunk on the North Wall and — off with them. Had no papers and so could not go up to Paris . . . and came home, armed with bottles of Pernod, 200 franc ex-bond, which was what I principally came for.

This is the first reference to the book which was to make Brendan famous. As early as 1942, writing from Mountjoy Prison to Bob Bradshaw, he had mentioned writing a novel on the bombing campaign called *The Green Invaders*. But it took Paris to make him begin it.

The Dieppe reference is to an incident when Brendan and a friend, who he was with literally fell onto an Irish fishing boat in the Dublin docks, dead drunk, and found themselves next morning on the way to Dieppe. They were quite broke. His friend remembers that, in despair, they decided to go into a church and pray. On their way in Brendan noticed a church collection box near the Holy Water font. With speed and skill he robbed it, reciting aptly as he did, the Irish proverb: 'Is giorra cabhair De na an doras' (the help of God is nearer than the door).

It was arranged that Vail would publish extracts from the novel in the winter edition of *Points* in 1951. But there was trouble about some of the language Brendan used in his manuscript. Brendan wrote to Vail:

> For the 'fucks' and so forth, could you not manage an initial and a dash? It is an extract from a novel. Why shouldn't it read like that? You must excuse

the terrible typing. It was not my fault. I had to do it myself. No typist in Dublin would look at it. A woman that used to do a bit for me, I fell out with. I have no copy of that MSS. I wonder would it be a terrible big thing to ask you to do whatever excising you would think necessary?

Poems of mine in Gaelic are being broadcast from Radio Eireann, but apart from not understanding Irish, Radio Eireann is but barely audible in the pub next door.

In the same letter he complains about the conditions for a writer living in Dublin as opposed to Paris:

Sometimes I will explain to you the feeling of isolation one suffers writing in a Corporation housing scheme. The literary pubs are not much good to me. I prefer to drink over the north side where the people are not so strange to me. Cultural activity in present-day Dublin is largely agricultural. They write mostly about their hungry bogs and the great scarcity of crumpet. I am a city rat. Joyce is dead and O'Casey is in Devon. The people writing here now have as much interest for me as an epic poet in Finnish or a Lapland novelist.

Writing a few years later in *Vogue* Magazine, Brendan recalled the effect his bohemian habits were having on some neighbours in the building scheme.

Sometimes there were literary parties . . . and I'd come home in the dawn, with my head filled with Portuguese Burgundy and Cork gin, a little unsteadily but happy, the sounds of old ballads and Pisan cantos still in my ears, and hear our neighbour, risen on her elbow from beside her sleeping lord, screech from the bedroom window: 'Are you on the night shift these times?'

As it became clear to her that I had no intention of painting any more, and that I had resigned from the building trade, she'd shout sadly after me, as I fled down the road towards Grafton Street, 'Do you ever think of your poor mother?' and 'Are you going in with them that will neither work nor want?' That was one evening she saw my name in the Radio Eireann programme, and thought I had become an actor or a commentator on Gaelic Football matches.

Eventually the first chapter of his new work was published and came out that winter in *Points*. Hard-core swear words appeared in hyphenated form. The extract, which he called *Bridewell Revisited*, is almost identical with the final version as incorporated in the first chapters of his best-seller *Borstal Boy* six years later.

What one encounters immediately in this extract is an

individual style. There is the sure touch of a writer able to produce exact dialogue. Brendan has a clever ear for regional dialect which he was able to reproduce by accurate phonetic renderings. The characters come to life through what they say as much as by description. There is a constant interior monologue which is personal and involved and makes no concession to the reader's background. For instance

> Oh, Cathlin ni Houlihan, your way is a thorny way. Much you knew about it, Yeats, yourself and Maud Gonne, bent over a turf fire reading Ronsard,

contains in two sentences, a quote from O'Casey, a reference to Yeats's first play in which Maud Gonne appeared, and a play on Yeats's poem 'When you are old and grey', in which there is an image of bending by the glowing fire and is generally thought to have been inspired by Ronsard's famous sonnet.

Brendan can bring one inside the prison cell with its emptiness and loneliness:

> I lay down, put my head on the pillow and wrapped myself in the blankets. The pillow was too much for me. I reversed and made a pillow of my jacket. Then I wanted to use the lavatory. It was in a corner. I stood over it, my bare toes touching the concrete floor. A church bell pealed away in the city. I thought it the dreariest sound that ever defiled the ear of man. It made misery mark time.

After releasing the strain on his nervous system in the traditional manner of solitary prisoners, he lies back and wonders did Irish patriots before him do the same thing. But in the final version as published in book form he leaves out the *names* of the patriots, one modern and one historical, knowing well that there are certain deified national figures that an ex-I.R.A. man, no matter how far he travels in fiction, may not traduce.

Though he refers to this work as 'the novel' it is obviously autobiographical. This had a double advantage for Brendan. He could make himself into an anti-hero and at the same time appear modest, as he knew quite well he was already established in popular legend in Dublin, as he later would be in England, as the youngster who tried to blow up shipyards in Liverpool. When the screws arrive in his cell to give him a beating for being cheeky he sees very quickly the difference between himself and the other patriotic prisoners that had been before him in English prisons.

> At home, give us back the martyred, mangled mortal remains of our dead hero. Drums muffled, pipes draped. When but a lad of sixteen years, a felon's cap he wore and in an English prison Ireland's cross he proudly bore. Lot of good all that to the poor f——er in the box.

In June, 1952, he writes to Vail that he is still hard at work on 'the novel'. He has left the Dublin set temporarily and has gone down the country determined to get a full length book off his chest. There is a reference in this letter to drinking, which is repeated in another written shortly afterwards. We can see the difficulty he was having in working and living in Dublin, where talk and social intercourse, lubricated by alcohol, take up much of the time which writers elsewhere spend in writing. It is clear than Brendan is worried for the first time that drink is getting the upper hand in him. He excuses himself by saying that it is due to free-lance writing and the effort of having to interview people. But we can sense that he is worried because for the first time he has realized that he is beginning to use drink as a means of bolstering up his nervous system and is becoming dependent on it.

> I decided to go to work as a free-lance writer to get enough money to finish my novel in peace. That's an easier trade than house-painting, that is . . .
> I made a packet, and very nearly lost my sanity in the process: I was drunk night, noon and morning. Now, outside of reform school and Borstal, I have been a steady drinker from the age of fifteen, but this wasn't that sort of drinking. It wasn't even like going in for one into the Babillon or the Reine Blanche (one bit of Paris I do not miss), and finishing in Les Halles the next morning, or in the rue Cordellières (up at Port Royal, at the Salvation Army—a bit more usual for me): it was just 'Givvez three thousand on — Brendan, will you? Usual rates, guineas a thousand and the shillings for meself' . . . 'Do iz an ould proagramme for the Easter Commemoration and I'il see Sean about the other.'
> And I finally said, to hell with it. I'll go down and do my own which is what I'm doing now, and am broke, and it is a matter of some scoff for next week. The mountains are lovely. I wish I had a snap, and this is an old hideout of the I.R.A. There was a man shot dead by the Free State Army at the very window I'm writing this at. And for all I run down the I.R.A. in my writing they were the only damn ones, when I had no place

to write in peace, to say, 'That's all right Brendan, you go down there and use G . . . it's no good to us now, it's too well known.' So here I am and very happy and I'll have the novel finished in its entirety before Christmas, and I'll submit to you a few thousand words.

It was while Brendan was living in the 'hideout' referred to in this letter, that he paid a visit to J. P. Donleavy, who had a pad nearby in Co. Wicklow. Donleavy not being in, Brendan made himself at home, mixing himself an enormous bowl of raisins, cornflakes, porter, butter, eggs and flour, which he later drained in a few gulps, to the astonishment of his host who had then returned. Donleavy was annoyed to find that in his absence Brendan had been altering the draft of his own manuscript of a novel on Dublin (later to become *The Ginger Man*) and had added his suggestions and corrections in ink. Later however, Donleavy recognized that many of the corrections were justified, and retained a number of them in the final draft. Brendan also showed him a draft of *Borstal Boy* that day which revealed to Donleavy for the first time Brendan's talent as a writer.

A month later, in another letter written to Vail in October 1952, Brendan is complaining about the literary set he has to mix with in Dublin.

A piece of verse in Gaelic I had in the *Irish Times* Saturday book-page, with accompanying translation by Donagh MacDonagh, was about the death of Wilde in the Hotel d'Alsace. It was much praised by the local mandarins or mandarineens, and then the next issue, Monday, had a most vicious letter attacking it as 'brutal' and 'ugly' . . . Jesus help my wit, didn't I think I was a great man altogether, when complete strangers would go to the trouble of abusing me thus (for, as you know, it's better to be adversely criticised than ignored), till I discovered the fucker that wrote the letter was someone that disliked me on grounds purely racial and social, and thought it a disgrace that the likes of me should be allowed into print at all, unless it would be into the criminal intelligence.[1]

[1] This letter appeared in the *Irish Times*, September 24, 1952:
Sir, When Oscar Wilde was dying in Paris—'beyond my means,' as he character-istically remarked—he disliked the hideous wallpaper of his room, and said: 'One of us had to go'.
He would have disliked another sort of paper with a brutally ugly verse about him in it today, and this time, if one of them has to go, it will not be Oscar Wilde.

County Dublin,   Yours, etc.,
September 20th, 1952.   'SALOME'

It's a thing we all do. I had a story rejected by — here at one time and went round the city saying the Editor was long known to the G.H.Q. of the I.R.A. as an agent of the British Government.

Things here are much as usual, except that Paddy the wanker, poet and peasant, is in London, which is as near home as he can get, not having the fare to Boston or New York. The disciples he left behind him still line the bars and give me an odd pint of malt, if I can listen respectfully enough to the old chat about Angst. A generation or so ago, they were arsing around the bog and a bowl of stirabout and a couple of platefuls of spuds would have cured all the Angst from here back to Norway: but since the change-over in Twenty-two, when they got well down to the porridge pot, there's no holding them. It started off with top-hats and white ties, and getting into the gentry, and then to chatting about the servant problem with the Horse-Protestants, and it went from that till late dinner, and now it's Angst, no less.

The 'poet and peasant' referred to here is Patrick Kavanagh, who regarded Brendan as 'incarnate evil'.

In the same letter to Sindbad Vail, Brendan had further news about his novel:

I have about 50,000 words done. I haven't done much to it lately, because I'm writing a play for the Abbey and have had to do some jobs for the radio and various journals to live. As it turned out, the strain of meeting the sort of people who have to do with journalism was so great that, for the first time in my life, I drank from pure nervous strain. I have a feeling I told you all this before. (So have you, more than likely, by the time you get this far.)

. . . I'm Jesus well starved of any kind of contact at the moment. The worst feature of the angsters is that they have it mixed with fox-hunting and meeting horses. I never knew a horse (to speak to, I mean) till I went to the nick in England and they put me ploughing on the farm because I was an Irishman. The end of my tussle with the horse was that I ran away and a warder fired at me, he thought I was trying to escape. So I was, from the bloody horse.

If he had, in fact, completed 50,000 words, this was not bad by Dublin standards in a little over a year.

Brendan had two short stories published at this time; one, *A Woman of No Standing*, in *Envoy* in 1950, and another, *The*

Confirmation Suit, in the *Standard* in 1953. They are an indication that he had learned to write and re-write, pare his work down to the minimum until he obtained the exact effect on paper that had first come before him as a picture in his mind. Both these stories are seen through the eyes of a little boy who tells them in the first person. The world that passes before his eyes is different from ours. He discerns the exceptional where the adult cannot, and is puzzled that what appears clear to him is not so to anybody else. The first paragraph in *A Women of No Standing* catches the mood immediately. The phrase 'this person' immediately establishes the central figure as an outsider:

> 'And the priest turns round to me', says Ria, 'and says he': 'But you don't mean to say that this person still goes down to see him.'
> 'I do, Father.'
> 'And brings him cigarettes?'
> 'Not now, Father, not cigarettes, he's gone past smoking and well past it, but a drop of chicken soup, tho' he can't manage that either, these last few days.'
> 'Well, chicken soup or cigarettes', says the priest, 'what really matters is that this person continues to visit him—continues to trouble his conscience—continues as a walking occasion of sin to stand between him and heaven. These Pigeon House people must be, shall be, told straight away. They'll be informed that you, and you only, are his lawfully wedded wife, and she is only—what she is. Anyway, this way or that, into that sanatorium she goes no more.'

The child overhears the grown-ups discussing the affair between 'this woman' and another man—'the ruined version of what was once the gassest little ex-Dublin Fusilier in the street'.

When the man dies, all that concerns the nun and the women was that he had abjured his lover and that 'he'd no mortal sin on his soul to detain him in torment for any longer than a few short years of harmonious torture in Purgatory'. At the funeral, the child is anxious to see the strange woman who seemed to have so much power and whom he had conjured up as 'dolled up to the nines, paint and powder and a fur coat maybe'. But there was only a poor creature, bent in prayer, in a ragged coat:

> 'Fur coat, how are you', said Ria scornfully, 'and she out scrubbing halls for me dear departed this last four years—since he took bad.'

She passed quite near us and she going out the door of the pub after-wards—her head down and a pale hunted look in her eyes.

In the *Confirmation Suit* Miss McCann, the central figure, is also an outsider. She is a seamstress of genteel background who lives in a tenement room. We can be sure that her character is based on one of those collected under the benevolent despotism of Mrs English, Brendan's granny, who in return for the surrender of their pensions would give them their keep and a room in one of her tenement houses. We sense from the child's account that Miss McCann is different in some way from other people in the neighbourhood.

> Miss McCann worked a sewing-machine, making habits for the dead. . . .
> Sometimes girls from our quarter got her to make dresses and costumes, but mostly she stuck to the habits. They were a steady line, she said, and you didn't have to be always buying patterns, for the fashions didn't change, not even from summer to winter. They were like a long brown shirt, and a hood attached, that was closed over the person's face before the coffin lid was screwed down. A sort of little banner hung out of one arm, made of the same material, and four silk rosettes in each corner, and in the middle the letters I.H.S., which mean, Miss McCann said, 'I Have Suffered'.

The child's Granny commissions Miss McCann to make him a suit for his Confirmation. The story turns on his fear that she will design him an old-fashioned suit remembered from her genteel days and make him a laughing-stock in front of the other boys. There is an excellent sketch of Mrs English herself in the story, and the efforts made by relatives to get her to wash more often ('My grandmother took a bath every year, whether she was dirty or not, but she was in no way bigoted in the washing line in between times.') and make her eat sensible food:

> Aunt Jack was very much up for sheep's heads too. They were so cheap and nourishing. . . .
> But my grandmother only tried it once. She had been a first-class gilder in Eustace Street, but never had anything to do with sheep's heads before. When she took it out of the pot, and laid it on the plate, she and I sat looking at it, in fear and trembling. It was bad enough going into the pot, but with the soup streaming from its eyes, and its big teeth clenched in a

very bad temper, it would put the heart crossways in you. My grandmother asked me, in a whisper, if I ever thought a sheep could look so vindictive, but that it was more like the head of an old man, and would I for God's sake take it up and throw it out of the window. The sheep kept glaring at us, but I came the far side of it, and rushed over to the window and threw it out in a flash. My grandmother had to drink a Baby Power whiskey, for she wasn't the better of herself.

When the suit is produced, the child's worst fears are justified.

The lapels were little wee things, like what you'd see in pictures like *Ring* magazine of John L. Sullivan, or Gentleman Jim, and the buttons were the size of saucers, or within the bawl of an ass of it, and I nearly cried when I saw them being put on, and ran down to my mother, and begged her to get me any sort of suit, even a jersey and pants, than have me set up before the people in this get-up.

With great resource, he finds a solution to satisfy all. He wears the suit, but keeps his overcoat on as well for the Confirmation ceremony, where at the finish he faints from the heat.

Sunday after Sunday, my mother fought over the suit. She said I was a liar and a hypocrite, putting it on for a few minutes every week, and running into Miss McCann's and out again, letting her think I wore it every week-end. In a passionate temper my mother said she would show me up, and tell Miss McCann.

The boy can't believe his mother will let on to Miss McCann about him. But one day he rushes in as usual in his confirmation suit to tell the seamstress he is going to the theatre:

She was bent over the sewing-machine and all I could see was the top of her old grey head, and the rest of her shaking with crying, and her arms folded under her head on a bit of habit where she had been finishing the I.H.S. I ran down the stairs and back into our place, and my mother was sitting at the fire, sad and sorry, but saying nothing.

I needn't have worried about the suit lasting forever. Miss McCann didn't. The next winter was not so mild, and she was whipped before the year was out. At her wake people said how she was in a habit of her own making, and my father said she would look queer in anything else, seeing as she supplied the dead of the whole quarter for forty years, without one complaint from a customer.

At the funeral, I left my topcoat in the carriage and got out and walked in the spills of rain after her coffin. People said I would get my end, but I went on till we reached the graveside, and I stood in my Confirmation suit drenched to the skin. I thought this was the least I could do.

Out of a seamstress and a working man's fancy woman, Behan has created a pair of anti-heroines. Both stories are carefully constructed with the pace accelerating at exactly the right time. The language is pared to the bone. From these two stories we can see that he had learned to work on prose as he worked on poetry, re-writing till he got his effect, instead of ripping it out of the typewriter without correction. *The Confirmation Suit*, with its Maupassant-like insights into Dublin working class life, may have been the best single piece Brendan ever wrote.

CHAPTER FOURTEEN

From 1950 onwards, Brendan made his living by writing. His two regular sources of income were from Radio Eireann and the *Irish Press*.

At Radio Eireann his patron was Micheál O hAodha, Assistant Director of Drama, who quickly spotted his talent and proceeded to employ him in the Programme 'Ballad Maker's Saturday Night'. This was a ballad programme which Brendan not only scripted, but sang in as well. In this way his splendid tenor voice became known to thousands of Irish people in pre-television days.

His repertoire of ballads inherited from his mother and uncle, was invaluable for this programme. It was noticeable that he never sang from the script, but always relied on his flawless memory to sing in Gaelic or English.

Micheál O hAodha thought that Brendan might be able to do some radio plays on the lines of the stories he told so marvellously over a drink in the pub across the road from Radio Eireann.

The result was two playlets, *Moving Out* and *The Garden Party*.

The first deals with the Hannigan family's move from tenements in Town to Kimmage, and the adventures of the head of the family who is left behind and has to find his way through a maze of unnamed suburban roads. It is based on an incident that actually occurred to Stephen when Kathleen moved the whole Behan brood to Kimmage without him rather than wait on her procrastinating spouse.

The second, *The Garden Party*, is also based on a characteristic of Stephen's, his reluctance to dig the garden of their new home at 70 Kildare Road. In the radio sketch, Brendan arranges for

Mr Hannigan to have his garden dug for him by pretending that there is stolen bullion buried in it, so that the police are forced to dig the patch in their effort to regain the swag.

Moving Out and *The Garden Party* are merely sketches. But they show a gift for dialogue and for telling a story within the limitations of dramatic form; it was clear that Brendan had a talent for play-writing if he wanted to develop it. An excellent example of his gift for descriptive stage dialogue occurs in *Moving Out*. One of the neighbours tells Mrs Hannigan of her experiences with the pork butcher.

> Says I, says I, it's a while now since we had a pig's cheek and himself was always partial to a bit, especially the ear, but there's pig's cheek and pig's cheek in it. The one old Daly handed me was the most ugly looking object you ever put an eye to. It was after being shoved up again the side of a barrel by all the other cheeks and was all twisted. A class of cock-eyed, ma'am, if you follow my meaning. 'God bless us and save us', says I in my own mind, 'if I put that up to him with the bit of cabbage, and that twisty look in it's eye, when he goes to put a knife in it, he'll throw me out.' So I says to old Daly, says I, 'God bless us and save us, Mr Daly', says I, 'but that's a very peculiar looking pig's cheek.' And says he, 'What do you want for two shillings', says he, 'Mee-hawl MacLillimore?'[1] The impudent ould dog. Says he, 'Hold on a minute, and I'll see if I can get you one that died with a smile.'

Brendan would usually arrive for rehearsals accompanied by one or two hangers-on, who would wait quietly in the studio while he performed, murmuring appreciatively in anticipation of the gargle to be supplied when the performance was over. He was always on the look-out for ready payment. Once his work was done, he wanted the money to spend it as soon as possible. On one occasion when Micheál O hAodha tried to point out that it was difficult for a state body to pay in advance, Brendan looked round at his companions and muttered darkly, 'There is an awful lot of glass around here'. For years he kept Micheál O hAodha and other actors entertained with his stories in a pub across the the road from the Studio. Eventually Brendan was banned from the pub there when the owner, a pious teetotaller, heard him lift

---

[1] Micheál MacLiammóir, the distinguished Irish actor best known for his One-Man Show on Oscar Wilde, *The Importance of being Oscar.*

the phone after it had rung and say, 'This is the Archbishop's fucking palace'.

He had a curious loyalty to his drinking companions. Some of them were hangers-on of no special merit. Others, like 'Spike' McCormack, a former British middleweight champion, were genuine friends. Once Brendan went into a bar on the quays with 'Spike' for a drink. Brendan was on the dry for a change, but the barman refused to serve 'Spike'. Brendan was outraged. He knew perfectly well that until recently the pub had been a notorious hang-out for prostitutes. One of them had been murdered and, frightened by the subsequent publicity, the pub owner in a sudden fit of piety, brandished his Rosary beads and banned the girls.

Then out of the corner of his eye, Brendan saw a man going to the lavatory. 'Watch out you don't pull the chain too hard', he roared at him, 'or you'll be drowned in a confetti of contraceptives'.

In 1953, Jim McGuinness, then Editor of the *Irish Press*, one of the three Irish national dailies, suggested to Brendan that he did a column in his paper. He was to write about the Dublin he knew, and would be paid £5 a week. This was a fortune for Brendan in those days.

It also brought him status.

Under McGuinness, the *Irish Press* had begun to employ writers as well as journalists in their columns, a rare enough occurrence in an Irish daily.

Lennox Robinson, the Abbey playwright and director was among the regular contributors, so it was a heartening recognition of Brendan's talent that he should be asked to join such company. He had to contribute three columns a week. Writing to a deadline was excellent training for him. He cultivated a pride in his ability to produce material at short notice. It gave him a sense of being a professional. Donal Foley, at that time London Editor of the *Irish Press*, remembers being approached by Brendan in London for an advance on his articles. Foley was advised by his head office not to give the advance until Brendan had produced three articles. When he told him this, Brendan with a breast pocket full of pencils and a quire of foolscap, retired to a sunny corner of Lincoln's Inn Fields. He returned triumphantly five hours later with four articles finished, and collected his advance.

These articles in the *Press* were later to be collected in book form and published under the title of *Hold your Hour and Have Another*. Taken as a whole, they appear to stand the test of time and survive as essays of city life in the Hazlitt or Leigh Hunt tradition. The denizens of Brendan's pub world have nicknames like Duck the Bullet, Red Jam Roll, Waxy Doyle, Rasher Campbell, Whacker Kinsella, Jewels Loughrey. There is mad Mrs Mountpenny who came back from Howth fishing village in 1927 thinking she was a lobster and ever since shrieks 'murderer, torturer who murdered my poor brothers and sisters' when she passes a fishmonger and looks at the crabs 'and cousins'. There was Aloysius Giltrap who always clapped in chapel, thinking he was at the theatre and ex-Provost Sergeant Coonee, who gets his wife up at three o'clock in the morning to do pack-drill and bayonet practice with a sweeping brush.

The dialogue is the genial, relaxed chatter of the Dublin market pubs where the fish-women and vegetable sellers go after their day's work. The market pubs open at six in the morning to accommodate cattle men and those connected with the daily supply and sale of fresh food to the city. The street vendors, often women of some property, are known as 'oul wans'.

Brendan, the I.R.A. man, records faithfully the British Army tradition that runs through Dublin's slumland. Since Waterloo, when many of Wellington's soldiers had been Dubliners, there had been a tradition of foreign military service among the working classes of Dublin. Most families had relations in The Royal Dublin Fusiliers in the Great War. Brendan had two uncles in the 'Dirtyshirts', as that regiment was known, and tales of Ypres and Gallipoli, Guinchy and the Somme feature in the talk he records.[1]

---

[1] One of Brendan's favourite books as a little boy had been a biography of Fr Willie Doyle, S. J., chaplain to the Dublin Fusiliers in the First War. The Dubliner in him reached out to the padre's account of the Irish lads in the trenches in France singing the Adeste in their Dublin accents before going over the top at Christmas, though he would scarcely have admitted such sentiments to his Republican comrades.

Some of the 'oul wans' had relatives in the Boer War; Maria Concepta describes how her husband Hogger perished:

'And more so, Brending Behing. The War Office had no news of him for weeks, and thought he might have been a prisoner and still alive. Though in the heels of the hunt, we gave up all hope.'

She sniffed into the butt end of the tumbler.

'Ah, yes. When they found six Dubling Fusiliers' buttings in a lying's dem.'

'Them lions', said Maria, 'you could never trust them.'

'And there was boings with the buttings.'

'Buttons and Bones', said I.

Another character, Fusilier Kinsella, recalls an 'encounter' with Field-Marshal Lord Roberts in the Boer War.

' "Wipe your bayonet, Fusilier Kinsella, you killed enough." '

'Go on', says I.

'That's genuine', said Kinsella, 'that's what Lord Roberts says to me in Blamevontame in 'nought one. I knew him before, of course, from the time we were in Egg Wiped.'

' "Shifty Cush!" says Bobs when he seen me on parade. "Is that you, Kinsella?" "It is" says I, coming smartly to attention, "Who were you expecting?" '

' "You've killed enough of bores", says Bobs.'

Maria Concepta and another lady Mrs Brennan are stock characters who appeared each week in the stories. So is Mr Crippen. (Crippen got his name from having had the reputation of serving such bad drink as a Mess Sergeant in the Free State Army Mess during the Civil War, that he was said to have killed more of his own men than the opposition did.)

Mr Crippen's venture into verse is well received by his pub audience.

'A bit of order now', said Mrs Brennan, 'and let the man show us his soul and his heart.'

Crippen lowered the half and projected his gaze far through Michael's window. Or to be precise, to the other side of East Arran Street, ten yards distant, to the wall of the cabbage factory. He spoke in the agonized tones of one who had seen much, and didn't fancy any of it.

That's the way he spoke:

'There is a sadness in my sadness when I'm sad.
There is a gladness in my gladness when I'm glad.
There is a madness in my madness when I'm mad.
But the sadness in my sadness
And the gladness in my gladness—'
  'And the madness in your madness', murmured Mrs Brennan respectfully.
    '—Are nothing to my badness when I'm bad.'
  There was a moment's silence and Mrs Brennan shook her head in the direction of the poet.
  'Mr Cripping', she sighed, 'you're rotting. Rotting with braings.'

Brendan was, of course, a talented impersonator, and there were few regional accents which he could not give a good imitation of. For his writing, he devised a phonetic system of his own which enabled him to reproduce for the reader's eye, the way people talked in the market pubs. If the following sentence is read out loud, it gives an almost perfect reproduction of the way Dublin people talk.

'Iz a mazzive pit-chewer', said the Granny Carmody in Grenville Street language. 'Yez zee all the poo-war japs and the coming offa the Brizidge battle chips and been mone dow-in in the wawdher.'

Translated this means:

'It's a massive picture', said the Granny Carmody in Greenville Street language. 'You see all the poor chaps and they coming off the British battleships and being mown down in the water.'

About this time Brendan was supplementing his income with occasional voyages to France on smuggling trips under the aegis of an Englishman who had been a safebreaker before the war and had then become well known as a double agent during it, receiving a pardon for his patriotic activities. On one of these visits to France in November, 1952, Brendan decided to visit his compatriot Samuel Beckett, who was at that time engaged in the production of the world première of *Waiting For Godot*.
One morning at 6.30 a.m. Beckett was awakened by a tremendous ringing of the bell in his flat. He found Brendan at the door, covered in mud and blood, but otherwise in cheerful enough mood. Brendan insisted on coming in and chatted

amiably for the next three hours. Beckett found the first half hour of the monologue fascinating, but grew understandably fatigued as it continued unabated. Then he realised he would have to be at the Théâtre Babylon for rehearsal at 9.30 a.m. He took Brendan with him on the Metro and managed to deflect him to the office of *Merlin* a magazine run by Christopher Logue and Dick Silver.

Later Beckett went to Brendan's lodgings in rue des Feuillantes and paid some rent due to a landlord who had been threatening Brendan with eviction.

His smuggling adventures gave Brendan material for a novel which he turned into a serial for the *Irish Times*. He asked the editor, R. M. Smyllie, for an advance. But Smyllie, knowing Brendan's habits, refused him. Brendan set out for the Aran Islands to write, and in a few days had produced enough material to extract £90 from Smyllie.

The Scarperer (scarper is prison slang for an escape) as the series was called, appeared in 1954 and was published under the name of Emmett Street. It deals with an English prisoner in Mountjoy Prison, Dublin, whose escape is arranged because he is the double of a French gangster, Pierre Le Fou. When he has been sprung from the prison, the scarperer is dumped overboard in the English Channel dressed in French clothes and with a passport to indicate, when the body is washed up, that it is that of Pierre Le Fou. The murderers are caught in a bizarre manner when a tweedy, middle-aged spinster from 'The Irish Society for the Defence of the Horse' mistakes them for horse dealers exporting horses from Ireland under cruel and insanitary conditions and reports them to the French police as 'murderers of our dumb brothers'. The police take her literally and a vivid shooting match ends the novel.

The Scarperer is not an important work. It shows, however, that Brendan could write mild fiction at this stage and sustain a plot at novel length.

The violent episodes are well described in short, spare sentences. But he thought so little of it that it was not until his publishers suggested it in 1962 that he considered having the serial assembled and published as a novel.

While Brendan was in the Aran Islands, he and Fr Tadhg Moran, the Curate on Inisheer, became firm friends. Brendan made the little priest his private bank, making him promise never to give him more than £5 out of the £90 he had got from the *Irish Times*, when he would come looking for it in a state of inebriation. They had some heated arguments but on the whole Fr Tadhg managed to make Brendan keep to their agreement.

Fr Tadhg remembers that Brendan was meticulous about attending Mass and Benediction when he was on the Island. They had many discussions about religion, walking on the Atlantic strands of the last Island of Europe.

A few years later, at Carraroe, on the mainland, Brendan gave Fr Tadhg a copy of *The Quare Fellow* with the words: 'Tuigeann an tAthair Tadhg Brendean O'Beachain.' (Fr Tadhg understands Brendan Behan.)

As he wrote this down, Brendan warned Fr Tadhg not to let the Bishops see the book or he would never become a Parish Priest.

R. M. Smyllie, of the *Irish Times*, had been very helpful to Brendan in this period. Indeed, Brendan was lucky in that he had the editors of two national newspapers taking an interest in him at this time, and giving him an outlet for his writing.

Smyllie, one of the notable editors of his time, has appeared in numerous reminiscences and has been portrayed in detail by two of his protégés, Brian Inglis and Patrick Campbell (now Lord Glenavy). Smyllie had piloted the *Irish Times* through its difficult period, when it had to make its adjustment from being a paper which represented the Unionist Ascendancy, to that of a Protestant Liberal one representing the minority point of view, and at the same time identifying to some extent, with the changes which were taking place in the new Ireland. During the war the paper was unashamedly pro-British in its alignment and many stratagems were adopted to beat the censor. The most famous was on the day the war ended, when the front page of the paper contained ordinary news releases which were displayed in such a way as to form a huge V.

Smyllie sang his editorials in a form of plain chant while they were copied down in furious haste by his office staff, and at the same time sharpened his thumbnail with a razor so that it had grown to resemble a pen nib, as Keats had done. He, the West-British editor, and Brendan, the former I.R.A. dynamitard, struck up a close friendship.

One of Smyllie's more hilarious wheezes was to send Brendan to Paris in June 1953 to write a column on the French reaction to the radio commentary on the France-Ireland soccer International that was to be played in Dublin at the end of the week. It was arranged that Brendan should fly to Paris as he was still prohibited from landing in England under the Deportation Order served on him in 1942. Unwisely however, Smyllie had handed Brendan the money for the air fare without buying the ticket, with the result that Brendan and a former Golden Gloves boxer friend of his, Ernie Smith, got roaring drunk the night before he was due to leave for Paris.

Brendan's only means of getting to France now was to go by boat to England. He raised just enough money to go to England where his brother-in-law, Joe Paton, gave him enough to go to Paris by way of Newhaven.

At Newhaven the Customs officer questioned Brendan closely as to what papers he wrote for. Brendan denied vigorously that he was related to Brendan Behan. At this the Customs officer lost his temper and gripped him by the arm screaming 'You are Brendan Behan'. He was taken to the headquarters of the Sussex police and Lewes jail, where he went through the familiar routine of finger-printing and being searched, and afterwards found himself in even more familiar surroundings: the lavatory bowl, the bare bed and the spy-hole for the 'screw' to observe him.

Next day he was cross-examined by Special Branch men who were anxious to find out if he was on an I.R.A. mission. Their failure to extort anything out of him seemed to please the local police who were guarding him. The next day he was brought to court where the magistrate remanded him for three days.

After he returned to his cell, the police were kind enough to give him pen and paper and he was able to make copious notes which he knew he could put to good use in the book on prison life he was writing. Jack Molloy, Counsellor at the Irish Embassy, paid him a visit and arranged for a barrister named Carter to defend him.

The case was heard by a woman magistrate. She listened sympathetically to Brendan's explanation. He was fined £15 and costs. An interesting aspect of the case is that Brendan's barrister, during the course of his address to the court, declared that the Irish police had applied to have the Deportation Order on Brendan revoked. For some time Brendan had been agitating to have this done and he had actually formally renounced his membership of the I.R.A. He was anxious to be able to travel back and forth to England without being in constant fear of arrest. As a result of representations made on his behalf by the Irish police, the Deportation Order was revoked in 1954.

After he was released from jail, Brendan was free to go to France and was escorted to the boat by a police officer who turned out to be a Dublin man.

When he arrived in Paris, he looked up Desmond Ryan the *Irish Times* correspondent, who got him into a hotel at the back of the Luxembourg. There, next day, he listened to what he could understand of the French commentator's account of the match, from Dublin. Ireland won, the French commentator said, because the French team was terrified by the 'Dalymount' roar.

Brendan was terrified to face Smyllie on his return. But the kindly editor put his arms round Brendan's shoulder and said: 'You will kill yourself more with drink, Brendan, than the I.R.A.' As he left, Smyllie handed Brendan an envelope. Brendan opened it later in the pub across the road. 'Jasus, it's a blue one', the barman said, as a tenner fell out.

When Smyllie died two years later, Brendan cried like a child. Said Stephen Behan of his own son, 'Brendan loved old Smyllie like a father'.

Constant work helped Brendan to consolidate the habit he had acquired in France, of writing rather than talking. But now he had a regular flow of money it meant that he drank more often and in greater quantity. Physically, in these years, he underwent a great change. Gone was the slim boy of eleven stone, of 1948, good-looking with black hair, blue eyes and flawless skin, and not a pick of extra flesh on his lean body. His face fattened and his whole body had coarsened between 1950 and 1953. There was a sudden change. Besides the increase in the regularity and size of his income, this was also related to his diabetic condition which remained undiagnosed until 1956.

Brendan was disturbed at this change in his appearance. But he used to joke about it to his friend, Mattie O'Neill, an I.R.A. man who had been in the Curragh with him, and say, 'I don't care what happens as long as I keep my teeth and hair'. He was to keep his hair, but some of his front teeth were knocked out in a fight in 1959. He never replaced them.

Drink had come to mean a lot to him—the larger he grew, the more his body needed nourishment. Reared since he was a boy of eight by his Granny, on the belief that porter was nourishing, and drinking it since that age, he didn't need much encouragement when he had money, to spend it on heavy drinking with his friends. It became noticeable at this time too, that if he went beyond a certain stage in drink, he became savage. This is one explanation of the frequent outbursts he made against people, and for the numerous assaults that occurred in pubs at this time, when he was present.

Drink changed his personality.

On March 29, 1953, he refused to leave Roberts Café in Grafton Street. The police were called, and Brendan fought them in Anne's Lane nearby. He ended up spending the night in a cell with a broken ankle.

Next day he was convicted of drunk and disorderly behaviour, by Justice O'Flynn, in the District Court. He was sentenced to a week's imprisonment. His solicitor, James McGoldrick, said in his address to the Justice:

> Brendan Behan's political persuasions might not nowadays be tolerated, but at one time he would have been a political hero in this country. He could be totally misguided by the sight of a Guard in uniform.

When he arrived in Mountjoy Jail to serve his sentence,

Brendan was interviewed by his old friend, Governor Kavanagh.

Kavanagh was distressed at Brendan's appearance. He remembered him as a trim, athletic young man in 1948; now, five years later, Brendan had aged considerably and was three stone heavier, fat and flabby.

The genial Governor did not make him wear prison clothes; but gave him the freedom of his office and lent him *War and Peace*. Brendan brought the book out with him on his release and never returned it, which is the reason the Governor says today that he, himself, never got down to reading Tolstoy's massive work.

In January, 1954, Brendan had an encounter with another Kavanagh. Dublin erupted with one of its regular literary libel actions when Patrick Kavanagh, poet and novelist, took an action against the *Leader* magazine, claiming that he had been defamed in a profile written about him. During the course of the case, while Kavanagh was being cross-examined, Brendan's name was mentioned on a number of occasions and he received some notoriety as a result.

The bitterness between the two was generally thought to have begun during this action, but from the beginning there was a rivalry between them which is not easy to understand between men of similar temperament who should have had interests in common.

One distinction was that Kavanagh was a countryman (from County Monaghan) while Brendan was city bred. Behan summed up the antagonism between rural and urban writers in Ireland in an article for *Vogue* in May, 1956:

Those of the bogmen who could speak Irish I could exchange greetings with, but I could not understand the English-speakers very well. I speak Dublin, Belfast, Cockney, Geordie, rhyming slang, but like Nehru, I have no common tongue with the majority of my countrymen from the interior. Especially when they had a few issues of *Horizon* digested and mixed the names of the English literary great into their speeches:

'Hah sure Aydit is a naice semple wamman at the back avitt, aye shewerly, Aye. And more betoken and where would you have

163

Satchamarverell? And Aveleen Waw has the Ting, aye, an' Sirril, aye, and Graves—aye but you wouldn't be sure a Raine, owenly sometimes.'[2]

I didn't know whether I had the Thing or not. What I did know was that whatever about the pen being mightier than the sword—it's lighter than the stockbrush.

It was this libel action which first made the antagonism between Behan and Kavanagh known to the general public. During the course of the trial Kavanagh was asked about Behan and replied:

> I hate to say anything really cruel, but there was always something in Brendan Behan that to my mind was not good. I have been friendly with him hoping that I would be free from the horror of his acquaintanceship.

In court the following day Kavanagh was handed a copy of his novel *Tarry Flynn*, autographed to 'my friend Brendan Behan'. Kavanagh was nonplussed.

Actually, Behan's brother, Rory, without Brendan's knowledge, had given the book to the Defence. Brendan was furious with Rory for doing this, and told him he should never interfere between writers.

It has become clear from a recently published letter included in *Lapped Furrows* (Peter Kavanagh Hand Press, 1969) that Kavanagh believed that part of the article alleged to be libellous was written by Behan. I have been assured by the author of the article that this is not true.

A year later, Kavanagh's obsession with Brendan preyed so much on his mind that before he went into hospital for a serious operation he wrote a memorandum to be issued after his death in case he did not survive:

> Behan was closely involved with the writer of the Profile for months before the case and acted as a sort of agent provocateur racing after me, leering at me, till in the end the opposition knew that they had only to

---

[2] This is obviously meant to be Kavanagh speaking. It is an excellent phonetic rendering of the Monaghan accent. In English it reads:

> Hah sure Edith (Sitwell) is a nice simple woman at the back of it, aye surely, aye. And more betoken where would you leave Sacheverell? And Evelyn Waugh has the Thing, aye, and Cyril (Connolly), aye, and Graves —aye but you wouldn't be sure of Raine, only sometimes.'

mention his name to get me angry. There appears to be in me a kind of reserve of dignity that makes people like Behan raving mad; they try to get through and are repulsed when they come up against that area of impenetrable defence which defends the soul.

Later on, Behan mellowed towards Kavanagh and would never let anyone denigrate his work in his presence, considering him the greatest living Irish poet. Kavanagh, on the other hand, continued to regard Behan with hatred even after Behan's death.

He may have resented Behan's inherent capacity for publicizing himself, sensing that if Brendan got a platform at all he could become a world figure. Though Kavanagh himself savagely desired recognition, he was never prepared to compromise himself in any way to get it. With a toss of his head and a whinny like a horse, he would spit at those who offered to help him for reasons he despised. He cultivated the lonely isolation of the artist, though his letters show how pleased recognition of his work outside Ireland would have made him. When he died in 1967, though he had some recognition in England, he was virtually unknown in America.

But Patrick Kavanagh was a poet and should have been able to see beyond Behan's pose to the sensitive personality beyond. Yet he chose to see one side only, closing his mind to the other, an example of the bitterness that divides writers everywhere, but that Dublin especially thrives on.

CHAPTER FIFTEEN

By 1954 Brendan had a reputation in Dublin, but he was quite well aware that it did not extend outside the city. With his flair as a publicist, he knew instinctively that he could launch himself on the international scene if he got the right platform. A play or a novel would do it and in that year he completed the work which was to make his name known outside Ireland.

It was a play, later to be called *The Quare Fellow*, which he had originally drafted as far back as 1946 when he was interned in the Curragh.

It's original name was *The Twisting of Another Rope*. This was a pun on the title of a one-act work by Douglas Hyde—*The Twisting of the Rope*, which was the first Gaelic drama to appear on the Irish stage.

The Twisting of Another Rope was based on Brendan's prison experiences and dealt with the reactions of the inhabitants of a prison—warders, governors and prisoners—to the hanging of a condemned man in their midst. When Brendan was at Mountjoy, the prisoners used to refer to the man in the condemned cell as 'the quare fellow'. One of these was Bernard Kirwan, convicted of the murder of his brother, who had said to Brendan the night before he died, 'I will be praying for you in Heaven tonight'. It was on the events surrounding his hanging that Brendan had written his play.

Early in 1954 he sent the play to the Abbey Theatre, where he had sent his first play, *The Landlady*, in 1946. The Managing Director, Ernest Blythe, who had originally suggested that Brendan rewrite a radio script he had shown to him into a full-length play, now found *The Twisting of Another Rope* too long and, after consulting with Lennox Robinson, a fellow-director, asked Brendan to shorten it. Instead, he took it along to the other leading Dublin theatre, The Gate, run by Hilton Edwards and Micheál MacLiammóir. They, too, turned it down. But, by chance, Sally Travers, a niece of Micheál MacLiammóir, read the manuscript and, becoming very excited about it, recommended it to Alan Simpson and Carolyn Swift of the Pike theatre. They were delighted with the play and decided to stage it after they had got Brendan to agree to work on it with them.

The Pike had been presenting avant-garde works in Dublin since 1953. It was a pocket theatre which held only fifty seats. Besides being the first company to obtain the English language rights of *Waiting for Godot* by Samuel Beckett, the Pike had introduced Dublin audiences to playwrights like Ionesco, Betti and Fabri, often before these authors' works had been performed on the English stage.

Carolyn Swift immediately set to work on the script to pare it down and make it suitable for a theatrical performance.

> I had to transfer passages from one part of the play to the other, as it was rather confused. Also, it was grossly over-long. Brendan had a special habit of writing subordinate clauses that did not connect with the main sentence in the audience's mind, but we cleared all that up soon enough.

Brendan was extremely co-operative, she remembers. He approved the changes and quickly re-wrote any passages that he was asked to.

It was Alan Simpson who suggested the title *The Quare Fellow*, which was the name the prisoners used for the man in the condemned cell. Later when *The Quare Fellow* played in the West End and was produced by Jose Quintero at the Circle in the Square theatre in New York, it was to give Brendan an opportunity to emerge from the obscurity of Dublin. By 1960 his exploits and vivid personality had made him better known internationally than most living writers. But unless he first of all had made an impact as a serious writer, he would not have achieved the notoriety he did.

As a play, *The Quare Fellow* lacks climax. The hanging of the condemned man which takes place off stage in the last few seconds of the play, fails to sustain the atmosphere of horror which has been built up before it. Some of the minor roles are more caricatures than characters, such as the prison visitor and the middle-class prisoner convicted of sex crimes. But the main characters, the two lags, Dunlavin and Neighbour, and Warder Regan, are well observed and have the richness of personality which is found in O'Casey, Lady Gregory and Synge.

Slowly, through the conversation of prisoners, warders, government officials and the hangman himself, the paraphernalia of judicial killing is brought before the eyes of the audience. It induces its atmosphere of horror and doom precisely because of the detachment with which the playwright presents the theme. The characters are not divided into heartless warders on one side and kind criminals on the other. Some of the most vicious condemnations of the 'Quare Fellow' man come from the other prisoners. The hero of the play, on the other hand, is a warder whose function it is to oversee the condemned man's last hours and to spend the night before the execution with him.

It is what Harold Hobson, in the *Sunday Times*, was later to call the 'terrible, trivial and impressive ritual' that precedes the taking of human life under the supervision of the State that creates the sense of awe among the audience. The play survives today, despite the absence of the death penalty in most countries, because it deals with a theme which is connected not merely with hanging but with the whole problem of the infliction of violence upon people with or without legal authority, and the corrupting effects of penal correction on those who administer it.

The hero of the play is Warder Regan. He is a devoted Catholic who advises the prisoners to pray to the Blessed Virgin. But he is a humanist, not a puritan. He accepts the system because the Church and Society tell him that it is a moral one; but the humanity in him rejects the hypocrisy in it. He is kind, but given to sarcasm when the occasion demands it. There is a good deal of Brendan's own mixture of religion and humanism in him. Regan, in fact, is Brendan's ideal of the decent Dubliner.

The play had its first night at the Pike Theatre on November 9, 1954. There were some doubts beforehand as to whether Brendan would get drunk on the night of the opening and interrupt the performance. During rehearsals he had usually gone to sleep, but occasionally woke up to shout advice at the players. Tom Willoughby, the manager, and Stephen Behan, however, devised a plan by which Brendan was to be fed as much drink as would keep him immobile during the performance, but not make him so stocious that he would be prevented from making the final speech to the audience if the play was a success.

They need not have worried. *The Quare Fellow* got a tremendous reception. After the final curtain, Brendan came to the front of the stage, made an excellent speech and sang a few ballads. Then he was brought away by the Simpsons to a restaurant to wait for the morning papers. The critics could hardly have been more enthusiastic for a first play. Gabriel Fallon (a director of the Abbey) wrote in the *Evening Press* that:

> When Mr Behan finds himself technically, the Irish Theatre will have found another and, I think, greater O'Casey.

The *Irish Independent* said:

> It could well be the first essay of a great playwright, still fumbling with the mechanics of his art.

while the *Irish Times* critic wrote:

> It produces in retrospect something horribly true to life in its apparent pointlessness.

The Quare Fellow ran for six months in the Pike. Because of the small seating capacity, however, and a large cast, it lost ten shillings a week. Brendan made £25 profit.

Through *The Quare Fellow* he made his name in Dublin. He became an accepted literary figure with a solid work behind him. His literary status improved to such an extent, in fact, that he was consulted by one political party for a suitable election slogan. At one discussion, a member suggested:

> How about 'With Labour from cradle to grave'?

Someone else came up with:

> With Labour from womb to tomb.

Brendan improved on these with:

With Labour from erection to resurrection.

His advice was not acted upon.

One night at a performance of *The Quare Fellow* in January, 1955, Brendan met Beatrice ffrench-Salkeld. She was a young botanist, aged twenty-three, who was employed as an assistant in the National Museum. She had finely-cut Norman features as if she had stepped out of a Plantagenet tapestry, rather like a good-looking version of Edith Sitwell. They had met before at her father's house—Cecil Salkeld being a well-known painter. One day he had heard Brendan announce in Davy Byrne's public house: 'A job is death without dignity', and was so impressed he immediately invited him home to his house in Morehampton Road for a drink, an invitation which was repeated. Brendan for his part was impressed when he heard Salkeld define existentialism as 'teaching that man is sentinel to the null'.

Brendan had first heard about Cecil Salkeld in another context years before. At the Bombing School in Killiney one of the leaders, Paddy O'Flaherty, used to read out selections from Flann O'Brien's *At Swim Two Birds* in which one of the characters, Cashel Byrne, was modelled on Salkeld.

When he first met Beatrice at her father's house, Brendan had been put off by her manner, mistaking her shyness for snobbery; and once had been downright rude to her, calling her 'a bourgeois snob'. Later they had met again when she was staying on Inishmore, one of the Aran Islands, and Brendan had come over for a party from the next Island of Inisheer. He had been banned from Inishmore for locking the local sergeant in a cell and throwing away the keys. Now, at the Pike, while her boyfriend went out for a coffee break at the interval, Brendan made an appointment to meet Beatrice the following week. They went out a number of times in the next month and decided to get married six weeks later.

One night, after they had really got to know each other, at the first night of *Waiting for Godot* at the Pike, he had whispered to her, in between some periods of horseplay with the audience: 'You know, I'm really respectable', and she had replied: 'I don't care whether you are or not.'

The wedding took place at Westland Row Church. It was celebrated by Father Tomkin. The wedding breakfast was at the Morehampton Hotel. Afterwards the bride and groom and most of the guests paid several visits to public houses. At the Lincoln Inn in Lincoln Place, Brendan encountered a street fiddler and asked him to play his favourite air, 'The Coolin'. Brendan sang it at the top of his voice and all round the windows opened and heads peered out.

It was an unusual marriage for Dublin. In a small tight-knit society, the middle-classes and professional classes tended to marry among themselves. Though Brendan's background could fairly be said to be one with genteel overtones, yet the image he had presented to the public, and the manner in which they recognized him, was as a house painter from the slums who had pulled himself up by writing, but who still indulged in drunken outbursts and public horseplay.

Beatrice, on the other hand, was on her grandmother's side a ffrench-Mullen of Galway. They were landed gentry. Her grandmother, Blanaid Salkeld, was a well-known poetess who had been one of the political gentlewomen of the 'twenties. Her father, though—to put it mildly, a man of Bohemian habits (he went to bed in 1957 and got up only once after, for Brendan's funeral) was associated in the public mind with an upper-class background.

Brendan's marriage was a well-kept secret. His parents only learned of it after it was over. He went up to see Kathleen in a taxi with Beatrice and her sister Celia the morning of the marriage. When he came to the door, Kathleen gave him two shirts he had asked her to iron for him and sat him down for a cup of tea. After chatting for a while, she inquired mildly: 'Who are the two little girls in the taxi outside?' 'That's my wife, Mother', Brendan said, bursting into tears and throwing his arms round her, 'but I'll never love anyone the way I love you'. Kathleen told him: 'Sure, Brendan, you know I just love to see people happy.'

When the 'little girls' were brought in, Kathleen was charmed by Beatrice.

'Beatrice is lovely', she would say afterwards, and she did not just mean the physical appearance of this strange girl, but the serenity and stoicism which had enabled her to understand, as Brendan's mother understood, what went on beneath his rough exterior.

When the news of the marriage broke, it seemed impossible that a demure being like Beatrice could cope with Brendan's extrovert personality and his wild drinking habits. It became obvious after a while, however, that this unusual girl had established a measure of control over him. She could be seen sailing serenely in front of him, like a pilot boat guiding a tattered steamer, as he was ejected cursing and roaring from pubs and hotels. When he got into brawls the fact that she remained calm and unruffled seemed to help to restore order. There had been a history of heavy drinking in her family, so she had experience in handling drunkards before she got married. One thing she didn't do was to nag Brendan or reprove him in public. This would have been fatal. The fact that Beatrice made allowances for his outrageousness and put up with him was the surest sign to him that she had seen beneath the mask, and knew him for what he was.

That she had recognized the real Brendan was sufficient for him. She loved him for his stories, his songs, his magnetism, his ability to enthrall any audience he chose. With an artistic temperament herself, she understood his desire to succeed at all costs as a writer. She was his best fan, who saw him in the raw and took him for what he was. He, in his way, loved her. Later he was to rant about Beatrice's middle-class background, that she wanted him to be out on Sandymount Strand every day with the dog, instead of living the life of an artist. This accusation was unfair. What she wanted Brendan to do, above all, was to write and follow his profession. It was when his drinking and carousing began to make writing impossible that she showed her disapproval.

There is no doubt, also, that he was anything but distressed by

Beatrice's social background. She was an artist who was at the same time a lady, in his eyes an ideal combination. He seems to have felt, subconsciously, that the Behans were getting back nearer to where they belonged and away from the council houses in Kimmage. He would never, of course, admit this in public. In outbursts of inverted snobbery, he used to like to show that he was well acquainted with the public school and rugby-playing classes, but that he was not at all impressed by them and really more at home with working-class people even though his company was sought in the highest circles.

In the next few years he was often confused by old allegiances. His I.R.A., Communist and working-class background were to weigh him down, since, though he no longer belonged to any of these categories, he was reluctant to jettison them for fear that he would be accused of betraying old loyalties. They had been woven into his image, and that would have suffered if he had spoken forthrightly on issues like these. In numerous public appearances and in letters to the newspapers, he salved his conscience by defending all three against what he regarded as their detractors.

For the first two years after his marriage, Brendan managed to establish regular habits of work and eating. He and Beatrice took a flat in Herbert Street, a pleasant Georgian backwater, with a narrow pathway opposite which had once been reserved exclusively for nurse-maids and their prams. He would get up in the morning at seven, no matter how late he had been in bed the night before, and work steadily till twelve. He came home regularly for his meals. With this routine his drinking had less influence on his life as a writer than it would have had if he was living on his own. Now he could drink and produce. Articles, stories, essays, broadcasts poured out and all the time he was working at and polishing his Borstal memoirs.

A problem that Beatrice had to cope with after her marriage was that Brendan was capable of obsessional untidiness; when he was drinking he could allow his personal hygiene to deteriorate to a primitive level. On the other hand, he loved to purge himself in the sea as often as he could and roll around like a porpoise in

Dublin Bay, shedding the grime with joyful enthusiasm. Beatrice encouraged him in this. If the weather was at all mild, she would pack him off most days in the summer to the beaches near the city. He especially liked the Forty Foot, a male bathing place at Sandycove where priests, doctors, lawyers, writers and working men meet in the common fellowship of hardy all-weather swimmers. Once, when the water was unusually low, Behan stood on the diving board for a second, then roared to his schoolteacher friend, Sean O'Shea, 'Here goes fuck all' as he launched his sixteen stone frame into the air, breaking water almost three minutes later with a huge grin.

Dublin is a city, as George Moore says, 'wandering between hill and sea', and Brendan made full use of its natural advantages. The sea is only a mile or so from the centre of the city and the rosary of mountains which ring the town could be reached in fifteen minutes from the Behans' home in Kimmage. Later in his affluent days he would roar into number 70 Kildare Road and pull his mother out, saying to the taxi driver he had kept waiting: 'Up to the hills me mother loves.'

With his sense of other people's needs, he recognized that the hills provided an instinctive sense of release for older Dublin people reared on hardship, and he was always surprising 'oul' wans' he knew, by giving them the treat of an afternoon up the Dublin mountains.

His aunt, Maggie Trimble, told Brian Behan once:

> Your Brendan, God love him, was here yesterday in a great big car, and he nearly tore the house down knocking. 'Brendan', I says, 'what's wrong?' 'Nothing', he shouted. 'Get your coat, you and me mother are coming out for the day'. 'Oh Brendan', I said, 'I'm too shabby, look at the cut of me, I can't ride in that big car.' He only roared like the town bull. 'To hell with poverty, we'll kill a chicken.' And out he dragged me, Brian. And away the three of us went up the mountains drinking and eating to our hearts' content. Ah, God love him for thinking of an old woman.

Regular meals were important to him. It was not until a year later that he was diagnosed as a diabetic. But the condition had been incipient for some time. He was a very mild type of diabetic and did not require insulin, but his diet had to be balanced and if he drank and did not eat, as his doctor said 'He went to hell altogether'.

But with the regularity of the life Beatrice provided for him, his health improved and something of his old pride of appearance revived under the care she gave him. In the four years before his marriage he had put on almost three stone. His face had lost its clean-cut appearance, his looks had begun to vanish in layers of fat. There was always a strong narcissistic streak in Brendan, and when he was unable to cut down on his drinking he was secretly horrified at the effect it had on his appearance. It was all very well for journalists to refer to his Roman Emperor features. They were talking of Nero, the debauchee, not of an Augustan profile. Between 1955 and 1957, after his marriage with Beatrice, neatly dressed and, when he was not drinking, cleanly turned out, it was possible to see that he was still a good-looking man.

This was a purposeful Brendan, even if he still went on skites; a writer working at his trade who showed every evidence of having learnt the lesson that an artist, if he is to be worthy of the name, must produce work.

In the year before his marriage, there had been a sharp increase in his drinking habits and it was only through luck that he had not been in prison more often. He compensated for this by slipping into the role of 'character', with his episodes making good stories in the only too eager Dublin mouth. But with the success of his play, a congenial regular column in the *Irish Press* and Beatrice's care he had a chance once more to allow the real Brendan to emerge over the image of the town clown and let the air out of his balloons.

CHAPTER SIXTEEN

In January, 1956, Brendan learnt that Joan Littlewood and Gerry Raffles of the Theatre Royal, Stratford East, London, were anxious to stage *The Quare Fellow* at their theatre. This was a big opportunity for him.

Brendan had, however, sold the London rights in the play to the Simpsons. This did not prevent him from selling them to the Stratford company as well in the hope that he could later fix it up with the Pike theatre. Though they were extremely disappointed, Alan Simpson and Carolyn Swift made no effort to enforce their option. They were glad, for Brendan's sake, that the play was to have a wider audience. Three years later, when the Simpsons were being prosecuted under the obscenity laws in Dublin for a production of *The Rose Tattoo*, Brendan came up to them with a sheepish grin: 'I admit I did you over *The Quare Fellow*. He pressed a £100 note into Alan's hand for the defence fund that had been set up to support the Simpsons in their fight against the Attorney General—which they later won.

The Stratford East production was scheduled to open in May. In the meantime, Brendan worked with Joan Littlewood on alterations in the script. She wanted to tailor it to give it the maximum appeal for English audiences.

The Quare Fellow, with its grim realism and cast of working-class criminals, was ideal for the English theatre of the middle 'fifties. Though it retained Shaw as its intellectual conscience, the English theatre generally had tended to remain out of touch with European developments. The theatre of Pirandello, Brecht and O'Neill had made little impact, while drama which reflected what the critic Edward Milne called 'England through the eyes of the deb's mum' dominated the West End. It is hard to realize now that Brecht was not played commercially in London till 1956, that Beckett and Ionesco had their works first produced there in 1955 and that Genet was not performed commercially in England until 1957; and even these tardy performances would probably not have reached the theatrical public had it not been for the emergence of the New Wave drama which had its focal points in the Royal Court Theatre, Sloane Square, and the Theatre Workshop at Stratford East. John Osborne's *Look Back in Anger* was the opening salvo for the new playwrights. This play, with its lower middle-class anti-hero, had taken London by storm just two months before *The Quare Fellow* was presented at Stratford.

It was the Dublin playwright who was to get carried along on the first wave of Osborne's success. Curiously enough, the social realism of *The Quare Fellow*, while it had a novel quality on the London scene, was in the tradition of Irish play-writing since before the First World War. The Abbey Theatre directors had encouraged Irish dramatists to write about their own lives and situations and a large output of realistic works had appeared on the Abbey stage in the 'twenties and 'thirties. While the acting techniques required for a realistic play of this kind therefore would have caused no problem in Dublin, there were a limited number of companies in England who could have given it an adequate production in the 'fifties.

Brendan was fortunate in that he had come in contact with Joan Littlewood and her Theatre Workshop Group. She had been a pioneer in trying to free the English stage from the destructive effects of drama schools and R.A.D.A. accents and bring it in contact with the techniques which had been developed in the European theatre since the 'twenties. Starting with a travelling company in 1944, made up largely of actors who had pooled their war gratuities, she had toured the industrial north for some years, working men's clubs and little theatres, before finding a home at Stratford East. Here the company began to make its name with an extremely varied repertoire—Aristophanes, Shakespeare, Marlowe, Johnson, Molière, Webster, Marston, Lope de Vega, Ibsen, Chekhov, Pirandello, O'Casey, Synge, Shaw, Gogol and Brecht. Though at the Paris Festival in 1955 the Littlewood Company won a first prize with *Volpone*, there was still reluctance to recognize the merit of her realistic techniques, in a London theatre world dominated by hidebound, drawing-room comedy traditions.

Littlewood sought an immediate and *total* communication between the actors on the stage and the audience. Everything, even the theme of the play itself, was subordinated to this purpose. Having extracted the central emotion of a work, she devised situations by which the cast could indulge this emotion freely before they ever put their hands on a script. In a rehearsal for one famous modern-dress *Macbeth*, for instance, the actors began playing cowboys and Indians, moved to an improvised battle, and only then were given the first scene of the play with Shakespeare's text.

The result of the Littlewood approach was that the impact of a play, when it did come off, could be electric. For *The Quare Fellow* she determined to extract the maximum drama from a work which suffered to some extent from lack of action in the plot.

In the first weeks of rehearsal, she brought the cast up on the roof of the theatre, so that the grim slate and stone there would give them the atmosphere of a prison yard. She then formed the artists in a circle and made them march round and round as if they were prisoners taking exercise. One of the actors has recalled the effect this had on the cast:

Round and round we trudged for what seemed like hours—breaking now and then for a quick smoke and furtive conversation. Although it was just a kind of game, the boredom and meanness of it all was brought home. Next, the 'game' was extended—the whole dreary routine of washing out your cell, standing to attention, sucking up to the screw, trading tobacco, was improvised and developed. It began to seem less and less like a game, and more like real. By degrees the plot and the script were introduced, although some of us never knew which parts we were playing until half-way through the rehearsals. The interesting thing was that when she gave us the scripts we found that many of the situations we had improvised actually occurred in the play. All we had to do was learn the author's words.

One scene, lasting forty-five seconds, they rehearsed for four weeks. When the warder passes through the prison yard with the condemned man's food, the prisoners scurry round to see it. The secret passing of notes, the prisoners sniffing at the bacon, and then the warder coming out and breaking up the group, were all rehearsed separately and then rebuilt into one fluid moment of theatre.

Brendan was excited at the prospect of success for *The Quare Fellow* in London. He knew that the venture could open up other opportunities to him. If he became known through a successful play he could exploit his gifts as a talker and entertainer as well. He might become a famous personality, as other talkative Dubliners with similar gifts had been before him.

Oscar Wilde, Bernard Shaw, Thomas Moore, Charles Lever, Richard Brinsley Sheridan, Oliver Gogarty had set a pattern and it was natural for Brendan to wish to emulate it. 'You have got to feed people or shock people to get into society', Wilde had said. The Dubliner, being too poor to feed people was not averse to using shock tactics, recognizing that once he had the public's attention he could retain the limelight by wit and originality.

It was a willingness to play the harlequin that distinguished the Dublin talker from English conversationalists like Sydney Smith and Samuel Johnson, who would never have indulged in the Irishmen's antics. Wilde with his knee breeches and lily in his hand, Shaw with his Jaeger suits and vegetarianism, Yeats with his cloak and black hat 'resembling an umbrella left behind at a picnic' in George Moore's description, had all used outrageous accoutrement to catch the public eye. Again Wilde, lying night after night outside Lily Langtry's door, greeting Sarah Bernhardt at Dover with his arms full of lilies, falling down with supposed fright in his black velvet suit and salmon-coloured stockings at a country shoot each time the gun went off, is as un-English as Shaw on a tour of the Western Front hoping that he will be blown flat on his face so that he can perform his clown's trick of getting up again as if an invisible agent was picking him up by the slack of his trousers. Gogarty would jump up on a table to imitate a stalker, in an anecdote about a shoot.

Philippe Jullian, Wilde's biographer, has remarked that Wilde, like Shaw, believed that the English accept sarcasm from people they believe to be their intellectual superiors. The dashing Dubliner with his picaresque flair traded on this licence to deliver pronouncements which, if they had been made by an Englishman, would have been received with derision or looked on as bad taste.

Of course it was their skill in social intercourse that enabled Wilde and the others to get away with it. They were born story-tellers and knew how to hold an audience with what Philippe Jullian has described as

> the Irish gift of beautifying truth for the unimaginative—of being able to give an extraordinary quality to the events of everday life.

Brendan, with his prodigious memory for details which he could weave into the text of the story he was telling, his lightning switch of subject to hold the listener's attention, each new anecdote joined to the last by a slim thread of relevance, his vast repertoire of quotations and allusions, his inexhaustible flow of language as if each sentence had been prepared the night before, was in the tradition of those who had preceded him. He could act out his stories and impersonate the central characters. He was always on the lookout for an opportunity to turn the occasion into an uproarious evening with ballads and music.

Essentially Brendan's gift derived, as did that of the others, from the Seanachaidhe or Irish traditional story-teller. Louis Gillet, the French critic, who noted with astonishment that James Joyce could surprise his friends with a superbly told fairy tale, has described the art as 'that of the oldest story-telling race in Europe'. Because it is ephemeral in its effect, it is almost impossible to create an impression of the story-teller's art on paper. But to see an Irish Seanachaidhe in action—the marvellously mobile features and exquisitely inflected voice conveying every nuance of the tale he is telling so that you are no longer looking at a man relating a story but seeing pictures pass before the eye—is to understand the success of the Irish Talker in other parts of the English-speaking world.

The week before *The Quare Fellow* opened, Brendan was

interviewed by Edward Goring of the *Daily Mail*. The interview was headed 'Ex-I.R.A. Man Returns as Poet'.

Brendan Behan, the poet known as the Dylan Thomas of Ireland, was back in England yesterday—a free man at last. This ex-I.R.A. man, who was banned from Britain in 1939, has returned for the London premiere of a play he wrote based on his years in jail. Gaelic-speaking Behan has spent eight of his 33 years in prison for I.R.A. activities. When he tried to return to Britain six years ago, he was arrested at Newhaven and deported to France. His last attempt to visit this country three years ago also failed.

'I was surprised and delighted when the British Embassy in Dublin said I was not likely to be arrested this time', he said last night.

Yesterday he made a 'sentimental journey'—to a Borstal establishment in Suffolk. He was sent there for three years for possessing explosives in Liverpool.

'Heath the murderer was there and objected to my bad language', laughed Behan. He laughed, too, when he recalled the 14-year sentence he received for shooting at two detectives in Dublin.

'The judge sent me an electric coffee-pot as a wedding present', he said. 'I joined the I.R.A. at the age of 14 and worked for them in Liverpool, Dublin, Belfast and Cork. I don't think I would like that sort of thing— shooting at policemen—now. I have finished with the I.R.A. But I still have many friends in the movement.'

The reference to Heath is a good touch. Neville Heath's savage crimes (he had sadistically beaten two women to death) had appalled England at the time. To have been a Borstal-mate of his and to have shocked him with bad language made Brendan a pretty naughty boy indeed.

However, this was mild compared with the tenor of the other newspaper reports and press releases that were circulated at this time. A pattern runs through them; the slum boy born in the back room of a brothel who has done years in jails for throwing bombs at the English and shooting coppers in Dublin. There is no mention of his brilliant mother or talented dad, his Abbey Theatre uncle or his mother's brother-in-law, Actor-Manager P. J. Bourke of the Queen's Theatre. Brendan preferred to be a flower that had blossomed in the mire despite early deprivations, rather than emphasize the truth about his background. This image was ideally suited to the temper of the time. Sympathy with the under-dog was fashionable. The classless man was about to emerge. Social barriers were being shattered.

Brendan was one of the first of the statue breakers.

The Quare Fellow opened on May 24, 1956. It succeeded beyond the wildest expectations. It was to run for three months at Stratford. Later it transferred to the Comedy Theatre in the West End. Not only was this the first play to transfer from the Stratford Theatre to the West End, but Brendan became the first Irish playwright to have a success there. Despite the international fame of the Irish theatre, none of its famous playwrights—Yeats, Synge or O'Casey—had been successful with West End audiences. In fact, O'Casey's three masterpieces had never been performed at all in the West End, and the only play of his that had appeared there—*The Silver Tassie*—when it was produced under C. B. Cochran, had been a failure.[1]

The mixture of grimness and gaiety in *The Quare Fellow* enthralled the audience. When the curtain went up on the first night at Stratford, a superb set by John Bury showed the stage open to the back wall, so that the bricks and central heating pipes of the theatre gave the impression of the bleak interior of a prison. Then Brendan's ringing voice, with poetry hidden somewhere in its stridency, intoned the opening song, 'The Old Triangle':

> A hungry feeling came o'er me stealing
> And the mice were squealing in my prison cell,
> And that old triangle
> Went jingle jangle,
> Along the banks of the Royal Canal.
>
> To begin the morning
> The warder bawling
> Get out of bed and clean up your cell,
> And that old triangle
> Went jingle jangle,
> Along the banks of the Royal Canal.

The *Daily Mail* reported that in the audience were men whose prison sentences totalled over 300 years. 'There were fifteen

---

[1] *The Quare Fellow* was staged at the Abbey in October, 1956.

recognized leaders of the Republican Movement in the theatre.' The audience became aware of their presence when the Irish National Anthem was played as part of the play in the middle. The I.R.A. rose from their seats and stood to attention but conversely remained seated when 'God Save the Queen' was played at the end. At the final curtain, Brendan made a speech and sang 'The Old Triangle' again.

The notice which really made *The Quare Fellow* was Kenneth Tynan's in the *Observer*. As a critic, Tynan exercised wide influence on the public taste at the time. He fell head-over-heels for the play and called it 'theatrical history'.

> The English hoard words like misers, the Irish spend them like sailors and in Brendan Behan's tremendous new play language is out on a spree, ribald, dauntless and spoiling for a fight. In a sense of course this is scarcely amazing. It is Ireland's sacred duty to send over every few years a playwright who will save the English theatre from inarticulate dumbness. And Irish dialogue almost invariable sparkles.

What impressed Tynan was that Behan could 'move wild laughter in the throat of death, playing with the horror of hanging in a way so that you sometimes laughed but still felt the drama of it'.

> The tension is intolerable. But it is we who feel it, not the people in the play. We are moved precisely in the degree they are not. With superb dramatic tact the tragedy is concealed beneath layer after layer of rough comedy.
>
> The curtain falls but not before we have heard the swing and jerk of the drop. I left the theatre feeling overwhelmed and thanking all the powers that be for Sidney Silverman.

The critic of the *Times* said that it was

> . . . a powerful portrait of life in prison. Mr Behan allows the lags to present themselves as warped citizens of an unnatural community.
>
> Had they been English, their intrusion would have been leaden but they are not: they speak a seductive dialect, rich in puns, invective and paradoxical commonsense, that contemplates the world from a window of a barrack room or a doss house.
>
> There are swift alliances and enmities and absorbed obsession with humour.

The same critic noticed that the 'deafening military music' (the Irish National Anthem) brought half the audience to their feet.

W. A. Darlington in the *Daily Telegraph* called it 'an unusual evening' and said 'it was the most effective kind of propaganda play in which the propaganda is implied and not stated'. Tynan's praise and the word of mouth ensured the financial success of the play.

Later when *The Quare Fellow* opened in the West End in the Comedy Theatre. Harold Hobson, in the *Sunday Times*, seems to have felt that he had not paid enough attention to it on the opening night at Stratford and now wrote:

> Brendan Behan takes a place in that long line of Irishmen, from Goldsmith to Beckett, who have added honour to the drama of a nation which they have often hated.
>
> Mr. Behan has one of the finest qualities of the polemical dramatist — the quality that Shaw had in abundance. He is generous to his opponents.
>
> Detail by detail he reveals the ritual to us—the digging of the grave, the holy oils with which are anointed the feet of a condemned Catholic, the bacon and eggs on the day before the execution, the calculations about the height of the drop, the thickness of the victim's neck, and his weight, his ration of cigarettes, the avoidance of telling him the time, so that he will never know how long he has still to live, the games of draughts with the warders, the euphemisms whereby he is called always the quare fellow and the hangman only 'himself', the slitting of the hood, the weights under the ears, and, finally, the processional march to the execution shed.
>
> This thing that is taking place in the prison may be wrong, it may be barbaric, but that is not what Mr Behan is primarily thinking of. It is its enormity and the solemnity that oppress and inspire him, like the ritual of a religion or of the killing of the bull or the matador.
>
> *The Quare Fellow*, like Garcia Lorca's lament—'Llanto por Ignacion Sanchez Mejias'—is a ritual elegy written in a prison yard. There is nothing else like it in London.

On the week after *The Quare Fellow* opened, Brendan agreed to appear on the B.B.C. *Panorama* programme in an interview with Malcolm Muggeridge. He arrived in good time at the B.B.C. studios in Lime Grove, but had obviously had a few drinks before he went into the rehearsal room to await the call for the programme. There he was given a bottle of whisky, a somewhat unwise procedure where he was concerned. As a result, when he went on the programme, he was quite stupid with drink. He seemed half asleep and replied to questions in incoherent murmurs which Malcolm Muggeridge did his best to interpret for the audience. Brendan did manage to get his Heath bit in, however. He was asked if he had met anyone important in prison and replied, 'I met Heath. He objected to my bad language'. Muggeridge then said, in a state of alarm, 'You are not going to use any bad language here, are you?' Brendan replied, cheerfully, 'All right', and then went on smoking his cigarette.

This became one of Television's most celebrated interviews. That a cheeky Dubliner could get drunk on the box and poke fun at the establishment, seemed beyond the expectations of the average English viewer. Brendan became a folk hero overnight.

Donal Foley, who was working as London editor on the *Irish Press* at that time, remembers the reaction:

> He became the toast of every Cockney pub overnight. They identified themselves with the rumbustious Irishman who refused to conform to any pattern. To flout B.B.C. conventions in those now far off conventional days was, of course, something. The morning after the broadcast, Brendan was walking up Victoria Street when a Cockney newspaper seller approached him and grabbed his hand enthusiastically: 'You were great, Mr Behan—I didn't understand a word you said but I didn't know what Mr Muggeridge said either.' It was the latter part of the remark that tickled Brendan. He was aware of his own lack of articulation that evening but pleased that Mr Muggeridge's well phrased and well modulated accents meant as little to the Cockney ear.'

Brendan realized quickly that there was capital to be made out of this indiscretion and, by the time he met Vincent Mulchrone of the *Daily Mail* next day, he had a story well in shape for public consumption.

> The rumbustious, sixteen-stone Irishman threw back his dark, curly head and laughed at the furore caused by his first TV appearance.
>
> 'Of course I was drunk', he said. 'I had a bottle of whiskey—good Irish whiskey—inside me before I went to the TV studios. I went there at five o'clock, and they kept me locked in the place until I went on the air at about ten. I had a few drops of Scotch there—but I'd better not say too much about that for I don't want to let the B.B.C. down. Anyway, there

I was getting a fair sup of the ould stuff in the B.B.C. What happened then was my fault, not the B.B.C.'s. I usually drink stout at home, and bitter in England. But last night I'd had plenty. So I made an exhibition of myself.'

But Behan said last night, 'Nervous? Not a bit of it. You can put me down as a ham actor if you like, but I wasn't nervous'.

To prove it he sang a couple of verses of O'Casey's song *Red Roses for Me*, to the delight of the saloon bar.

'I'm sorry', he said, 'if I've let the governor of my old Borstal down and sorry if I annoyed Malcolm Muggeridge—a real English gentleman. And *they*', he added, 'are a rare breed nowadays'.

When he returned to Dublin in June, Brendan had made a discovery. You could get drunk in public in England and, provided you played your cards well, it could make you rather than break you. The image of the 'roaring bhoy' with the pen of fire was on its way to being born.

One aspect of Joan Littlewood's presentation of *The Quare Fellow* might have worried Brendan if he had not been carried away on the whirlwind of success.

In tailoring the play to make it more acceptable to a cosmopolitan public, Joan Littlewood had altered the character of Warder Regan by cutting sections of dialogue from the script. She had also left out a number of passages which helped to project Regan as the major character in the play, a position he does not occupy in the Littlewood presentation. Of course it can be argued that the play is a series of tableaux in which the ritual of hanging is unfolded and that the inclusion of a fully drawn character would overbalance it. On the other hand, Regan is the most striking of the characters which Brendan created for the stage. He is a Christian humanist with an Irish sense of irony which enables him to walk a tightrope between duty and compassion. It is difficult to see how the play could benefit from having the following passages altered which were left untouched in the Pike Theatre production, but not in the Stratford one. The dialogue is between Regan and the prison visitor, Mr Healy.

HEALY I can't see how society could exist without hanging. Don't you believe in it?

REGAN Well, I've seen such a lot of it, sir, that I suppose familiarity breeds contempt. But do I believe in it? Well, it works. I've never seen the fellow that could go out and drink a pint afterwards. You mean we kill people to stop other people killing other people?

HEALY And because they have killed other people.

REGAN Oh sir, we never mention that part of it in the business. That'd be revenge.

HEALY But we give a condemned man every spiritual facility. I venture to say that some of them die holier deaths than if they had finished their natural span.

REGAN But that's not our reason for hanging them, sir. We don't advertise 'Comit a murder and die a happy death'. You want to be very careful in what you're saying, sir, or you'd have them all at it. They take religion very seriously in this country, sir.

HEALY The fact remains, the condemned man does get a priest and the Sacraments, more than his victim got maybe.

REGAN Well, sir, maybe it would be more of a deterrent if we gave them no priest and no Sacrament.

HEALY That, my man, is ridiculous talk.

Later, when Healy says he has never seen a hanging, Regan replies[1]

REGAN I'm sure you didn't, sir. Not much sense in keeping a dog if you have to bark yourself. But the priest does make it easier on the man that's to be hanged, except in one little way, sometimes.

HEALY What way?

REGAN A person so near death and having all his trouble settled—they'd sometimes cry, sir. Not from fear of the rope, but because they see now what they might have done to please God at such little cost to themselves. When they were in their health, so to speak. They could have made him a free gift of an odd little thing now and again, during their life, and now they have only a few minutes to love Him in. But they'll have anyway that couple of minutes. More nor you nor I'll have, sir. We won't be hanged, I don't suppose.

HEALY I should suppose not.

REGAN We'll only croak out and reach a drowning man's grip on the candle.

When Healy remarks that we are all God's children, Regan replies:

REGAN Certainly we are. But no more than them. God won't lower Himself either to back up the murderer in killing or to back us up in

[1] Neither this passage nor the following one (with the exception of one sentence) are included at all in the Stratford version.

killing. God won't interfere, any more than a father of a family will take sides in a row between his children, except be sorry for all, and ready to forgive the lot.

HEALY If you think that way about it, I wonder you stop in the service at all.

REGAN I don't know; it's a soft job between hangings. (*Thoughtfully*) At least I better put up with it, for I'm not likely to get another one at this time of life.

HEALY You know Regan, in Rome or France or on the Continent, they'd hardly take you for a Catholic at all.

REGAN Well, if they were giving anything for it, I could show me baptismal certificate and my marriage lines.

HEALY It's the penalty of isolation, I suppose. You see, Regan, you are what might be termed an Irish Catholic.

REGAN I don't get much chance of being anything else, sir, unless it would be an Irish Protestant. A decent enough class of people, but I believe the Protestants in England find something the matter with them, or I might have been an Irish Jew, but I suppose the Jews in America find something the matter with them. But sure none of us can help it, sir. I suppose the lot of us, Catholics, Protestants and Jews—we all would have been born some better place if we'd known about it in time.

Joan Littlewood's problem in cutting these passages was that she had to keep a London audience entertained by an Irish play. To ensure its commercial acceptance she had, in some way, to internationalize the local atmosphere of *The Quare Fellow*.

Would her audience have accepted a 'philosophical' warder as portrayed in the original version of *The Quare Fellow*? Perhaps not; on the other hand, if a character is well drawn, it should coerce an audience into accepting its reality, even if it seems unusual to them.

Later, Brendan's willingness to allow his plays to be worked over at Stratford East in order to accommodate popular taste was to have a serious effect on his development as a writer.

CHAPTER SEVENTEEN

BACK in Dublin, Brendan went on a drunken spree that landed
him in hospital. He now found that he was such a celebrity in
England that even his illnesses were news. The British dailies ran
stories on his comments from his hospital bed. He told one
reporter he had drunk fourteen pints of stout or two bottles of
whiskey a day for the past ten years. 'Now that is over with.
I'll never be the same man again.' He had twelve volumes of
Proust's *Remembrance of Things Past* beside his bed to show
reporters he was taking his work seriously.

In hospital, a discovery was made that was to affect his mode
of life from then on. A series of tests revealed that Brendan was
a diabetic.

This was one explanation for his constant thirst. It also, to a
certain extent, explained his violent fits of temper when he had
drink taken. But it meant for the rest of his life, to be properly
in control of himself, he would have to keep to a strict diet and
avoid taking alcohol to excess. He could control the illness with
pills and by balancing his intake of certain foods. If, however,
an imbalance was set up, he would be liable to fall into a diabetic
coma. To return to bouts of heavy drinking again would be
dangerous, as his diet would go by the board and a coma could
ensue.

In fact, when he got out of hospital, he returned to the hard
work and routine life of a writer. He wanted to finish the account
of his Borstal period that he had first talked about as a boy of
twenty-one years in Mountjoy Prison in 1944. Valentin Iremonger,
the poet who was at that time First Secretary at the Irish Embassy
in London, had read part of the manuscript and encouraged
Brendan to finish it as quickly as he could. Later, Iremonger

mentioned it to Ian Hamilton of Hutchinson who came over to Dublin in the summer of 1957 to meet Brendan and inspect the manuscript. He was delighted by what he saw and signed Brendan on a contract with a generous advance of £350.

Brendan had been keeping himself going on *Borstal Boy* since 1956. He sold extracts from it to John Murdoch of the *Sunday Dispatch* in the summer of that year as a serial. The following year, he sold the same sections of it to the *People* without taking the trouble to inform them that they had already appeared in the *Sunday Dispatch*. Now, with a firm contract, he determined to get it finished somehow.

He would get up early in the morning at seven o'clock and write through until about twelve. Then he would feel he had done enough to have the rest of the day to himself. No matter how much he had drunk the night before or how late he had got to bed, he stuck on the whole to this routine of early rising and morning work. The result of this was that he had a certain amount of work under his belt before he submitted to the temptations that Dublin provides for self-employed citizens after opening time.

He was most meticulous about his diet during this period. There would be vociferous complaints to Beatrice if the food put before him at meals didn't conform exactly to the diet cards prescribed by Dr Childers. He knew he had a fine book inside him. It was coming out as he punched his typewriter while the milkmen rattled their carts below, and he was happy.

John Montague, the Irish poet, lived a few doors down from the Behans in Herbert Street at this time. He remembers Brendan as 'Nearly happy and working at his best.' Brendan used to drop in to Montague's flat nearly every day and talk French to Madeline, his wife who was from Paris. When Madeline Montague's Niece was over on holiday, Brendan would call with sweets for her every day.

'For myself as well as Madeline,' Montague recalls, 'these few years were a joy, despite the occasional awkwardness of dealing with Brendan. I was very fond of him. He seemed to me half angel, half beast. On the one hand a very handsome little man with delicate feet and hands and a quick intuitive mind: on the other, a beast, with a crooked mouth that spat poison at people. Never at me, however, though I had to put manners on him several times. I think he always respected people who stood up to him.

He was at the height of his powers in 1957, a formidable little bull crackling with energy and affection for the world.'

At this time Brendan wrote *The Big House*, a short play for radio, commissioned by the B.B.C. Home Service. It was broadcast in Spring 1957. It proved to be below standard with a number of stock characters who were bad caricatures of the Anglo-Irish.

In March 1957, he was drinking in a pub, McDaid's pub in Harry Street, with Riobard MacGorain, who had published him in *Comhair*, a Gaelic magazine of the 'forties. MacGorain was an executive of Gael Linn, a forward looking organization which has as its aim the revival of Irish culture and language. MacGorain suggested that Brendan write a play for their Gaelic-speaking theatre, at the Damer Hall, which was situated under the Unitarian Church in Stephen's Green. Frank Dermody, a former Abbey producer, was directing outstanding performances there at that time. These were frequently translated from Italian or French into Gaelic, works by Fabri, Betti, Sartre and others.

Brendan agreed to write this play on commission and was given an advance. It was to be more than a year before he finished it. It came in in dribs and drabs. MacGorain recalls, however, that Brendan was quite meticulous about his payments and that he remembered exactly what he had received and what he was owed for each draft. When they were discussing the play in McDaid's, Brendan had given MacGorain some idea of what it was to be about. He had heard of a British Tommy captured by the I.R.A. at Ballykinlar Camp in County Down during a raid in 1955. The I.R.A. had been conducting guerrilla forays into Ulster in a renewed campaign at that time. Brendan had been struck, too, by a tale he had heard about this time of the Black and Tan War in 1921, when a group of young Tommies had been mowed down in an ambush. His play would be about the futility of war: it would be, although he did not recognize it at the time, his final renunciation of revolutionary nihilism, the full swing from the young boy of nineteen who had shot to kill at a policeman in April, 1942.

Brendan used as a background for his play a house in Nelson Street, owned by a Madame Rogers. She was a genteel revolutionary who gave hospitality to anyone with the remotest connection with revolutionary activity. On her large horsehair sofa could be found any evening the recumbent forms of remnants or embryos of revolutionary Ireland; in fact anybody who had been in prison at all had a good chance of winning her sympathy, as she had a generous streak of anarchism in her nature which allowed her to include among those fighting for Ireland anybody who had been in conflict with the police. The resident revolutionary of Nelson Street was an ancient Anglo-Irish patriot, who spewed hatred of the Saxon in an Oxford accent, mixed with Gaelic phrases. Later, as he was writing the play, Brendan changed the milieu somewhat and blended the background with Kitty Mulvey's 'hotel' a few hundred yards away down Parnell Street where girls brought men in search of transient joy and were admitted by two homosexual doormen, Fonsey and Freddy.

Brendan says himself that he wrote *An Giall*, which was later to become *The Hostage*, in twelve days. This is true in the sense that the last drafts were produced in a frenzy as the production date at the Damer Hall drew near. In fact, I remember meeting Frank Dermody, the play's director, in a night-joint in the last weeks of May and hearing him complain how the final revisions were coming in 'scrawled on the backs of cornflake bags'. Brendan was to complain later that he did not like Dermody's Abbey Theatre naturalism in the direction of the play. But Dermody had worked at the Abbey in the 'forties with actors of the calibre of Siobhán McKenna, Cyril Cusack, Maureen Delaney and F. J. McCormick, and besides had just returned from London where he had directed the record-breaking West End success *Reluctant Heroes*.

One reason that Brendan wrote *An Giall*, as he was to call the play, in Irish was that it had been commissioned by an Irish-speaking theatre. But after having had a London success with

The Quare Fellow, it is an indication of how much he was still attached to the 'Irish thing' that he should have decided to do his next play in Gaelic. He seems to have felt that he could express himself in Gaelic at least as well as he could in English and that, by writing in this language, he might touch on some mood that he would have been unable to produce in any other language. 'Irish is more direct than English, more bitter', he explained to a reporter. 'It's a muscular fine thing, the most expressive language in Europe.'

Brendan was docile during rehearsals and made whatever changes in the play that were suggested to him. However, he got the jitters on the first night and did not attend. After he had read the first-night notices the next day however, he wanted to make a speech on the second night, but Dermody refused to let him, on the grounds that he had not enough confidence in the production to come on the first night—'You were too bloody cowardly, Brendan'.

An Giall opened on June 16, 1958, and was favourably reviewed by the critics. The *Irish Independent* critic said he found the play so moving that he was in tears at the end of it. The *Irish Times* critic wrote:

> *An Giall* is a very cleverly written play. Indeed, in the first act the writing was possibly too clever and the dialogue was overloaded with witty lines that were of little use to the play as a whole. However, this was a small fault and did not detract from the over-all picture of excellence. The play is set in a lower-class Dublin brothel owned by a fanatical Gael, the son of an Anglican bishop, who was educated at Oxford, and managed by a one-legged old I.R.A. man willing to use it for his own ends. A young English soldier, stationed in Armagh, is kidnapped by the I.R.A., brought to Dublin and imprisoned in the brothel. It is only by accident that he discovers that he is a hostage and will be executed by the Republican soldiers if a young man, under sentence of death in Crumlin Road Jail, Belfast, is hanged. He falls in love with the maid in the house and she with him, and they find that both have more or less the same background—that neither cares a straw for any war or battle which Ireland and Britain might have had in the past or would have in the future. The manager of the place also understands the futility of carrying on the 'Old Fight', but he is powerless to intervene.

On the first night, it was apparent that this was an important moment in the theatre. There had been periods during the play, particularly during the love-scene between the soldier and the maid, when there was that breathless attention from the audience which signifies that something remarkable is taking place on the stage. Edward Golden, the Abbey actor and producer, who was present, recalls:

> Though the action of the play took place in a brothel, there was an extraordinary air of innocence about it. At the end I felt as if there had been a falling of flower petals through the air. I could almost smell them. It was uncanny.

At the end of the run at the Damer Hall, Brendan got an offer from Joan Littlewood. If he would translate *The Hostage* into English, she and Gerry Raffles would stage it at her Theatre Workshop at Stratford.

Though he had worked hard on his prison memoirs since he had signed the previous January, he had not completed the manuscript by mid-July 1957. He had been dispatching, in the meantime, pleading letters to his London publishers full of his own special brand of blarney, carefully adapted to suit Scot or Saxon as the occasion demanded it. Rae Jeffs, the publicity officer at Hutchinson, was 'little rae of sunshine'. Ian Hamilton, a Highland Scot, was addressed as 'A Chara', and there were constant references in the letters to him emphasizing the kinship between Scottish and Irish Gaels. Eventually Brendan forwarded a completed manuscript on December 20, 1957. It required a good deal of editing and consultation with lawyers on legal matters before it could be released to the printer.

He and Beatrice set out for Sweden in August, 1958, to translate *An Giall* into English and to put the finishing touches to the proofs of *Borstal Boy*.

There, at the country home of Dr Olaf Lagerlöv, on an island near Stockholm, he worked happily on these jobs and on August 15 he sent back the page proofs to London remarking, 'No wonder Charles Dickens used to drink two glasses of port and an egg before he'd start work in the morning: navvying couldn't be much worse than writing in longhand'.

He was not so successful in completing the translation of *The*

Hostage and by the time he went back to London, where news of his various enterprises had preceded him, he had very little work on the play completed.

All the same, the next few months looked exciting for the boy from Russell Street. In October, *The Hostage* was due at Stratford. In November, Jose Quintero was to stage *The Quare Fellow* in the Circle in the Square, New York. It was also to be produced under the title of *Le Client du Matin* in Paris at the Théâtre de l'Oeuvre after Christmas and in the Schillertheater, Berlin, in February.

The excitement and the attention from the press now made it more difficult to get Brendan down to work on *The Hostage*. The Theatre Royal, Stratford, was in bad financial straits at this time. Most of the grants, including one from the Arts Council, had been withdrawn and they really needed a successful run to put them on their feet again. Gerry Raffles, the manager, finally managed to induce Brendan to sit down and finish the translation. By the middle of September he had done so, but in a rather ramshackle way, leaving gaps in the dialogue and plot that were to be filled in as the play went into production.

It was Brendan's own fault that portions of the play had to be extemporized after he had delivered the manuscript to Theatre Workshop. He had been woefully late with the script. But his procrastination left him open to pressures which it would have been much better to avoid. As rehearsals proceeded, it became clear that what was emerging was a different work from the one he had written in Dublin. Additional characters were written in who had no special relevance to the theme. Rio Rita, a homosexual navvy, and 'her' Negro boyfriend, Princess Grace, materialized, to use a phrase of Alan Simpson's, 'somewhere between Stephen's Green and the King's Road'. They belonged to Chelsea camp, not Dublin bawdy. Miss Gilchrist, a social worker, and Mr Mulleady, a Civil Servant, two other additions, are caricatures of English and not Irish prototypes.

This was Littlewood's method of working. Once she got a script, she went into instant collaboration with the cast and, as their views of the play unfolded during rehearsal, she allowed them to interpolate suggestions for dialogue and even scenes that were later incorporated in it. She once told Charles Marowitz, the director, that she did not believe in 'the supremacy of the director–designer–actor or even *the writer*'. She relied a great deal on intuition and sudden flairs of inspiration. Sometimes this worked and it heightened the effect of what the playwright was trying to say. Sometimes it destroyed its meaning. One thing, however, she never lost sight of: that there were people beyond the footlights who had to be entertained, and no matter how irrelevant or destructive to the theme the interpolations were, they were always ones geared to attract an audience's attention and keep them in a state of expectancy.

Not unnaturally, because of her methods of working, Little-wood was to come into conflict with playwrights from time to time who resented having their scripts subjected to this treatment.

Wolf Mankowitz, the English playwright, recalls the difficulties he had with her when she produced a play of his to get her to keep to the original script.

> Joan took a play to pieces and she put it back together again with actors inserts, ad libs and catch phrases. Sometimes it worked, sometimes it didn't. Often in rewriting, the original idea was lost. I had to fight her for the survival of script. It was still only fifty-fifty in the end.
>
> Brendan didn't care. He was pissed out of his mind anyway when half the changes were made. It was only when you saw *The Quare Fellow* you realised what a good writer he was and how much better his work could be than the changes he accepted from Littlewood. A lot of the non-sequitur scenes were invented by Joan.

Mankowitz later co-produced *The Hostage* with Joan Littlewood and Gerry Raffles at Wyndham's Theatre.

Daniel Farson who later had a scenario he wrote on Marie Lloyd, the Music Hall star of the Edwardian era, produced by Littlewood, maintains that the work was changed against his will almost out of recognition by the time it reached the boards.[1]

[1] Farson at the same time has immense admiration for Joan Littlewood. 'With a few strokes she can create miracles' he says. 'One forgives her for everything because of the genius she brings to her productions. But she puts the actor before the playwright. As I am a writer this seems a pity.

A revealing account of the Littlewood method comes from Frank Norman who made his name and a great deal of money with *Fings Ain't Wot They Used t'Be* which had a record run at the Garrick Theatre in 1961. Norman, a Cockney, who had been brought up in an orphanage, gave his play, which dealt with the Soho underworld, to Littlewood in June 1959. She decided to adapt it for a musical. Norman admits it was a great success under her direction. He alleges, however, that what emerged was 'a load of schmaltz which had very little to do with what I had written about'.

> I'm often accused of not being grateful enough to the actors for ad libbing their parts so well, or to Miss Littlewood for her magnificent production, without which the show would most likely have run for not more than three days. This is far from the truth. I am indebted to them all for the money they have earned me. However, I still feel very strongly that the theatre is a place for playwrights first, actors second, and then producers, for without the original idea no one can do anything at all. However, I will endeavour to persuade the directors of any future plays that I may try to write to give a truer interpretation of my work than was done with 'Fings'.

Norman resented the manner in which actors were allowed by the director to ad lib and add lines.

> The actors start adding lines which have nothing to do with the play, such as remarks about Krushcev, Tony Armstrong-Jones, the Lord Chamberlain, the Duchess of Argyll, Franco, parking meters, deb's delights, football teams, the weather and even myself, also anything topical which might get a laugh. I reckon this is a bit dodgy because the action of the play took place ten years ago when the characters in the play would in fact have no interest whatever in the aforementioned people, objects or subjects.

Of course, all this ignores the chemistry that Littlewood put into a production. If the play suffered, the audience did not. The plays were hailed by the critics and the audiences poured in. In the early 1960's, Joan Littlewood had three plays running in the West End. Shelagh Delaney's *Taste of Honey*, *The Hostage*, and Frank Norman's *Fings Ain't Wot They Used t'Be*. Later, she and Gerry Raffles were to have another resounding West End success with *Oh! What a Lovely War*.

The Hostage opened on October 14, 1958 at the Theatre Royal, Stratford East. On the first night, to everyone's surprise, Brendan appeared in a dress suit. He glared around with a certain amount of disdain as he walked down the aisle, at the open-neck shirts around him. 'This is not an effing Socialist meeting, you know', he muttered to Joe Hone. Commenting on the number of beards in the audience, he said audibly as he settled in his seat, 'What's going on here? A meeting of the Explorers' Club?' The programme note was geared to remove all suspicion that Brendan, as a former I.R.A. revolutionary, was attacking the British.

> He has hatred for the political forces who divide and subject Ireland. But for the people, even if those people are the instruments of antagonistic political forces, he has only love and understanding. If a stranger attacks Britain, no one will support this country more strongly than Brendan Behan.

The fair-minded English in the audience could feel that here indeed was a jolly Gael, who had seen the light and discovered that the English were fine fellows after all. The plot was clear and easy to follow, owing to the Littlewood rearrangement. It made the mirage of Anglo-Irish relations relatively clear to the uninitiated. Joan Littlewood's production really had the audience going after the first act. It was obvious half way through that the play was going to be a success.

At the final curtain there was thunderous applause. Brendan, in a modest speech, paid tribute to Joan Littlewood and described her as the best producer in the world, and her company as the best company in the world. He said the play was 'a comment on Anglo-Irish relations. As to what it is about, you will find out from the critics in the morning'. Next day, in the tube going up from Blackheath to London, Brendan read what the critics had to say. He was delighted. He read out extracts to the bowler-hatted passengers sitting beside him, accompanying the extracts with songs from the play as a further proof of how correct the critics were in their estimation of it. Some of the bowler-hat brigade barely raised their heads from their newspapers, but others were carried away by his enthusiasm. The *Times* critic wrote that

> the main substance of the rollicking fun is the outrageous fun poked at Irish types. *The Hostage* is an extravaganza with songs and dances. It is as formless as if it were being improvised on the spur of the occasion, but it is full of brawling energy and it treats past and present Anglo-Irish relations with a laughing impartiality which is almost anarchic. . . . It is a curious entertainment which has the vitality that excuses a multitude of shamelessly loose touches.

Milton Shulman of the *Evening Standard* described it as

> a rare and invigorating experience.

Kenneth Tynan in the *Observer* went so far as to say that Brendan might well fill the place vacated by Sean O'Casey:

> It seems to be Ireland's function every twenty years or so to provide a playwright who will kick English drama from the past into the present.

Penelope Gilliatt commented:

> Language hasn't had an outing like this since *The Quare Fellow*. The English habitually write as if they were alone and cold at ten in the morning: the Irish write in a state of flushed gregariousness at an eternal opening time. 'There are two kinds of men', says the caretaker in *The Hostage*, 'there's the earnest religious kind and there's the laughing boys'. *The Hostage* is a huge belly laugh that secretes enough morality for a satire. It puts politics where they belong, in the midst of life, where they seldom appear in the English theatre.

In the *Sunday Times*, Harold Hobson greeted it with an enthusiasm which would not have been exessive if it has been applied to the younger Strindberg:

> A masterpiece of magnanimity, Mr Behan's portrait of the young English soldier is magnanimous indeed. Life is what *The Hostage* is rich in. It shouts, sings, thunders, and stamps with life, and with the life of the un-selfpitying English orphan; as ever Mr Behan finds for him an epitaph that is classically restrained and beautiful. A girl drops on her knees beside the shot body and stills the boisterous tumult of this curious rowdy play with words of a staggering simplicity: 'He died in a foreign country and at home he had no one'. Nothing finer in this kind has been written for 2000 years. Nothing since:
>
> > Ante Diem Periet,
> > Sed miles sed pro patria.

The Irish, the Southern Irish, the I.R.A. Irish, have found in Mr Behan a dramatist in the line of Mr O'Casey. They should treasure him and be proud of him.

The Hostage ran at Stratford for some months. Princess Margaret went to see it, and—so the newspapers said—'laughed herself to tears'. After Christmas it was to be performed as the British entry to the Théâtre des Nations and later was to play in Stockholm, Berlin, Amsterdam, Copenhagen and Munich, as well as having successful production in the West End and on Broadway. Through it, Brendan became a world figure in the theatre. Without Littlewood's handling of it, *The Hostage* could not have been the instant success it was.[1] She succeeded in subduing the local element and giving it an international framework which made it comprehensible in Europe and America. Had it remained in its original as *An Giall*, it would have been noticed abroad eventually as a remarkable play—if it was fortunate enough to be translated. But its progress would have been slow and its audiences smaller, if more discriminating. Littlewood's Brechtian approach, the popular songs, the cabaret dialogue, the topical references, the theatrical surprises she provided, were acceptable to an international audience and helped to ensure the success of the play which otherwise might have failed commercially through being too local in its theme and treatment.

Nevertheless, *The Hostage* as it was performed in the West End and Paris version is a blown-up hotch-potch compared with the original version which is a small masterpiece and the best thing Behan wrote for the theatre.

[1] There was a genuine affection between Joan Littlewood and Brendan which made it easy for them to co-operate. She wrote to the biographer in 1968:

> Unfortunately I have been in India and am returning there this week having long since cut my connections with theatre. I have been distressed by the meanderings, purporting to be Brendan's writing, which have been published since his death. He was a marvellous, splendid, sad, shy human being and intensely proud of his craft as a writer. I cannot think it serves his memory to publish what must be some sort of reportage of his talk during his final illness. All that I knew of him went into my work with him. The story of his life would be very painful, probably hurtful—if the truth were told. Personally I have not been able to come to Dublin since his funeral.

The first production relied for its effect on a quality which is missing from the West End one. This is the contrast between the total innocence of the two central characters, and the atmosphere of violence and lust in which they become involved.

Leslie the soldier and Teresa the maid know nothing of the world. They are both orphans. She has just left a convent where she has been reared by nuns. He has been brought up in an institution in Macclesfield. It is their innocence which produces the catharsis. In *An Giall* they are two flower children baffled by violence, understanding love but not lust:

LESLIE Well, maybe I've put my arms round girls when we were dancing, but that's the first real kiss I've ever got. Every soldier isn't as bad as the soldier that mate of yours met.

TERESA What mate of mine?

LESLIE Jennie Galvan, or whatever her name was, who was giving you good advice about soldiers.

TERESA (*Bursts out laughing in spite of herself*) Oh, Sister Gemma Galgan, . . . Oh, (*Laughing*) if only she heard that. She's a nun. What would the like of her have to do with a soldier or with any man, young or old.

LESLIE I didn't know she was a nun. I'm always saying the wrong thing.

TERESA (*Herself again*) Oh, I suppose that's the blarney you go on with every girl.

LESLIE Straight, Teresa, I haven't got a girl. All the blokes in the billet barring myself had pictures of their people and their girl friends on the press beside their bed. Sometimes I've been near lifting a girl's picture and putting it there to try and show that I'd a girl friend, as well as anyone else. And I wanted to put a picture of a nice old fellow and nice old lady there and pretend they were my Dad and Mum—but in the long run it's what's written down on my paybook:

'Family. Information to be sent in case of death or illness to The Head Master, Boys' Home, Macclesfield, Lancs.' That's all the family I had.

TERESA Leslie. . . .

LESLIE Yes, Teresa?

TERESA Were you serious that time when you kissed me?

LESLIE I was . . . listen, Teresa.

TERESA Yes?

LESLIE Would you give me a photo of yourself—if you happened to have one to spare, like?

TERESA I would, Leslie, and I've a wonderful one of myself. Well, I'm not saying I'm wonderful, but. . . .

LESLIE You are, Teresa, you are.

TERESA Well, myself and a couple of other girls were down in O'Connell Street, and we went to this place, for a bit of gas, you see, and—but I'll go up and get the picture. I won't be long, Leslie.

The love treatment has been changed in the West End version so that the soldier has become a hardened sexual athlete, while Teresa is an experienced colleen who will hit the sack at the wink of an eyelid. They are no longer remote from what is going on about them. The contrast is gone.[1]

SOLDIER Don't go! Let's pretend we're on the films, where all I have to say is 'Let me', and all you have to say is 'Yes'.
TERESA Oh, all right.
SOLDIER Come on, Kate.
They sing and dance.

> I will give you a golden ball,
> To hop with the children in the hall,

TERESA
> If you'll marry, marry, marry, marry,
> If you'll marry me.

SOLDIER
> I will give you the keys of my chest,
> And all the money I possess,

TERESA
> If you'll marry, marry, marry, marry,
> If you'll marry me.

BOTH
> If you'll marry, marry, marry, marry,
> If you'll marry me. . . . .

SOLDIER
> But first I think we should see,
> If we fit each other,

TERESA (*To the audience*) Shall we?
SOLDIER Yes, let's see.
They run to the bed. The lights black out. Miss Gilchrist rushes on and a spotlight comes up on her.
MISS GILCHRIST (*Horrified*) They're away. (*To Kate*) My music, please! *She sings.*

> Only a box of matches,
> I send, dear mother, to thee.
> Only a box of matches,
> Across the Irish sea.
> I met with a Gaelic pawnbroker,
> From Killarney's waterfalls,

[1] Mr. Gerry Raffles of the Theatre Workshop, Stratford, London, feels that I have misunderstood the play by suggesting that the soldier has become a hardened sexual athlete. The full scene is on pages 68–71 of 'The Hostage', published by Methuen, and can be read in full by anyone interested in comparing the two passages. U. O'C.

With sobs he cried, 'I wish I had died,
The Saxons have stolen my. . . .'
Pat rushes on to stop her saying 'balls' and drags her off, curtsying and singing again—

Only a box of matches. . . .

In the Dublin version, the brothel was a bawdy, ramshackle Dublin 'kip', peopled by amiable eccentrics of the sort that Joyce wrote about in *Ulysses* and Gogarty in his ballads. In the Littlewood production it has become less a brothel than a platform for the queer camp current at that time. The two new characters written into the London production—Rio Rita, and Princess Grace—make an attempt to seduce the soldier. Miss Gilchrist, a highly improbable social worker, also written into the later production, throws herself in between them in an effort to save Leslie's heterosexuality by advocating the advantage of life as a ponce. This scene is characteristic of how remote the second version is from the atmosphere of the first one:

Rio Rita, Princess Grace and Mulleady sing:

When Socrates in Ancient Greece,
Sat in his Turkish bath,
He rubbed himself and scrubbed himself,
And steamed both fore and aft.
He sang the songs the sirens sang,
With Oscar and Shakespeare,
We're here because we're queer,
Because we're queer, because we're here.

MULLEADY   The highest people in the land
Are for or they're against,
It's all the same thing in the end,
A piece of sentiment.

PRINCESS GRACE   From Swedes so tall to Arabs small,
They answer with a leer,

ALL THREE   We're here because we're queer
Because we're queer because we're here.

PRINCESS GRACE The trouble we had getting that past the nice Lord Chamberlain. This next bit's even worse.
The song ends and the three queers gyrate across the stage, twisting their bodies sinuously and making suggestive approaches to Leslie. Leslie is about to join in when Miss Gilchrist throws herself at him.

MISS GILCHRIST	Would you live on a woman's earnings,
	Would you give up work for good?
	For a life of prostitution?
SOLDIER	Yes, too bloody true, I would.
MISS GILCHRIST	Would you have a kip in Soho?
	Would you be a West End ponce?
SOLDIER	I'm fed up with pick and shovel,
	And I'd like to try it once.
MISS GILCHRIST	Did you read the Wolfenden Report
	On whores and queers?
SOLDIER	Yeah, gorblimey, it was moving,
	I collapsed meself in tears.
	Well, at this poncing business,
	I think I'll have a try,
	And I'll drop the English coppers,
	They're the best money can buy.
MISS GILCHRIST	Goodbye, my son, God bless you,
	Say your prayers each morn and night,
	And send home your poor old mother,
	A few quid—her widow's mite.

At the end of the dance the Russian silently and smoothly removes Miss Gilchrist. The whores and queers melt away, quiety cooing 'Leslie'.

Brendan claims that he wrote one of the lyrics for *The Hostage* in six minutes while the manager of the theatre stood over him with a revolver. 'The Captains and the Kings', a lyric that was much praised at the time, contains verses he cannot have been specially proud of later on. He had found out somehow that the mention of Evelyn Waugh's name drew a laugh from a London audience, so it became a stock article in his plays and stories:

> In our dreams we see old Harrow,
> And we hear the crow's loud caw,
> At the flower show our big marrow
> Takes the prize from Evelyn Waugh.
> Cups of tea or some dry sherry,
> Vintage cars, these simple things,
> So let's drink up and be merry
> Oh, the Captains and the Kings.
> So let's drink up and be merry
> Oh, the Captains and the Kings.

> Far away in dear old Cyprus,
> Or in Kenya's dusty land,
> Where all bear the white man's burden
> In many a strange land.
> As we look across our shoulder
> In West Belfast the school bell rings,
> And we sigh for dear old England,
> And the Captains and the Kings.
> And we sigh for dear old England,
> And the Captains and the Kings.

Some of the interpolations in *The Hostage* are out of place in a serious work of drama. Before the play had finished its run, *The Hostage* contained references to the Queen, John Foster Dulles, Peter Townsend, Uffa Fox, the Virgin Mary and the Duke of Edinburgh among others. Some of those were shoved in as the season progressed. Others had been invented in rehearsal. Joseph Hone, grandson of the Irish writer, who was working behind the scenes during the early part of the production, remembers being asked about remarks which were being inserted in the script, 'Would they say this in Dublin'? Brendan was not present when a lot of this was being done, but it is quite clear that whether he was or not he would not have objected.

Jokes were stuck in like stamps in an album. This one is lifted from Joyce's *Ulysses*.

> MONSEWER A race occurs when a lot of people live in one place for a
> long period of time.
> SOLDIER I reckon our old sergeant-major must be a race; he's been stuck
> in the same depot for about forty years.

Some of the additions achieved a music hall quick-fire effect, without much taste. When someone says:

> 'Up the Republic',

the reply is:

> 'Up the Arsenal'.

This usually brought the house down. Another remark of this kind was:

VOLUNTEER There's something in that. My own father was in the Royal
    Irish Rifles.
OFFICER Mine was in the Inniskillings.
MEG: And mine was a parish priest.

References to Brendan himself were included in the play.

PAT That's if this thing has an author.
SOLDIER Brendan Behan, he's too anti-British.
OFFICER Too anti-Irish, you mean. Bejasus, wait till we get him back
    home. We'll give him what-for making fun of the Movement. . . .
SOLDIER (*To audience*) He doesn't mind coming over here and taking
    your money.
PAT He'd sell his country for a pint.

A good example of the sort of topicality that Littlewood sought
was an allusion inserted in *The Hostage* when it opened in New
York; the play's Russian sailor wore a jersey with 'Baltika'
written across the chest, the name of the liner which had brought
Krushchev to New York the previous Monday.

It is not that the Stratford version of *The Hostage* is undramatic;
it is that the drama is of quite a different quality from the original
Gaelic version of the play.

It was her flaunting of convention, the outrageousness of her
treatment, that drew audiences to Joan Littlewood's production
of *The Hostage*. The London stage was still subject to the strictures
of the Lord Chamberlain. The year previously Genet in *Le Balcon*
had created a sensation with his outspoken treatment of the
brothel-world. (One of the London critics confessed himself too
innocent to understand its full implications). It is hard to realize
in these days of *Oh Calcutta!* and *Hair*, that *The Hostage* was
virtually the first West End play to present high camp on the
stage. The posturing of the two homosexuals was a titillating
insight for many of the audience into a life that they had read
about in books and heard hinted at in the crime columns of the
newspapers—the high jinks of Soho and the Kings Road. Here
it was, all quietly de-Nazified under the auspices of the Arts
Council and respectable critics had hailed the play as a work of
genius. In a pre-Vassal and pre-Profumo era, it was still possible
for a play like *The Hostage* to have a succès de scandale: almost as

if the establishment were shaking off centuries of inhibition in a single night of guffaws.

The manner in which the I.R.A. characters are presented in the London production of *The Hostage* indicate how Brendan was influenced in the re-writing of the play. The I.R.A. men are depicted in it as rather nasty caricatures. 'Kevin Barry', an I.R.A. 'hymn' about an eighteen-year-old Republican boy hanged in 1920, was sung in a derisive way in the second act. Christopher Gore-Grimes, Brendan's solicitor, was disgusted when he heard the song mocked in this way, and wondered how Brendan could lend himself to it. Mattie O'Neill, a fellow-internee of the Curragh Camp days, nearly had a stroke when he saw *The Hostage*. 'My blood boiled. I thought I'd burst with anger'.

Why didn't the I.R.A. object? Probably very few of them saw it in the West End. Brendan knew perfectly well that any of them who did must have sensed that he had let them down.

Brendan never complained in public of the way his play had been altered, in fact he seemed to approve:

> Joan Littlewood, I found, suited my requirements exactly. She has the same views on theatre that I have, which is that Music Hall is the thing to aim for to amuse people and any time they get bored divert them with a song or a dance. While your audience were laughing their heads off, you could be up to any bloody thing behind their backs; and there was much we were doing behind their bloody backs that made your play great.

Yet no matter how much he blathered about the Music Hall, the transformation must have hurt him. *An Giall* had its roots in Ballyferriter, the Blaskets and the Atlantic; *The Hostage* in a commercial entertainment world Brendan had no real contact with. It was, in a sense, a betrayal not only of the I.R.A. whom he guyed in the play but of the instinct which led him to write the first version, the compassion of the artist for a human predicament he could personally identify with. One night during the successful run of the play at Stratford, when the theatre was packed, he turned round suddenly to his brother Brian and said, 'Fuck Joan Littlewood'. Brian recalls:

I was surprised and I looked at him closely. He looked suddenly as if he knew he had been 'taken for a ride', that he had been adopted as a broth of a boy, that they had played a three card trick on him. I think he suddenly had a moment of insight which was gone as soon as the next joke or drink came round.

It was a turning point in Brendan's career. Was he in future to write on demand? Would he allow the mask he wore, created by the mob, to influence the personality behind, by submitting his work to the public appetite instead of to his own judgment?

Back in Dublin Brendan's friend the painter Tom Nisbet, when he heard what had happened to *The Hostage*, commented: 'The difference between Brendan Behan and Dylan Thomas is that Dylan wrote *Under Milkwood* and Brendan wrote under Littlewood'.

Brendan's success with *The Hostage* alone would have been sufficient to establish his name. But four days after its premiere he was to unleash another work on the public which was to have as great an impact.

Borstal Boy was published on October 20. There had been outstanding previews of it. Frank Swinnerton, the essayist, who had written the authoritative study of the Georgian writers, thought that it was

> as precise a document and as personal a dream as a novel by Victor Hugo. I call this book a masterpiece.

Canon Collins described it as

> a vital and moving book. To anyone concerned about the British penal system, and surely this must apply to everyone who possesses a Christian spirit, this book is a must.

In anticipation of the book's success, the publishers held a party on October 18. Brendan behaved well on the whole on this occasion, and sang 'The Old Musheroon' with Patrick Campbell, a fellow writer, and 'The Old Fenian Men' with Hugh Delargey, M.P., besides swopping prison experiences with Emanuel Shinwell, M.P., who had spent some time in jail for his part in a strike in 1919. After the party, when they had adjourned to an Italian restaurant nearby, Brendan and Paddy Campbell got stuck into one another, Brendan becoming abusive because of some policeman ancestor of Campbell's who was only relevant in the context of Brendan's irritation and wish to insult a fellow Dubliner, which he succeeded admirably in doing.

The next day he was to do a television interview with Kenneth Allsop in Birmingham. Though very nervous, Brendan made an excellent impression. But the strain sent him back on to the bottle again so that Beatrice, Rae Jeffs and Allsop had to steer him into the train carriage on the return journey to Euston. When they reached London they had to forcibly remove him from the train after he had refused to leave the lavatory where he had locked himself. At length, a forlorn figure with his trousers down to his ankles, he was led along the platform by Beatrice to a taxi.

Two days later, on October 20, *Borstal Boy* was published. It had a splendid reception. Within a few days fifty-two papers in Britain and Ireland had reviewed the book and the first printing of 15,000 copies was sold out immediately. Cyril Connolly, though he had reservations that Brendan was unsure about his use of anticlimax, wrote in the *Sunday Times*:

> Mr Behan is a natural writer. His rare descriptions of scenery are poetic. His accounts of Christmas relaxation among the Warders and Prisoners is almost Dickensian.

Maurice Richardson in the *Observer* wrote:

> An excellent book, vivid, solid . . . very warm and full of human observation There are sharp sketches of fellow Borstalians in brilliantly characterised dialogue.

The *Times Literary Supplement* spoke of the book as

> a brilliantly evocative account . . . a stupendous gift for language.

Christopher Logue in the *New Statesman and Nation* said:

> The most important book of its kind to be published in this century.

Translation rights were sold in Germany, France, Italy, Spain, Sweden, Norway, Denmark and Holland.

Four months later it was published in New York and had a similar reception. Orville Prescott in the *New York Times* wrote:

> Mr Behan can write prose, that sings, or snarls, or chuckles.

Time magazine said that he had

> Gabriel's own gift of the gab, a cold eye for himself, a warm heart for others, and the narrative speed of a Tinker.

There was a second review in the *New York Times* by Brian Moore, the Irish novelist, who said:

> *Borstal Boy* is a fine memoir, amusing, clearheaded, vivid. But there is in young Behan an echo of some parts of *The Playboy of the Western World* forever peeping out of the prose and not very praiseworthy, saying, 'Look at me now, amin't I the fine fellow'. A desire to be loved robs the memoir of power.

In one month in New York it sold 20,000 copies.

Borstal Boy brought Brendan not only literary fame, it helped to fix his public image. What filtered through to the general public was an image of a young man of working class background whose early life had been crippled by crime and prison but who had survived to become a writer and playwright. Through this image he became an established writer with a right to thumb his nose at society, and be taken seriously by the intelligentsia at the same time—a picture which, let it be said, suited Brendan Behan down to the ground. He was a hidden persuader who worked overtime on a single account—his own.

There were obvious reasons for the success of *Borstal Boy*. It was an account of reform school life related vividly by a former prisoner and included frank language and dialogue of the type that almost a decade before had made Norman Mailer a notorious figure with *The Naked and the Dead*. What is less noticeable in the welter of Cockney dialogue, violence and comic episodes is the excellence of the prose style, especially in the descriptive passages. Here is how Brendan catches the atmosphere of summer on the Suffolk coast:

> He brought us down through an orchard and the leaves were heavy and glinted in the sun as if they had a coat of synthetic green enamel on them. We walked over some more sand heaps, and, at last, Jones stood on the top, looking down at the sea, as if he'd made it himself.
> We stood beside him and looked down at the sun on the water.
> 'Me life on you, Jonesy', said I. You're like "Stout Cortez when with eagle eyes, he stared at the Pacific"—and all his men looked at each other

with a "wild surmise, silent, upon a peak in Darien". By Jasus, this equals any fughing Darien'.

There was no beach, like Killiney, but a stony stretch of pebbles that would remind you of the people of the place, but the water, glittering and dancing, stretched away out in front of us, with no limit but the rim of the world and it was green and blue farther out; there was a bit of a concrete breakwater, that I picked for a dive.

538 Jones and Charlie and I dived and swam under water towards Joe, looking towards each other, as if this was where we'd always lived, a world of naked, waving limbs and silent, open eyes.

This is how he describes winter:

The autumn got weaker and beaten, and the leaves all fell, and a bloody awful east wind was up before us and we on our way to work in the morning, sweeping down off the top of the North Sea, which in the distance looked like a bitter band of deadly blue steel out along the length of the horizon, around the freezing marshes, the dirty grey shore, the gunmetal sea, and over us the sky, lead-coloured for a few hours, till the dark fell and the wind rose, and we went down the road from work at five o'clock in the perishing night.

Going back down the road I could see the moon, wild and hiding itself, behind an odd cloud, out over the mad grey sea, beyond the half-drenched marshes.

As in *The Quare Fellow*, Brendan is more concerned with presenting human beings as they are, rather than separating them into pre-conceived categories of good and evil.

Jean Genet in his autobiographical *The Miracle of the Rose* deals with the same themes as Behan does in *Borstal Boy* and *The Quare Fellow*. He describes his boyhood in the prison colony at Mettray and later on depicts the effect of the execution of one of the prisoners on the rest of the prison. But Genet makes no attempt at detachment. For him the Governor, Warders, and Chaplain exist only as vague phantoms of oppression necessary to kindle the fantasies by which he is able to enter his own personal dream world. The sun may have shone on Fontrevault and the sky have been blue. Genet will not permit this. It is the glance of the reptile through the glass.

Genet undergoes Yoga-like visions, through which he identifies with the condemned man. But there is no pity shown for the victim who is a little girl. The murderer might have bestrode a cheese for all the interest Genet shows in her reaction. Genet's glorification of evil and treachery as ends in themselves have been praised as presenting an existential view of life. But by rejecting their opposites he succeeds in categorizing existence so as to exclude an element of it which Behan has been coerced into accepting.

Borstal Boy is also a record of Cockney, Liverpool and Welsh working-class dialogue. With his ear tuned to the elaborate quality of Dublin speech, Behan was on the lookout for interesting forms of language in other people; and while a fault in the dialogue of the book is that it introduces at times a plethora of picturesque speech into single sentences so as to weaken the realistic effect, *Borstal Boy* remains one of the few authentic records in the English language of young criminals talking.

Brian Moore, the Irish novelist, writing on *Borstal Boy* in his *New York Times* piece, noted that the author's wish to see himself as a fine fellow, and his desire to be loved, robs the memoir of power. But though the desire to see himself as a central figure and a tendency to romanticize himself is a weakness of the book, nevertheless an important feature of *Borstal Boy* is that Behan has portrayed himself with his indigenous Dublin culture, against a background of an industrial proletariat without proper roots.

Woven into the tapestry of the work is the culture he has been bred from — Gaelic, Latin, Anglo-Irish, the Dublin of Swift, Sheridan, Wilde and O'Casey that gave him, as it gave Joyce in exile before him, the confidence 'that the expression "Dubliner" bears some meaning which cannot be said for such words as Londoner or Parisian'. As he comes back on the mailboat to Dublin after his release from Borstal, Brendan realizes what his native city means to him:

> The next morning I stood on deck while the boat came into Dun Laoghaire, and looked at the sun struggling up over the hills; and the city all round the Bay.
>
> . . . and I will make my journey, if life and health but stand,
> Unto that pleasant country, that fresh and fragrant strand,
> And leave your boasted braveries, your wealth and high command.
> For the fair hills of Holy Ireland . . .

212

There they were, as if I'd never left them; in their sweet and stately order round the Bay—Bray Head, the Sugarloaf, the Two Rock, the Three Rock, Kippure, the King of them all, rising his threatening head behind and over their shoulders till they sloped down to the city. I counted the spires, from Rathmines fat dome on one side to St George's spire on the north, and in the centre, Christchurch. Among the smaller ones, just on the docks, I could pick out, even in the haze of the morning, the ones I knew best, St Laurence O'Toole's and St Barnabas; I had them all counted, present and correct and the chimneys of the Pigeon House, and the framing circle of the road along the edge of the Bay, Dun Laoghaire, Blackrock, Sandymount Tower, Ringsend and the city; then the other half circle, Fairview, Marino, Clontarf, Raheny, Kilbarrack, Baldoyle, to the height of Howth Head.

I couldn't really see Kilbarrack or Baldoyle, but it was only that I knew they were there. So many belonging to me lay buried in Kilbarrack, the healthiest graveyard in Ireland, they said, because it was so near the sea, and I thought I could see the tricolour waving over Dan Head's grave, which I could not from the ten miles over the Bay. And I could see Baldoyle there, because it was the races.

In November, shortly after *Borstal Boy* appeared, *The Quare Fellow* opened in New York, directed by Jose Quintero at The Circle in the Square. It was well received on the whole, but it had nothing like the reception it had had in London. The *New York Times* and the *New York Herald Tribune* did not appear to think it had made a sufficiently deep impression on the audience, but John McLean of the *Journal American*, found it 'enormously beguiling' and noted that Brendan's new play 'rings with realism'.

As a result of the New York premiere, Brendan got a hefty piece of world-wide publicity in an interview which appeared in *Time* magazine the week the play opened:

A richly vocabularized ex-terrorist and convict named Brendan Behan is on the town. The night *Quare Fellow* had its off-Broadway opening, playwright Behan, a tousled Falstaffian figure of a man, celebrated by heading out on a glorious binge in Dublin. Behan (rhymes with seem') is the descendant of a distinguished line of eccentrics, rebels and house painters.

Behan's thunderous and immediate success was on the scale of another bedevilled elf, the late Welsh poet, Dylan Thomas.

For all his attachment to the spigot, Brendan turns it off during his writing bouts. Not that it is easy to, now that the vagabond liver has money and fame. Brendan has started a novel about Dublin, but, he says 'I can't get on with it with all this blanking success'. Meanwhile, since his *Borstal Boy* was banned as 'obscene' by the Irish Government, he strides about bellowing (to the tune of MacNamara's Band):

Oh me name is Brendan Behan, I'm the latest of the banned,
Although we're small in numbers, we're the best banned in the land;
We're read at wakes and weddins, and in every parish hall,
And under libr'y counters, sure you'll have no trouble at all.

After Christmas he learnt that *The Hostage* was to transfer to the West End in August. It would be Brendan's second play to be staged there. Even more exciting was the news that it had been chosen as the British entry for the Théâtre des Nations Festival in Paris, which was to open in April. There would be twenty-three countries represented from all over the world competing for the Prix des Théâtres des Nations. As well, four days later *The Quare Fellow* was to be presented in translation at the Théâtre de l'Oeuvre in the same city. In February it would be staged in the Schillertheater, Berlin, in a German translation.

Brendan had not been exactly an anonymous writer when *The Hostage* had its premiere at Stratford in 1958. He had previously had a play staged in the West End. But now in the space of three months he found himself the author of a best-selling book, translated into eight languages and of two plays, one of which was to be staged in Paris and Berlin in the original languages of those countries, and another which had been selected above other productions in England as an entry for a major theatre festival.

To be accepted as a writer in Paris was specially exciting for him. He had gone there to become a writer in 1948. For him, it was *the* writer's city, the school where Scott Fitzgerald, Hemingway, Henry Miller, Beckett, and many others had learnt their trade—the artistic capital of the world. He had been known to a small group there in the 'forties, including some French journalists. But now he was to return in triumph to a city where he had been one of thousands of anonymous writers looking for recognition less than ten years before.

Before he went away, he decided to get some writing done. In the middle of February he took a room in the La Touche Hotel in Greystones, a town seventeen miles from Dublin, noted for its peaceful atmosphere, ultra-respectability and Protestant quiet.

With a day's hard work behind him, Brendan was drinking in the bar of the hotel when a man sitting on the next stool asked him if he could join him for a drink. Brendan agreed in good-humoured fashion, and then found out that his new companion was a retired policeman. This unleashed some inner fury in him and he roared that he wouldn't accept a drink from any 'effing copper'. When the man remonstrated, Brendan hurled a bottle of stout at him. The manager of the hotel, David Fitzgerald, a human being of infinite tact who has been known to quiet drunken professors with quotations from Horace, managed to steer Brendan out of the hotel into the cold night. He sent someone after him to make sure he was all right. Fitzgerald is quite convinced that Brendan was not drunk at the time he left the hotel, he was just extremely angry.

Sometime later, Brendan was found by a policeman, lying on the ground and talking incessantly to himself. When the policeman questioned him he became abusive and a squad car was called. Three policemen took him to the Station at Greystones, where, according to the evidence given later, he referred to the police as 'bloodhounds and murderers'. If he was looking for publicity he certainly got it. British and Irish papers carried detailed reports of the case after he appeared in court next day.

Brendan, at the start of the proceedings, resorted to the ingenious stratagem of insisting that the case be heard in Irish. This was his right under the Irish Constitution, which presumes every State official to be bilingual. This is not necessarily so and Brendan knew quite well that it might embarrass the prosecution if he was to continue to insist on his right to have the case tried in this way. He was heard at Bray District Court, in front of District Justice Manus Nunan. When the case was called, Brendan said in Irish: 'I want this case to be heard in Irish, please. According to the Constitution of this country I have a right to be heard in Irish'. The District Justice, caught unawares, told him in Irish to sit down, and the Inspector added, though it was not in order for him to do so, 'Be quiet', also in Irish. Brendan continued, 'I have a right that only the Irish language is used in this case'.

The first Guard to give evidence, Guard J. A. Molloy, began in Irish and said that on the morning of March 4 he got a call from a civilian, named Terence O'Riley, that a man was lying in Church Road, Greystones. At 12.45 a.m. he went to Church Road where the defendant, Behan, was. Brendan then interrupted in Irish: 'Justice, can I speak to you for a moment?' The Justice replied, 'No'. Brendan continued in Irish: 'According to the Constitution of the State I can speak in Irish and have a right to be heard in the language which is the first official language of the State'.

The District Justice again said: 'Sit down', The Guard tried to continue his evidence in English, but Brendan interrupted again: 'That man is not talking in Irish. I want the case to be heard in the first official language of the country'.

Guard Molloy, continuing his evidence in English, said that he asked the defendant what he was looking for. He was lying down. The local doctor, who was also on the scene, told him that Brendan was not ill and that he appeared to be a case for the police. The witness said: 'He said that he was looking for his wife and added that she was in one of the local houses. He was dishevelled and appeared to have been in a struggle. He said: "Here are the — bloodhounds" and "You are — murderers".'

BEHAN Correct.

WITNESS He then left the scene, and went towards another hotel, where he hammered on the door to gain admittance. I remonstrated with him, and he used vile language. Then I telephoned for a patrol car, and two Gardai came along in it.

BEHAN (in Irish) Well, at least you know one word in Irish, 'Gardai'.

WITNESS He said that we were bloodhounds. He resisted violently when we tried to arrest him, and used foul language. You could hear him all over the place.

BEHAN (in Irish) No doubt it was not the Irish language.

Guard Molloy then went on to say that Brendan had to be forced into the patrol car, and had to be forced out of it again at the police station. He was forcibly searched, and then forcibly put into a cell. He added: 'He kicked at the cell door from 1.30 a.m. to 4.30 a.m. He said that the police were murderers, and said: "You are no good". He was discharged at 8.00 a.m. when he was still in the same tone of voice'.

BEHAN As I always am.

Guard Molloy said that when he attempted to take the defendant into custody he had no idea who he was. Brendan then cross-examined the Guard in Irish:

BEHAN When I asked you for a drop of water during the night, did you give it to me?
WITNESS Yes.
BEHAN You gave it to me five minutes before I left in the morning. Now you know I have no great love for you, don't you? You are a perjurer.

Addressing the District Judge, still in Irish, Brendan continued: 'This Guard said to some of the others, "We have the quare fellow now".' The Inspector jumped to his feet at this juncture: 'I must ask you, Justice, to treat this behaviour as contempt of court. He has abused this Guard and called him a perjurer. This should not be allowed.' The Justice, however, made no comment. The next Guard, Denis O'Leary, said he came in a patrol car and that the defendant had called him a bloodhound. Guard L. G. McEntaggert alleged that when he tried to get Brendan into the car he called him a guttersnipe. The District Justice remarked: 'It would be hard to translate that one'.

BEHAN I'll do it for you.
WITNESS His language was vile and could be heard all over Greystones.

Brendan then cross-examined him:

BEHAN Did you recognize me?
GUARD MCENTAGGERT I did not know him and I do not know him. I have never heard of him and never read him.

Brendan then asked: 'Can he read at all?'

Asked to make his defence, Brendan, speaking in Irish, said:

I went to the Grand Hotel, Greystones, on the evening of March 3, because I wanted to do some writing for a film. I was in the bar and was having a few drinks. I had booked into the hotel for a couple of days. While I was in the bar a man, who said his name was Charlie Reynolds, came up to me. He wanted to drink with me. He told me that he was an old policeman. I told him that I would not give a drink to any policeman, new or old.

Then I went out into the open, and the police came. They put me in the car. They would not even give me a drink of water. I have been in jail in Belfast and Britain, and have never been refused a drink. I am on my oath now, so I must admit that I was drunk on this occasion.

Beatrice Behan then gave evidence for her husband and said that he had gone down to Greystones to work, so that he wouldn't be interrupted, and when the Justice suggested that it was obvious that Brendan had gone down for a skite, she denied that this was so. When the Justice remarked that Beatrice did not seem to be able to control him, she said: 'I would have if I had been there'.

The Inspector said that if the case had been carried on in a proper fashion he wouldn't press it. It was a shame that an otherwise talented man should behave like a blackguard. He was drunk when he was found and he behaved very badly.

DISTRICT JUSTICE   Will you make an apology for your behaviour?

BEHAN   (*in English*) How can I make a sincere apology? I regard you as a representative of the Irish people. But I will apologise for my language.

DISTRICT JUSTICE   Is that an apology?

BEHAN   Which would be the greater insult—to apologize if I was not sincere, or not to apologize?

DISTRICT JUSTICE   That is a matter for your own conscience.

BEHAN   All right, I will apologize.

DISTRICT JUSTICE   Fined forty shillings.

An aspect of the case which shows how observant Brendan could be when he was looking for publicity, was that he must have found out somehow or other that the press reporter taking shorthand notes was bilingual. If this hadn't been so, there would have been no point in Brendan's speaking in Irish, as he would have lost all publicity value if the reporter had not been able to understand what he was saying.

What is curious about the affair is how Brendan got into the condition he appeared to be in, if he was sober when he left the hotel. He couldn't have got drunk anywhere else at that time. Was he acting? Had he conceived some Machiavellian plan to deceive the police and cause trouble for them that misfired when he lost his temper? Is it possible that he was staging a scene that he hoped would hit the world press? From now on there were to be so many repetitions of his 'Muggeridge' act, that it became increasingly difficult to discover which were genuine manifestations of inebriation, and which were engineered for the purpose of obtaining world publicity.

He was due in Paris for the opening of *The Hostage* in the second week in April. He decided first to go to Berlin for the German premiere of *The Quare Fellow* on March 16 and then continue on to Paris to arrive there ahead of the rest of the cast.

The Berlin visit was a fiasco.

On the opening night, at the Schillertheater, Brendan tried his usual antics on the stage. This did not appeal at all to the stolid Germans. He received the next day from the critic Friedrich Luft in *Die Welt* what must be one of the most vicious notices ever written about a play:

This is a report of a flop, the notification of a complete artistic washout. The critic on the wailing wall of theatrical failure. It has seldom been so hard to keep one's seat as now in the Berlin Schillertheater during the German premiere of Brendan Behan's *Der Mann von morgen früh*.

This author enjoys in England an aura of interesting infamy. He is Irish. He was born in the slums of Dublin. He spent his youth in the back room of a brothel. He was to have been a house-painter like his father. At a tender age he associated himself with bombthrowers among the angry Irish.

The first time in Bristol he was put into a reformatory for three years, when explosives were found in his pockets. Then he was sentenced to 14 years in Dublin for the attempted murder of two policemen: he was again arrested in Manchester, held for four months, and sent to France.

In France he ripened towards literature. He sang songs to the lute, wrote a book about his experiences in prison and worked the same experiences into a play. The latter, unfortunately, has just come into this country.

Probably due to an old misconception: If an author has personally experienced scandal what he makes out of it must in any case be scandalously interesting. Wrong! Dickens was never in the poorhouse, nor Dante in hell—despite that both have given us glowing descriptions of these places.

In his prison play he pleads against capital punishment. The boredom which this produces is, however, mortal. Many painful varieties of active theatre sleep could be seen in the Schiller stalls. Snoring from all sides. What makes the play so ineffective? Its poor dramatic form! Behan wants to get rid of his pleading against capital punishment. But while he writes he forgets the purpose of the play. He gives us only Dönekens out of the memories of an old prison-inmate. . . .

What poor character-sketching he attempts does not become funny, hilarious or macabre. Often enough even whole characters are lost in the course of the action. Badly played characters go by the board. Behan is already rushing on to other convict types.

And a three-hour treatise was not necessary to convince us that there are some seedy, some cute, some wretched and some foolish. We also see them as such. To show that they are out to cadge cigarette butts and dupe the warders is not an evening's entertainment. Interest is soon lost.

It dies completely when the author in the middle of jejune and uninteresting observations still far from the core of the work finally forgets his main theme. He intended—admittedly with good grounds—to argue against capital punishment. But that escapes him due to dramatic clumsiness. . . .

If no tragedy had already occurred, an unintentional satire followed promptly, when the author, tempted by a little polite applause, tottered onto the stage in a state of imperturbable drunkenness and, reeling and stuttering, collected himself to address a sort of speech to the audience which had only with difficulty awakened. We learnt that he was opposed to the East–West conflict. Then he and the rest of his speech were tactfully cut short by a tactful lowering of the curtain.

And then—at last—came the the first, liberating whistles.

A year and a half later, when *The Hostage* had its German premiere in Ulm, smoke bombs were hurled in protest by bored members of the audience. It is obvious that Brendan's image as a slum rebel who had fought the English was a bad one to try on the Germans.

The prospects in Paris seemed decidedly better, however. There his play had already been selected as the British entry for the Théâtre des Nations. It could hardly receive anything approaching the treatment the German critics had given *The Quare Fellow*.

He arrived in Paris a few days before *The Hostage* was to open on April 3, 1959. Columnists from England, including David Nathan of the *Daily Mail* and Leslie Mallory of the *News Chronicle*, went over specially to cover his Paris visit. Brendan was besieged by requests for personal interviews. Radio and Television were after him. Magazine editors wanted features.

He met the Theatre Workshop Company on the day of the performance when they arrived at Le Bourget Airport. He drove in with them in great form, and pointed to a poster where the words: 'Under the patronage of the British Ambassador' had been overprinted by a notice saying that His Excellency would not attend. 'Sure, haven't we plenty of oul' Ambassadors, anyway', Brendan said. This was true. That night, the American, and Polish Ambassadors were among the crowd who jammed the doorways of the Sarah Bernhardt Theatre, and the British Ambassador did arrive—late. Among others there were Lady Diana Cooper and Jean-Louis Barrault.

There were ten curtain calls. There was a three minute ovation from a crowd of 1200 people. Desmond Ryan, writing in the *Irish Times* described the scene as the curtain went down:

> On Friday night, Paris discovered another B.B., which it took to its heart with perhaps not quite the same sentiments, but with almost as much enthusiasm as it affords to the luscious Mademoiselle Brigitte Bardot. But after all Brendan Behan is equally eye-filling from certain points of view and takes up more space.
>
> When, after half-a-dozen curtain calls at the end, there were enthusiastic demands of 'Author, Author,' he appeared on the balcony and paid a gracious tribute in his individual brand of French (not at all inferior, I noticed, to Sir Laurence Olivier's on another occasion here) to 'the most civilised people in the world!'

Later that night at a party at La Méditerranée he kept to his decision not to drink.

Next day the notices were excellent. Jacques le Marchand in *Figaro Littéraire* thought the play brought to mind 'the felicitous reversals of Menotti's plots'.

> A tragedy—yes; but the youthfulness, generosity and comedy which transform this tragedy into a musical comedy without detracting from its meaningfulness, endow this treatment of a tragedy of our time with a novelty and liberty which make it extremely provocative.

Robert Kasters wrote in *L'Express*:

> If Claudel's *L'Otage* is a tragedy of spiritual liberty, this Hostage is the bitter farce of an anarchic liberty. This play takes on much force because it

is said without ceremony, with music-hall songs, doubtful jokes, a sort of healthy vulgarity. No compliments, no oratorical circumlocutions to satisfy morality, religion or nationalism, nothing but solid, continuous derision.

Four days later *The Quare Fellow* was presented in a French translation by Jacqueline Sundstrom and Boris Vian at the Theatre de L'Oeuvre. Robert Kemp, writing in *Le Monde* found it 'a joyous and delightful evening', even though he noted 'that anguish streams across the footlights and grips us'.

Jean Jacotier in *Le Figaro* wrote:

> The author, while seeming to show us a photograph is in fact revealing a work of art. The dialogue is powerful, nervous, coloured, sarcastic: under a false front of humour and purely external burlesque, it is, in reality, biting, and we are all seized by this icy comedy which conceals genuine sentiment and deep emotions. Brendan Behan has succeeded in conferring a universal value on the individual emotions of a well-defined microcosm.

Brendan's picture was in so many papers that the manager of the Hotel d'Angleterre rushed over with *Le Figaro* in his hand and insisted on Brendan staying as his guest for the rest of his time in Paris. 'Any other time I would have thought he was pointing me out to the police', Brendan remarked.

Jean-Louis Barrault gave a dinner in his honour. Brendan got drunk and misbehaved for the only time during his visit to Paris.

David Nathan remembers how happy Brendan was at this time. He was sober and in control of himself. He had recognition in a city where he most wanted it. One evening, he and Nathan, Leslie Mallory, Beatrice and Nathan's wife, Norma, went to a fish restaurant. Afterwards they drifted out into the warm Paris Spring night and settled down in a café in Saint Germain des Prés. Brendan was in famous form. David Nathan remembers:

> I have never heard anything like it. He started to compose couplets about the writers and painters who had lived in Paris in the 'twenties. I can only remember a few of them, but it went on for an hour and a half, each better than the next. One was:
>
> > Say, my friend, what have you missed
> > In not seeing Scott Fitzgerald pissed.

Another one was:

> If you had seen André Gide,
> Chasing boys on a Rapide.

Nathan also remembers how Brendan suddenly seemed to realize that he might be offending Nathan's wife, Norma, with his bad language. He turned round as they were walking down a street and said 'I'm sorry, but all this swearing must be annoying you'. Nathan remembers that for at least ten paces Brendan didn't use a swear word until the reflex began to assert itself again. Norma had become accustomed to it in Brendan's case and was touched by his sudden consideration for her. One result of being with him for such a long period was that on the journey back she asked an astonished hostess on the 'plane: 'Get me a glass of fucking milk'.

Art Buchwald interviewed Brendan for his column in the *New York Herald Tribune*.

> We met Mr Behan at high noon at his hotel. He was wearing a blue tie: 'I wear a red tie for my school', he told us, 'a green tie for my country, and a blue tie when I have a hangover. I have been partial lately to blue ties'. Mr Behan has had several minor scrapes with the French police. Once he made a row out at Orly about getting on an aeroplane: 'The newspapers quoted me as saying I did not want to die for France. What I actually said was, I did not want to die for Air France'. He blames his troubles on his fondness for Irish whiskey and Guinness stout: 'I don't necessarily drink them together', he said, 'but there is a very short interval in between'. We asked Mr Behan if he was married: 'Yes, I am', he said, 'to a very dear girl who is an artist. We have no children except me'.

One aspect of his life in Paris he was anxious to keep out of the press. The author of a Theatre Workshop production and Brendan had been seeing a good deal of one another in the previous few months and she had come to Paris for the Festival, mainly to be in his company. She was a simple girl, who had no hesitation in telling Beatrice that she was in love with Brendan. Beatrice, with her usual seraphic resignation, did not show any resentment and continued to keep her usual watch over Brendan in order to minimise the chances of another breakdown through over-indulgence in alcohol and neglect of proper eating. 'I thought it was honest of her to tell me', was her comment. 'She was a nice girl to be so frank about it.' Of course, the press were avid for news of the affair. It was something to write about now that Brendan was off the gargle for a while.

Brendan was on Librium at this time to help him resist his compulsive urge towards alcohol. But before he left Paris his good intentions gave way, and he had a few hard nights' drinking. The strain showed when he appeared on a television programme with Derek Hart, on the B.B.C. *Tonight* programme on his way home to Dublin.

He didn't stay there long. After two days he was back in London again. He wanted the bright lights. Dublin wasn't enough for him after his months of fame. He didn't want to remind himself too much of the council home in Kildare Road or the hardships of his early upbringing. It was all right to play the working-class boy when he was away. When he was at home he wanted to be accepted as a world success. In Dublin, city of professional knockers, this was not easy.

For two weeks he drank himself round London, then suddenly he announced his intention of going home. At the beginning of June he and Beatrice set out for Carraroe, Connemara, where there was a little cottage they rented each year from Paddy Griffin. It was a wild, isolated, Irish-speaking district. Nothing could have been worse for Brendan at this moment. In the west, they are great talkers and great drinkers. Their likes were Brendan's likes; talking in Irish, drinking and singing and telling yarns into the small hours.

What Brendan really wanted was a place where he was totally unknown, where he couldn't speak the language—sun, too, instead of the inconstant weather of the Irish west with its sudden changes from dazzling blues and greens to sodden, drizzling grey—inevitable drinking weather. He was pursued by reporters everywhere, even when he went on a visit to the Aran Islands by steamer. Worst of all, the habits of regular food to control his diet that Beatrice had managed to build up since their marriage were beginning to break down. Perhaps after the Paris affair she had not as much influence over him as before. He was drinking now and not eating, though occasionally she managed to get a raw egg in milk into him in the morning, before he went out on a skite.

It was obvious that Brendan was finding it harder and harder to settle down and concentrate on writing. He had become a world figure overnight. Money had flowed in, in amounts beyond anything he had ever thought he could earn. For six months, since October, he had been on show. He had shot off witticisms for press men to make the news next day, done countless radio and television interviews, and generally concerned himself with propagating the legend of Behan. His talking sessions were marathon ones. In drawing room or bar, he had held audiences for four or five hours with uninterrupted monologues of stories, songs, poems and jokes. Such activity makes large demands on the psychic and physical resources of those who practice it. A room full of people have to be conquered, and drawn into orbit—people of different temperament and background—while the talker competes against the clink of glasses and the chatter of conversation. It is only subtly, and with gradual skill that he can conquer the room, eliminating less powerful competitors, till by the sheer force of personality and mesmerism his words begin to form pictures in front of his listeners and a captive audience is created.

Brendan, at his eloquent best, was the equivalent of a one-man show—except that he had no script and the run was unlimited. Unlike a stage actor when his performance is over, Brendan's obligation to his art did not cease when he stopped talking. It was then he should have settled down to serious writing. But in his public performance he had syphoned off so much energy that he was often too exhausted to lift a pen. This was to be his great dilemma. If he indulged the extrovert side of his character, he lessened his chances of doing the only thing in life that really mattered to him—writing.

Oscar Wilde and Dylan Thomas were other victims of this double gift. They were entertaining Celtic necromancers who could not resist the desire to entrance. This undermined their ability to write, so that in Wilde's case the last four years of his life were spent talking rather than writing, while Thomas gathered the torn shreds of his nervous system together to recite a hastily-prepared *Under Milkwood* to a frenzied audience in New York shortly before succumbing finally to the strain of being an artist in two spheres. Scott Fitzgerald, whose Celtic reaction against the despotism of fact was tempered by a streak of Yankee pragmatism, was detached enough to see himself slipping into a public role half way through his writing career and reacted from it:

> I had become identified with the objects of my horror or compassion. My life had been drawing on resources I did not possess . . . I had been mortgaging myself physically and spiritually up to the hilt.

Brendan, alas, instead of reducing his overdraft continued to extend it. He told Kenneth Allsop:

> Success is damn near killing me. I think a man should be allowed success for one month and then given a pension and allowed to retire.

He did not go over for the first night of the West End production of *The Hostage*. A *Daily Mail* reporter interviewing him in Connemara recorded Brendan's reaction to the premiere:

> Rumpled, rumbustuous, Brendan Behan was downing whisky and stout chasers here tonight, despite the fact that he should have been in London's West End for the opening of his play, *The Hostage*, and despite doctors' warnings that if he keeps on drinking it will kill him. Between the drinking and singing, he told me: 'You are right, I am not well. I sometimes feel terrible. But I don't know what the trouble is, so have another drink'. His wife, Beatrice, says: 'It is too much for anyone. He drinks too much and won't eat a thing at all'. And in the Malthouse in Galway, he flung his arms around my neck, ignored the serious matter of his health, and, with a thumping fist, announced loudly: 'Kingdoms fall, Empires crash, but we shall rise again, I will go.'

One day at Carraroe he had gone for a swim without togs on. He wallowed in the Atlantic for almost an hour and when he came out he found that a number of the Abbey Theatre Company who were on holiday in Connemara had come to the beach to swim. Brendan wasn't the least embarrassed at his nakedness, for as he said: 'The one half of you is actors and other other half is 'actresses'.

Beatrice wrote to Rae Jeffs to tell her what was happening to Brendan:

> I'm worried to death, but no one can control a man like Brendan. It is too much for anyone. He drinks too much and won't eat at all. He has been told to stop drinking completely. But what can I do with him? He is ruining his health. I wish he would stop for a little while.

A day or two later he returned to Dublin from the country. He had been complaining about a pain in his left ear at this time. One afternoon out in Dun Laoghaire, a handsome Dublin suburb, with an Edwardian facade overlooking the sea, Brendan took what amounted to an epileptic fit. It was an epileptiform seizure, contributed to by alcohol and had all the symptoms of a genuine epilepsy. When it was to happen again, Beatrice had to teach herself to put a pencil between his teeth when the frightful seizures overtook him so that he would not bite his tongue off. Terrified on this occasion, she took him to a local G.P. who immediately got him to Baggot Street Hospital, where he was seen by his own doctor, Terence Chapman. He was put to bed in a ward and sedated immediately. However, two days later, on July 14, gathering his clothes, he scampered from the hospital and set out for London. Later he told the press he wanted money and he knew he could get an advance in London on the spot, out of the proceeds of *The Hostage*. But it is more likely that what Brendan wanted was to be around to share the glory that was emanating from the West End success of his play.

The first night, which took place on July 11, 1959, at Wyndham's Theatre, could not have gone better. The critic of the *Times* wrote:

> Mr Brendan Behan's *The Hostage*, has the roaring vitality of an extravaganza which has made up up its mind to have no truck with form of any sort. The story is really only Mr Behan's excuse for taking a fling at past and present Anglo-Irish relations with a rollicking, almost anarchic, impartiality. Mr Behan's irreverence for the established rules of society strikes us as going deeper than Mr John Osborne's. He is not so good a playwright, but his flouts and jeers, however outrageous, are essentially warm-hearted. The wounds inflicted are never poisoned. He can arrange for one of the characters to sing a bitter anti-English ballad and turn away

the offence by putting into her mouth the comment 'Why doesn't the author come up here to do his own dirty work?'

The *Manchester Guardian* noticed that the play was an immense improvement on the original Stratford production:

> The show is directed by Joan Littlewood and it would be beyond the power of the most expert exegetist to decide where Brendan ends and Joan begins. But the simplest spectator can see that *The Hostage* by the broth of a boy friend Behan deserves to fill Wyndham's for a long, long time to come. Most of the songs, the programme asserts, were written by the author, some of them by his uncle. Others are 'trad' or from the music-hall. Together they make the evening something less than the ordinary musical and something much more than the ordinary play. For once it was an occasion which would have been heightened if the author could have taken his deserved call. But he is ill in a 'foreign land' and will be welcome in London whenever he can come to see his own play so well done!

Mervyn Jones of the *Observer*, while praising the play generally, said that

> more than half the time it turns into undisguised cabaret; speaking and singing straight to the audience the cast gets splendid fun out of Irish traditions, English snobbery, Holy Church, racial intolerance, sex in all its forms, the H-bomb and whatever else you can think of. It's magnificent, but it isn't drama.

When there were shouts of 'Author' at the end of the play, an actor read out a card from Brendan: 'Tell the audience I was asking for them'.

The actor added: 'He's with us in spirit'. He didn't know that Brendan was to be with them sooner than they thought.

When Brendan discharged himself from Baggot Street Hospital he took a taxi and went straight to Dublin Airport. There he took the first available plane to London. After lunching at London Airport, and finding that his sister-in-law, Celia Salkeld, who was playing the lead in *The Hostage* and at whose flat he intended to stay, was out, he made for the bar of the Salisbury next to Wyndham's Theatre, already togged out in a dinner-jacket which he'd borrowed from his uncle, Seamus De Burca, before he left Dublin.

He went up to the busker who was singing to the queue outside the theatre and asked him for an Irish song. When the old man replied by singing 'When Irish Eyes are Smiling', Brendan roared: 'That's not an Irish song', took the hat off the busker, put it on himself, and sang 'Bold Robert Emmet'. The crowd were delighted and contributed generously when Brendan passed round the busker's hat. When it was full he returned it to the delighted street performer. Brendan then made straight for the box office, and after some trouble secured two seats, one for himself and the other for Kathleen Dennehy, a Cork actress who was sharing a flat with Celia Salkeld. At the play he proceeded to do his usual repertoire, shouting remarks to the actors and joining in the dialogue. He also sang the songs as they sang them and called the actors by name from the auditorium. Howard Goorney called out: 'Are you a member of Equity?' and Brendan replied, 'Are you in the N.U.J?' He roared at his own jokes in the play, made loud quips, according to the *Irish Times*, 'to the great delight of the audience'. The actors joined in the fun and began to improvise their lines. One of them asked Brendan to come up on the stage. Brendan couldn't have been as drunk as he seemed, because he made quite a genial summing-up of the whole affair to the *Irish Times* reporter as he left the theatre. The following morning, after reading the newspaper reports of the affair with great enthusiasm, he started off on a round of the pubs with Desmond MacNamara. Late in the afternoon he escaped from him and turned up outside the theatre again, where he was refused admission. Sir Bronson Albery the owner of the theatre and father of Donald Albery who had brought the play to the West End, had left strict instructions that Brendan was not to get in. Next day Brendan went to the flat of a friend, Tara Browne, in Mayfair, where he lay down on a couch and went into a coma. Later that afternoon he was arrested for being drunk on the street. The faithful MacNamara and Duncan Melvin, his press agent, bailed him out. But with that extraordinary cunning he used when he was in search of alcohol, he eluded them again. Next day they were relieved when he turned up in court.

Brendan was charged with being drunk. When the magistrate,

Mr Clive Burt, asked: 'Anything known?', Behan replied before the policeman could say anything: 'Not in this court'. He then interrupted: 'I was given fourteen years for shooting at two cops, but this black eye didn't come from the cops. They were very kind and very civil.' He was fined five shillings. His whole demeanour in court seemed demoralized. There is the tinker's whine in his attitude to the magistrate, a touch of 'the tip of the forelock'—any dodge to get out.

After the hearing, he immediately made for the airport, in a green suit, brown sandals and white shirt, borrowed from Duncan Melvin. He was followed by thirty reporters. He stopped at a pub on the way out and insisted on talking Irish all the time, thus giving them plenty of copy when they turned in their reports about the 'impossible' Irishman. It also put his friend Donal Foley, the London Editor of the *Irish Press*, in a strong position as he was the only one present who knew Irish (and Brendan recognized this) and who could translate for the rest of the reporters what he was saying.

Back in hospital in Dublin, he explained his position in an article written for the *People* four days later:

> For a start let me tell you that I am neither dead, drunk nor dotty. I'm just damn sick, but getting better all the time. My liver, I'm told, is like the sole of a hobnailed boot. My inside feels as if it has been scoured out with sulphuric acid and my head occasionally thumps like a pneumatic drill. But sure, I could be worse, and often I was. It is true, however, that I am an alcoholic, and that excessive gargle is responsible for my present position. I am a lonely so-and-so and I must have people around me to talk with. Bars are usually the best places because they are full of poor people, hardchaws, ex-convicts, chancers and tramps who'd lift the froth off your pint if you didn't keep your nose well in over the edge of the glass. I know I can cure myself from drink and that is what I am doing here in hospital, and I will take nothing until I come out a new man this week.

Though he had set his physical condition back considerably, Brendan couldn't help but realize that he had helped the run of the play. The publicity from his London escapades was world-wide. His uncanny gift for doing the wrong thing at the right moment had paid off once again.

In September Brendan was chosen to captain a football team composed of athletes and show-business personalities in a Charity match against a British team of T.V. and film stars, captained by Tommy Steele. The match was to be played at Dalymount Park, Ireland's leading football stadium. As the biographer was playing on Brendan's team, it would have been an excellent opportunity of meeting again. Alas, our captain didn't make an appearance until after the match. Then he collared Tony O'Reilly, one of Ireland's legendary football stars (6 feet 3 inches and 210 lbs.) as he was leaving the pavilion after a shower saying 'I was going to send Beatrice in after you Tony but when I saw what was on show in the shower, Jasus, I thought I would never get her back again'.

In November he appeared on American television for the first time. The programme was the Ed Murrow show, *Small World*. It was televised by the Columbia Broadcasting System. The subject was 'The Art of Conversation'. Besides Brendan, John Mason Brown and Jackie Gleason, the comedian, also appeared on the programme. After fifteen minutes Brendan disappeared from the screen, due to what Ed Murrow called 'Circumstances beyond our control'. He had been cut off. Later, Jackie Gleason commented: 'Behan came over one hundred per cent proof. It was not an act of God, but an act of Guinness'.

The *New York Daily News* described Behan's performance as:

A disgraceful exhibition. If the celebrated actor was not pickled, he certainly gave the best imitation of rambling alcoholism you ever saw.

The *New York Times* and *New York Herald Tribune*, however, did not mention drunkenness at all.

A spokesman for C.B.S. said next day that Brendan had been as sober as a judge at the start, but had made visits to 'another room' when delays took place as the camera was being reloaded. What appears to have happened then was that Brendan returned to the show, took it over and abused John Mason Brown. It is likely that he had a drink too many to steady his nerves and that, carried away on the first flush of his enthusiasm, he determined to repeat his Malcolm Muggeridge performance in the hope of hitting the headlines in America as he had done in Britain.

He had looked forward to the effect the show would have on the public, and was livid when he found himself exorcized from the screen. But he realized nevertheless when he read the reports the following day that, even by being expelled from the programme, he had made an impression on the American public which would be useful to him when *The Hostage* was staged the following September in New York.

Meanwhile a third Behan—Brian, his youngest brother—was hitting the headlines. Brian, who was working as a bricklayer in London, was the leader of a strike at the Shell Centre that had paralysed building on the South Bank of the Thames. Brian was at this time a member of the British Communist Party. Later, he resigned and became a Trotskyist and then an Anarchist. He had come to London like Dominic and Sean because of unemployment in Dublin. His energy and personality as a strike leader got him for a period almost as much press publicity as Brendan.

Brendan was delighted with the strike and went down in person to visit the strikers. He paraded around the pickets, congratulating them and handing out money here and there. After abusing the scabs who were working inside, he went round with some of the leaders to the 'Hero of Waterloo' and told Brian 'I am proud of what you are doing'.

Brian has written an excellent autobiography (*With Chest Expanded*) and drama for the B.B.C. He is the handsomest of the Behans, with a head of heroic proportions, well cut features and a mass of wavy, copper-gold hair. Less sentimental than either Dominic or Brendan, he has greater insight into the social forces that created the Behan family. He shares the Behan literary flair and gift for language. No wonder their father, Stephen, when a journalist asked him 'Why have you never produced a play?' replied 'I am too busy producing playwrights'.

Like Brian and Dominic, Brendan's other brothers, Sean and Seamus and his sister, Carmel, live in Britain today.

Seamus served in the R.A.F. during the war. Carmel is married to a Scot, Joe Paton. Sean, the half-brother and the eldest in the family, remains an ardent Communist. He lost his job in the Olympia Theatre, Dublin, because of his principles. He is a gentle person with a Dickensian sense of humour and a gift for perpetrating mild malapropisms and, like all his brothers, is drenched in the literary tradition of the Behan ménage.

It is ironic that Britain, the country their mother brought them up to regard as the source of all Ireland's misfortunes, should have become the place where five of the Behans live today; a reflection on the system under which they grew up, where education was available on the basis of family income and not on intellect or talent.

Early that autumn a plan was hatched from an unlikely source to try and halt Brendan's drinking habits. A young American journalist, Clancy Sigal, had visited Brendan in Dublin to do an article on him for the *Observer*. David Astor, the Editor, had seen *The Hostage* four times and was a fervent admirer of Behan's. Sigal sent in a somewhat alarming report to Astor of Behan's condition and they both determined to try and do something about it.

Sigal went over to Dublin again and made a further report. Having talked to a number of people who knew Behan well, he was convinced that Brendan would not under any circumstances submit to psychiatric treatment in Dublin, though there seemed to be a possibility that if he did he might have made a complete recovery. Sigal therefore proposed a plan to Astor. He suggested that Astor send over a London psychiatrist to confer with Brendan's physician. Brendan would probably be impressed by such a procedure, and it might induce him to undergo treatment. Sigal included in his letter a report from John Montague, the Dublin poet and author who had been helping him in his contacts with Behan:

I had been raising my courage for a visit to Brendan when he called upon me and we had a very amiable but sad session together. He's very depressed; first about his health and second his writing . . . Beatrice was also there and we drank a few light beers—Brendan sank one morose whiskey and then counted himself out—and as the conversation was running sweetly, with Brendan in a gentle and confidential mood, I broached the health question. . . .

It seems that besides the diabetic problem his liver is practically wrecked—which is why the doctors here won't try the anti-alcoholic injections on him. If he keeps to beer he has a chance; if he touches the hard he's done. And in a city like Dublin where pubs are the only sparks in grey winter dreariness and everyone expects you to have a jar. . . .

Nevertheless, Montague thought that Brendan would be quite flattered by Astor's interest in him. The result was that on November 27 Astor wrote to Behan:

Dear Brendan Behan,

Clancy has shown me your letter of November 24 and I want to say how very pleased I am that you are not, in principle, against the idea of a serious medical inspection in London.

Thank you for what you say about my offer—I am very relieved that you have taken it in this spirit. . . .

It will obviously be difficult for you to come to London for a thorough check-up and an even more difficult matter if you should decide to undergo a course of treatment here. This is very much your own affair. All I would like to say is that I would feel much honoured if you would allow me to be of help—and that is not just bally-hoo but what I really mean. . . .

Yours sincerely,
David Astor

Astor's interest in Behan was based on genuine admiration:

I admired him because of his tremendous humanity, his detachment. He seemed to me like George Orwell, incapable of prejudice against any class because it was a class. He was just in favour of people. He disliked injustice, no matter where it came from. In *Borstal Boy* the Governor is as much a hero as the Warder in *The Quare Fellow*. There are no conventional good chaps and bad chaps—just human beings. I wrote to him simply because I heard he was in a mess and I thought it was terrible to think of this marvellous man destroying himself.

CHAPTER EIGHTEEN

AFTER Christmas in 1960 Brendan began the first of the books that he was to produce by tape recorder. He had been commissioned by Hutchinson some time before, to do a book on Ireland with drawings by Paul Hogarth, the English artist. Hogarth had gone to Ireland and finished his part of the job, and was understandably anxious to see his illustrations in print, accompanied by a text.

Nothing had appeared, however, from Brendan, so Hogarth's agent suggested to Ian Hamilton that Brendan experiment with speaking his chapters initially into a tape recorder instead of writing them on a typewriter. It would be considerably less arduous for him, and with his remarkable flow of talk, might have the effect of capturing in print some of the exhilaration engendered by his talk. Ian Hamilton mentioned the matter to Brendan by telephone, who instantly agreed to the proposition, and Rae Jeffs was sent to Dublin by Hutchinson in January to begin the task of getting Brendan to talk literature into a microphone.

A series of questions intended to cover different sections of Irish life had been prepared by Ian Hamilton and Robert Lusty, and on the first day Brendan and Rae Jeffs rolled happily through 4,000 words. Brendan commented:

> If the Mycenaean Greek Poets could do it, then so can I. I do not set myself up as an authority on these matters, but if Homer is to be believed, the Greeks wrote their books by improvising them in talk. Now, I'm getting in on their act.

Though he had one or two falls from grace as far as drink was concerned, he managed to complete 40,000 words in three weeks. This, together with two short stories, translations of two of his poems and a letter slipped into the text as if it were spoken, made up, when it was finally edited, quite a sizeable book.

He was fortunate to get Rae Jeffs to work with him on the tape recorder. She believed implicitly in his genius and modestly rates the product of their collaboration well below the rest of Brendan's work.

'I think it would be appalling if he were to be judged by these books and not by his two works of genius: *Borstal Boy* and *The Quare Fellow*. The whole idea was to use the tapes as starting points for a book: but unfortunately Brendan never got down to anything then and so we had to piece them together as best we could.'

Brendan made such an impression on Rae Jeffs that even today she finds it hard to listen without tears to his recordings.

Before Rae Jeffs left, Christopher Gore Grimes—Brendan's solicitor—gave a dinner for her and Brendan at The Royal St George Yacht Club in Dun Laoghaire. This was a calculated risk, as 'The George' is the most conservative of Dublin clubs. Brendan arrived in an open-necked shirt, took one look at the portraits of British Royalty on the walls, and proceeded to the bar, where he drank soda water and launched straight off into some of his more scandalous tales. He was the recipient of outraged looks at first; but gradually a group began to form around him and when he left the bar for the dining-room he was followed by a large crowd hanging on every word as a stream of corrosive comment poured from his lips about each individual member of the Royal Family whose pictures hung on the wall. Christopher Gore Grimes remembers it as 'a triumph of Brendan's personality and gifts over what was potentially the most unreceptive audience I could think of'.

Brendan Behan's Island was to receive wide acclaim two years later when it appeared. 'One immediately likes Behan', wrote Cyril Connolly in the *Sunday Times* in October, 1962, referring to the book. 'He has more than charm, he has instinctive kindness and charity, a verbal grace, an unforced assertion of his strong personality that may even have a touch of greatness, a demonic energy that notoriety has not entirely dimmed.'

Louis MacNeice writing in the *Observer* commented:

As for Behan's text; anyone who has read *Borstal Boy* will know what to expect. He writes like a talker talking with plenty of hyperbole and emphasis, with humanity, gusto and formidable wit.

Gerard Fay in the *Manchester Guardian* went even further:

I seriously believe him to be the best thing in Irish writing since Sean O'Casey.

His 'Island Sketch Book' is endearing; it has its vivid, piercing, scurrilous blasphemous, sentimental, patriotic, anti-British, anti-everything passages.

In October 1962, *Brendan Behan's Island* was chosen as Book of the Month, and was also serialized in the *Observer*.

Compared with *Borstal Boy* or *The Quare Fellow*, Brendan's 'talk' books are not of great value, but they do preserve a record of the range and variety of his conversation. On one page the reader can be taken through history, poetry, politics or sport, all told in the special form of anecdote and humorous comment which was the keystone of his conversational technique, and strung together by the thread which the story-teller creates to unify the most diverse subjects, so that each tale seems to spring naturally from the one before it. As the reader is carried along, he can see how Brendan has ballads or poems at hand to quote or sing as illustrations to the flow of his talk. In the first chapter alone, for instance, he quotes from memory, the following ballads and poems: 'The Foggy Dew', 'Love is Teasing', 'Hooligan and Hannaghen', 'The Curragh Soldiers', 'The Workman's Friend', 'Joe Brady', 'The Zoological Gardens' and 'Master Magrath'.

Some of Brendan's favourite stories are here. They are usually illustrative of some character trait, regional, if possible. This is about a Kerry woman:

Near by, at one part of a very lonely road overlooking the bay, there was a shooting—about twenty years ago—and the police came down in droves but couldn't find out anything about it. So one policeman dressed as a tinker, and he went to an old lady living beside the house in which the shooting took place. The shot must have nearly deafened her.

'Would you give me some hot water', he said, 'for to make a cup of tea, if you please?' Which she did and they carried on a conversation in

Irish. During the talking he said to her: 'I'm a tinker' which aroused her suspicions immediately for tinkers, as a rule, don't speak Irish—but as she hadn't very much English he had to speak Irish to her. He talked about the weather, the crops and one thing and another and 'Tell us', he said, 'wasn't that a terrible thing that happened up in the house yonder when the man was shot?'

'Oh', says she, 'I never heard anything of that', though, as I say, the shot must have deafened her barring her being deaf already which she didn't seem to be. So he asked her a lot of questions and to each one of them she answered she didn't know.

'Tell me, ma'am', says he, 'do you know anything?' And he pointed out over the Atlantic Ocean to the Blasket Islands lying out in the bay and he said, 'Tell me, ma'am', he says, 'do you know the names of these three islands out there?'

'I couldn't tell you, sir', she said. 'They weren't there when I'd gone to bed last night'.

Another catches the flavour of Protestant Ulster:

I remember being up in Derry once with my wife and we went out for a picnic. We had cold meat, tomatoes, hard-boiled eggs and bread and butter, but the one thing we needed was a drink, but being Sunday the pubs were shut. I passed a chemist's shop, however, that was open for a couple of hours, and like many other chemist's shops, there was wine for sale in it. Usually it's Australian Burgundy sold medicinally for the amount of iron in it, for it turns your tongue and teeth black when you drink it. There was an old woman behind the counter and I asked her for a bottle of wine.

'I'm sorry', she said, 'but it's Sunday and I couldn't sell it. In the first place, it's against the law and in the second place it would be against my principles, for I'm a teetotaller and I only sell it as medicine'.

'Well, ma'am', I said, 'it's against my principles to drink anything else but wine, I'm not a Presbyterian but a Calathumpian'.

'Oh!' she said, 'I never heard of them. What are they?'

'Well', I said, they're a religion that would sooner eat the stalks of cabbage than the leaves. But another important part of our faith is founded strictly on the Bible, and, as a good Presbyterian, you know that wine was almost the only thing they drank in Biblical times'.

'What', she said, 'about milk?'

'It interferes with my digestion', I said: 'I'd be going against my doctor's orders if I drank milk, and I'd be going against my religion if I drank tea or coffee, and I'm just about to have something to eat and I need something to drink with my food'.

'Well', she said then, 'I won't interfere with any man's covenant with

God for the sake of any man-made law', and she gave me the bottle of wine, which was drunk by my wife and myself with humility and pious gratitude.

One of his stories mocks in a mild way, the I.R.A.'s reputation for assuming hierarchical titles.

Cork is a very affluent city with a good reputation for work, and it was there that Henry Ford in 1920 established their first European factory. Some time thereabouts the Cork Brigade of the I.R.A. were conducting some operations against the British that necessitated the use of motor transport—plenty, so a few of the I.R.A. went down and held up the staff and the manager and demanded some lorries in the name of the Irish Republic.

The manager of the works, being a very clever and quick-thinking man, announced, 'I'm sorry', he said, 'you can't have any in the name of the Irish Republic because these works', he said, 'are the property of a citizen of the United States of America with which the Irish Republic is not at war'.

But the commanding officer of the I.R.A., was what the times demanded of him, a quicker thinking man, and he turned away and wrote something on a piece of paper. He turned back to the manager and, 'Here', he said, 'read that'.

And the manager read out: 'In the name of the Irish Republic, I solemnly do as from this moment declare war on the United States of America'.

'Now', says the commanding officer, 'hand over them bloody lorries quick'.

Though the late Bishop of Cork, Dr Cohalan, was a sworn enemy of the I.R.A., Brendan couldn't resist an amusing tale about him:

The story is told that the late Bishop, the Most Reverend Doctor Daniel Cohalan—known affectionately to all Cork people as 'Danny Boy'—lay in his last illness. He was old—he must have been about ninety-four when he died—and his illness dragged on and on. What happened but the Protestant Bishop of Cork, a very much younger man, upped and died before him. The Monsignor brought the news to 'Danny Boy' and stood around waiting for the words of spiritual consolation that they would convey to the Protestant chapter. There was a long silence. After two or three minutes, 'Danny Boy' opened an eye, looked at the Monsignori and said to him: 'Well, he knows now who's Bishop of Cork!'

One story which Brendan loved to tell, and retold again and again, is reproduced in *Brendan Behan's Island*. It concerns a greyhound race that was scheduled to take place in a stadium immediately after a Rosary Rally there, conducted by an American priest had finished. Greyhound racing, like the Rosary, is very much part of the Irish scene. A variety of people, from priests (a cardinal's brother raced under the name of Mr Twyford) to members of Parliament engage in it.

Brendan was familiar with the devices employed to increase acceleration in dogs who were not proceeding at sufficient speed to guarantee an income for their entourages. Conversely, if the odds were poor and the dog a cert, it could be necessary to curb the beast's zest temporarily until the odds went up again. Nembutal was used in the latter eventuality, while benzedrine given in sufficient degrees would ensure, 'in the words of the poet that the dog would meet itself coming back after the judicious injection'.

These drugs were known as 'springers' and 'stoppers'. One danger of the 'springer' however, was that after it worked to its peak it began to work in the opposite direction, and in a short time put the dog asleep. After the race it was necessary to employ some haste to get the animal off the track and into a motor car before he sank publicly into the arms of Morpheus.

One summer evening, according to the story, Brendan and a friend set out with a dog named Molloy for Navan Greyhound Stadium. On the way down, Brendan injected Molloy with a 'springer'. The dog was to be in the second race at 8.15, and the dose was calculated to have him at his peak at that time.

> Fifteen minutes it would take until he got drowsy and sleepy, falling finally into a deep coma from which the noise of a hydrogen bomb or a Redemptorist preacher would not wake him. By that time, we figured he would be safely tucked up in the back of the car, bowling home on the rocky road to Dublin.

Near the track, Brendan realized to his concern that an American priest was holding a Rosary Rally on the track before the Greyhound Meeting. He tried to draw the owner's attention to this, but he was in a mood of high piety in anticipation of collecting the night's winnings later on:

'Nark it, Brendan, nark it. It is not a lucky thing to mock religion and we going out to do a stroke'.

'But they're holding the rally at . . .'

'Listen now, and for Jesus' sake and for the last time, it's all bloody equal to you where they bloody well hold their bloody rally. They're not interfering with you, and they're not asking you to go to it, and you know what these country people are. I suppose you want to get us run out of this kip the way you got us run out of Belcuddy the time you started arguing the toss about Ireland being sold to the English by Nicholas ——stick that you said was a Pope.'

'Nicholas Breakspear'.

'Nicholas any ——ing thing you like. Didn't the man prove to you there was no Pope called Nicholas any ——ing thing, and now you're trying to get us pitched out of this place.'

'I'm only trying to tell you that this Rosary Rally is being held in ——

The owner turned and roared at me: 'I don't care a fiddler's ——k where it's being held.' Then he softened and said: 'Now keep easy for Jesus' good sake, till I hand this dog over at the track here.'

I sighed and held my peace and we went down and he was a pleasure to see, making the other old bowelers look like an advertisement for Bile Beans if I didn't know what I knew.

The chap at the kennels took the dog, wrote in his book and looked up: 'Yous know, of course, about the Rosary Rally, men?'

The owner smiled ingratiatingly and said: 'Ah, yes, a great thing, too. I mean I'm not over-religious myself, God forgive me—'.

The kennelman nodded soothingly: 'Er-em-yes-er-em-we-all-shure-er-en-err . . .'

'But it's a great thing all the same. A man all the way from America'.

'Ah, yes', says the kennelman, 'shure we told the priest when he asked for the loan of the track; 'The dog men', says we, 'the dog men, they may take an ould jar and that'.

'True', said the Owner, owning up to it, 'It's true for you'.

'And sure', we told him, 'they may have their faults but there's not one of them will begrudge you the track for such a good purpose. And a..ter all', he turned to us, 'it only means putting racing back for an hour and a half'.

'What?' asked the Owner.

'They'll only have the track for an hour, and all the races are put back until it's cleared'.

He nodded and went towards the gate without saying anything with me following. As he let us out, the kennelman said, 'I suppose you can kill an hour in the hotel opposite', and he smiled and added, 'some of the dog men are going to pass the time even better—by coming to the rally'.

We went into the hotel and the Owner, always a fair man, said: 'One glass of whiskey and a glass of gin and tonic'. The gin was for me for I had spent some of my time among the Anglo-Irish of Scotland Road, Liverpool.

'I can see us eating an awful lot of porridge', said the Owner, 'when they find that dog asleep in the kennels at racing time. Twelve ——ing months'.

A notable characteristic of *Brendan Behan's Island* is that it confirms an attitude that had become apparent in Brendan's autobiography and plays—humanitarianism freed from the doctrinaire restrictions of his youth and early manhood. Though he regarded Northern Ireland as 'the last out-post of flunkeyism in the British Isles', he could write with humour of the situation there, which fifteen years before he could only have looked on with bitter resentment.

What is more striking for a former hard-core republican, he had come to look benevolently on 'Free-Staters'. This was the section of Sinn Fein who had voted for the Treaty in 1921 and governed the country until 1932 in spite of armed opposition from the I.R.A. The Left Wing of the I.R.A. looked on the first Irish Free State as a bourgeois reactionary group, which had splintered off from the real Revolution. Arthur Griffith in particular was regarded as an arch-deviationist.

Without Griffith and Collins the modern Irish State could not have come into being. Brendan had come to recognize this and now wrote of Griffith and Collins as 'honest and innocent men' in *Brendan Behan's Island*, the equivalent of a Stalinist praising Trotsky.

He quotes in the book the lovely ballad he wrote about Michael Collins, to whom his mother had given the title 'Laughing Boy' when she met him to tell him her husband was in prison for I.R.A. activities and he handed her £20.

Twas on an August morning, all in the dawning hours,
I went to take the warming air, all in the Mouth of Flowers,[1]
And there I saw a maiden, and mournful was her cry,
'Ah, what will mend my broken heart, I've lost my Laughing Boy.

[1] Michael Collins was killed in an ambush at Beal na mBlath in August 1922. Beal na mBlath in Irish means the Mouth of Flowers.

So strong, so wild and brave he was, I'll mourn his loss too sore,
When thinking that I'll hear the laugh or springing step no more.
Ah, curse the times, and sad the loss my heart to crucify,
That an Irish son with a rebel gun shot down my Laughing Boy.

'Oh, had he died by Pearse's side or in the G.P.O.,
Killed by an English bullet from the rifle of the foe,
Or forcibly fed with Ashe lay dead in the dungeons of Mountjoy,
I'd have cried with pride for the way he died, my own dear Laughing Boy.

'My princely love, can ageless love do more than tell to you,
Go raibh mile maith agat for all you tried to do,
For all you did, and would have done, my enemies to destroy,
I'll mourn your name and praise your fame, forever, my Laughing Boy.'

Brendan Behan's Island was both a literary and financial success.
Ironically, it may have contributed to the destruction of Brendan's
talent as a writer. After dictating the book he was to do no more
than two months actual writing before his death in 1964. The
'taping procedure' gave him a way out. He must have recognized
that if he was to get anything on paper again he would have to
revert to the disciplined life he had led when he was writing
Borstal Boy between 1956 and 1958. Now he discovered he could
produce books which were received with critical acclaim,
merely by talking into a machine. He produced two other
dictation books, *Brendan Behan's New York*, and *Confessions of an
Irish Rebel*, but the ability to shut himself off long enough to
write had deserted him three years before his death.

Outwardly, he didn't seem to mind. His publishers, naturally
pleased with the sales of the taped volumes, were not specially
alert to the danger this type of work provided for Brendan.
But inwardly, his failure to return to his typewriter ate into him
like an acid burn, and was one of the factors which contributed
to his final collapse in 1964. He used to say:

If I am anything at all, I am a man of letters, I am a writer, a word which
does not exactly mean anything in either the English or Irish or American
language, but I have never seen myself as anything else, not even from
the age of four.

He knew the taped volumes were not the product, but the
by-product, of a man of letters. Though he gave copies of

243

Borstal Boy and his plays to his doctor, Terence Chapman, he never gave him what he called his 'talk' books, which he spoke of in a disparaging fashion: 'They'd praise my balls if I hung them high enough', he told Brian when he mentioned the reviews the book received, and once, in a mood of despair, he told Chapman he wished he had never written them.

Was the tape recorder held to his mouth the temptation of Faust?

About this time a handsome equestrian statue of a British soldier, Lord Gough, was blown sky high in the Phoenix Park. There had been five previous attempts by armchair revolutionaries to destroy it. In one of the attacks the statue's head had been sawn off and thrown in the Liffey, from where it was recovered by a dutiful corporation and restored to its original position.

Though Brendan had contributed generously to the I.R.A. guerrilla campaign of the 'fifties, he regarded blowing up statues as a moronic pastime. He composed a ballad satirizing savagely the 'assassins' which was repeated with glee around Dublin.

The initial assaults are described:

> Neath the horse's prick, a dynamite stick
> Some Gallant hero did place
> For the cause of our land, with a light in his hand
> Bravely the foe he did face.
>
> Then without showing fear, he kept himself clear
> Excepting to blow up the pair
> But he nearly went crackers, all he got was the knackers
> And made the poor stallion a mare.

Finally, after many attempts, his Lordship goes heavenwards.

> This is the way our heroes today
> Are challenging England's might.
> With a stab in the back and a midnight attack
> On a horse that can't even shite.

Brendan kept his authorship of this poem a secret. There were still groups in Dublin who could take it out of him if they knew he had written it.

CHAPTER NINETEEN

IN February, 1960, Brendan got a shock. He learnt that his younger brother Dominic was to have a play produced at The Gaiety Theatre, Dublin. Brendan had been rather unhelpful to Dominic in his literary career, and if anything, had discouraged him. He was not in favour of other members of the family writing. He said sarcastically to Denis Dwyer, a housepainter friend of his, when he heard that Dominic's play was to be produced: 'What does Dominic think; that geniuses are born in litters?'

When, four years later, Brian produced a book of memoirs, Brendan snarled across the hearth to his father: 'The cat in No 70 will be writing next'. Stephen used to maintain that the reason Brendan was so fond of Rory and Sean, his half-brothers, was that they did not write books—they were no threat to him.

Brendan, however, mustered a show of enthusiasm for Dominic's play which was called *Posterity be Damned*. It had its premiere on February 28, 1960. At the end of the play, Brendan clapped generously and shouted at the players, though Dominic later alleged that Brendan said something quite different from what he was meant to have said from his box. The play, which dealt with disillusionment in the I.R.A., had a good reception, and it was booked to appear two months later at the Metropolitan Theatre, Edgeware Road, London, with the same cast.

One of the features of the opening night had been Dominic's appearance on the stage. He came out of the wings singing the theme song, 'The Patriot Game', a ballad which is now known throughout the English-speaking world. There was something extraordinarily touching in his appearance, his delicate fine-boned profile, his small, perfectly-proportioned figure, like an Italian of the Quattrocento. It was as if his natural breeding was a reproach to the injustices of society which had submerged his type and denied them opportunity to use their talents, a feeling which transferred itself to the song with its theme of idealism betrayed by the place seekers.

The hero of 'The Patriot Game' is Fergal O'Hanlon, a young I.R.A. boy who was killed in a raid on Northern Ireland in 1958. But the theme is not confined to Ireland. It has a meaning in any country where young men have died in war time.

> Come all you young rebels
> And list while I sing
> For the love of one's country
> Is a terrible thing.
>
> It banishes fear with
> The speed of a flame
> And makes us all part
> Of the Patriot Game.
>
> My name is O'Hanlon.
> I'm just gone sixteen.
> My home is in Monaghan
> Where I was weaned.
>
> I've learned all my life
> Cruel England to blame.
> And so I'm a part
> Of the Patriot Game.
>
> It's barely two years
> Since I wandered away
> With the local battalion
> Of the bold I.R.A.
>
> I'd read of our heroes
> And I wanted the same
> To play my part in
> The Patriot Game.
>
> This island of ours
> Has for long been half free.
> Six countries are under
> John Bull's tyranny.
>
> So I gave up my boyhood
> To drill and to train
> To play my own part in
> The Patriot Game.

And yet de Valera
Is greatly to blame
For shirking his part
In the Patriot Game.

And now as I lie here
My body all holes
I think of those traitors
Who bartered and sold.

I wish that my rifle
Had given the same
To those quislings who sold out
The Patriot Game.

Brendan determined to be in London for the premiere of *Posterity be Damned*. He arrived in London on March 20, having been on the drink in Dublin for the previous week. He proceeded with Rae Jeffs to the Salisbury Pub in St Martin's Lane where he indulged in wholesale abuse of the other customers and the English in general till closing time.

Next day he went to meet his parents at Euston Station. They were coming over for the premiere. He greeted them in a dazed condition, dressed in a suit thoughtfully purchased for him by Rae Jeffs in case the press should turn up for this reunion of the Behan clan.

After luncheon, Brendan went with Stephen and Kathleen to a rehearsal of the play at the Metropolitan Theatre. He slept through the rehearsal, waking up occasionally to shout critical remarks at the actors. At the end, all his resentment at Dominic and the play seemed to burst out. 'It's a load of nonsense', he shouted. 'There were no murderers in the I.R.A. The whole play is a load of muck.'

Dominic retorted, 'You were the worst murderer of the lot'.

A frightful row ensued in which the parents tried to calm their angry sons. Next day, needless to say, it made headlines in the news columns and most of the papers carried photographs.

Why should Brendan have resented Dominic's emergence as a literary figure?

Instinctively, his built-in sense of insecurity reacted against any threat to his position as a writer. The more writers who emerged from No 70 Kildare Road, the less glory would reflect on Brendan. It would become evident that the atmosphere he had grown up in was conducive to culture and not the squalid illiteracy of slum life.

The theme of the play touched him on the raw. It was a dismissal of the I.R.A. as a group of futile idealists misled by their leaders. Brendan considered himself the only person entitled to criticize the I.R.A. He had been in the organization and had suffered for it. If anyone was going to dismiss the Movement, it was he. Although by now he had lost any hatred of England and had come to dislike war and violence in general, he was tied by an umbilical cord to the I.R.A. It was interwoven with the tapestry of his youth and to cut it meant losing a part of him which he had never trained himself to do without, the memory of his boyhood. When Eamon Martin who had been in the Fianna with him asked him once 'Have you stopped being an I.R.A. man?' Brendan replied 'Do you stop being a priest? Thou art a priest for ever according to the order of Melchisidech'.

In 1957, when Seamus Byrne's play *Design for a Headstone*, which had an anti-I.R.A. theme, had a successful run at The Abbey, Brendan had been livid and got into a vicious fight in an I.R.A. friend's house one day because of it. He himself had been abused for guying the I.R.A. in *The Hostage* and he compensated for it in a guilty way by attacking anyone whom he thought was denigrating the Movement in a way that he disapproved of.

Both brothers claimed to have paid their parents' fare over to England for the premiere. In fact, neither had. The fare was paid by John Ryan of the Bailey Restaurant who backed the show. But that Dominic and Brendan should have claimed to have done so, shows how they were attempting to establish priority positions in the family.

Relations between Brendan and Stephen had declined at this time. Brendan used to give money to his mother, sometimes as much as £100 at a time, telling her to hide it from Stephen. Of course, Stephen would have used a portion of it on liquid nourishment. But it was his industry and tenacity that had kept the family in funds in the lean years. He was entitled to a reward.

Also, there is no doubt that he was hurt by Brendan's failure to credit him with inculcating a literary background in Brendan when he was a boy. Brendan rarely referred to this. It would harm his image as a working-class boy who had pulled himself up by his bootstraps.

Even when he gave Stephen money, the tension between them frequently resulted in a row over the transaction. One day, Stephen was working, painting a house in Fitzwilliam Square, when Brendan called up to him from underneath the ladder: 'Are you short of money?' 'I'm always short', Stephen replied, coming down from the ladder. 'Come to the bank, then', said Brendan, 'and I'll give you a tenner'.

Stephen took off his overalls, settled his bowler on his head and walked down Fitzwilliam Square with Brendan. Out of one of the elegant houses there, came the handsome wife of a Dublin anaesthetist. Stephen had done some work for her some weeks before and took off his hat and greeted her. He stopped to talk to her for a few minutes. Brendan, not introduced, stood sulkily aside. As Stephen said goodbye, Brendan said, so that the woman could hear him 'Who's that effing old prostitute you were talking to?'

Stephen made a spring for a passing bus that was just getting up speed and left Brendan standing open-mouthed on the footpath. Brendan started to run after the bus. The conductor tried to stop it, saying that it was Mr Brendan Behan that was trying to catch it. Stephen threatened the conductor, saying that if he let Brendan on, he would report him; with the result that his son was left panting out of breath and totally perplexed on the pavement as the bus drew off.

Stephen was not turning his back on Brendan, but on his image. The incident hurt Brendan deeply however, and only occasionally after it was there anything like their old relationship. Kathleen always took Brendan's side and this did not help in the relationship between the two when they fought. Stephen loved Brendan in his own way, and about this time actually floored a Trinity student who attacked Brendan in a pub off Grafton Street. Brendan, too, loved his talented and courteous Da, but between them there was a tension that seldom allowed any overt expression of affection.

Once, Brendan shocked a crowd of Dublin friends by insisting that you were finished with your parents after twenty-one. In Dublin, especially working-class Dublin, with its hierarchical family system, this was heresy, as it was considered that parents were part of the family circle till they died.

'You might as well', cried Brendan, angry at this reaction, 'expect a Ford motor car, coming off the ramp at Cork, to turn round and say thank you.' This is an aspect of Brendan, a realistic side, that contrasts with the sentimental side of his character; and his estrangement from his father in the last years was a symbol of his growing isolation from the optimistic and decorous Dublin that had bred him.

After the row with Dominic, Brendan went on a bash around London lasting three days. A physician, summoned by Rae Jeffs, recommended immediate hospitalization when he examined Brendan in a friend's flat where he had been staying and had collapsed. Brendan had an extraordinary habit of being able to remain in touch with the conversation around him even when his body was in a state of semi-coma and collapse. While they were getting Brendan ready to go to the Middlesex Hospital, Rae Jeffs happened to mention that she had heard from Brendan that the correct way to pronounce 'Parnell' was to put the emphasis on the first syllable.

Brendan opened one eye: 'That's what my father always said, and he should know.'

Later, just as he was about to leave for the hospital, he asked Rae Jeffs to telephone David Astor, the editor of the *Observer*, and to tell him that Brendan Behan was determined this time to cure himself and give up alcohol altogether. Rae Jeffs had never heard him speak of David Astor before, nor was she aware that Brendan knew Astor well enough for her to contact him on a personal matter of this kind. But Brendan had not forgotten Astor's offer of help the previous November.

After Brendan had been a week in the Middlesex Hospital,

David Astor visited him. Together, they discussed various cures. Astor thought Brendan should try Alcoholics Anonymous, but for Brendan the idea of having to listen to other people talking about themselves, with him taking his place in the queue to talk, was not an agreeable one. Dr Nabarro of the hospital, wanted him to enter the psychiatric ward.

Brendan was not willing to try this, however. He had a deep-rooted fear of psychiatrists. One reason for this probably had its origins in the Irish superstition that going to a psychiatrist is tantamount to admitting madness in the family. Confession is considered a sufficient panacea for anything that doesn't require a strait jacket. But another reason was that Brendan nourished a fear that if he allowed the mechanism of his mind to be tampered with in any way he might lose his ability to write. He preferred to be an original neurotic rather than a sober vegetable. 'This is the truth,' he once said, 'I'm a neurotic. My neuroses are the nails and harness which give me a living. If they cured me I'd have to go back to house-painting.'

After consultation with Beatrice he signed a note authorizing David Astor to supervise his treatment:

> I agree that David Astor should supervise medical treatment for me, and I authorize him to prepare such measures as he sees fit.
>
> April 2, 1960.
> Signed: Brendan Behan.

It was arranged by Astor that Brendan should enter a private home in Surrey, run by a Dr McKeeffe, after he convalesced in the Middlesex Hospital. Brendan was now determined to cure himself. His health got better, and he wandered round the hospital chatting to patients and cheering them up with his splendid talk.

Before he left the Middlesex he was visited by Alan Brien, then writing for the *Sunday Dispatch*, who found him in great form:

> Brendan must be the healthiest invalid ever to startle his premature mourners since the famous Finnegan sat up in his coffin to say: 'Leave a drop of the stuff for the corpus'.
>
> Brendan's face lit up a corner of the room like a stage sunset. His head, as ever, looked like a bust of a Roman Emperor baked in bright red terra-cotta and slightly battered by the shovels of the archaeologist's mates.

In the glow of his grin even the pretty pale nurses, crackling and rustling by, seemed drained by anaemia.

Could he ever stop the drink? He had been at it since he was eight. 'I never turned to drink. It turned to me', he used to say. 'I never remember when I wasn't drinking.'

It was not merely the stimulating effect of a pint of stout or a glass of whiskey on his highly strung temperament. Drink is part of the Irish pattern of social intercourse. The pastime he liked best—talk—was inextricably interwoven with public house drinking. To tear himself away from this environment would require enormous strength of will.

A major problem was that he now had what he never had before, money, and plenty of it. He once said:

> When I was growing up, drunkenness was not regarded as a social disgrace. To get enough to eat was regarded as an achievement; to get drunk was a victory.

For Brendan, to an extent, money meant the power to buy unlimited quantities of drink without being inhibited by the thought of lack of cash. His youthful desire for drink, and the absence of the wherewithal to fulfil it, had created a reflex by which, when he did come into money, the natural thing for him to do was to spend the major part of it on booze-ups.

Had he not been a diabetic, this would not have had the disastrous results it did. It is possible that without the complication of this disease Brendan might have become like many writers, a heavy drinker who regulated his hours of drinking to allow him to produce a certain amount of literary work each day. This may not have resulted in perfect health, but without the additional diabetic complication he could have lived a fairly normal life and had an impressive literary output as well.

It was gradually becoming clear to him that as a diabetic he simply must give up alcohol altogether. As soon as he turned to drink, his diet regimen disintegrated and a sugar imbalance was precipitated by his failure to eat regular meals, which resulted in frenzied changes of temperament, often followed by a collapse. All this was the result of chemical changes in his body, brought on by his diabetes.

The astonishing thing is that he did make the decision to give up drink, without help from others. He decided to return to Ireland and submit himself to a self-imposed discipline of walking, swimming and a teetotal diet. He left the Middlesex without seeing Dr McKeeffe in Surrey as he had promised. But a new determination had formed inside him. He spent the summer as he had intended, exercising and getting himself fit: swimming and running on the beaches in Donegal and Connemara. He didn't touch alcohol at all, sticking to soda water and milk. In September he was due to go to the United States for the opening of *The Hostage* on Broadway. He knew that he would be on show during his visit there. Like Oscar Wilde before him he would have to marshal all his exhibitionist talents together, in order to make the impression he ought to, on that vast Continent. It was to be a major test. Like an athlete in training, he got fit for it.

For nine months (with two minor lapses) he did not touch alcohol.

In those months all who knew him remember his gaiety and good spirits. The old Brendan had returned. His gift for talking seemed unimpaired.

If his reformation had lasted long enough for him to return to serious work, after he had indulged his gift for entertaining the public in America, the last four years of his life would have been very different from what they turned out to be.

CHAPTER TWENTY

BRENDAN was to take New York by storm. The New York press had faithfully followed his drinking escapades in England. His name had come before the public with the success of his *Borstal Boy*, published in New York in 1959, and he had achieved additional notoriety two years before with his drunken appearance on the Ed Murrow Show.

Now he was coming to New York with a play which the *Daily News* wrote had been delayed in its American premiere because of the unprecedented number of people who came to see it in London after Princess Margaret had laughed uproariously throughout the performance, especially at the references to her Royal relatives.

Brendan staged his arrival superbly. He got off the ship with a bottle of milk in his hand. 'I'm on the wagon', he told reporters. 'It's not easy to smile when you're drinking this stuff. I may need a stomach pump.'

When asked would he meet Gore Vidal, he said 'Who's he? An Indian?' But he added that he'd look forward to meeting Shane O'Neill, (Eugene O'Neill's son) and Norman Mailer. About New York police he had this to say:

> When St Patrick banished the snakes from Ireland they all went to the United States where they became cops or politicians, and there is still more to be held against them. Neither class buys theatre tickets; cops are too busy gambling after hours, and politicians reckon that they give such a good performance there is no need to listen to me.

When asked did he have a police escort in Dublin, he said 'Yes, but I'm usually handcuffed to them'.

The *New York Times* reported that since his arrival

> Mr Behan has not stopped talking in English, French, and Gaelic. He says the I.R.A. don't know whether to accept a charity performance of *The Hostage* or bomb the theatre.

In fact most of what Brendan said when he got to New York was finding its way into newspapers and magazines. He told the *Herald Tribune*:

> I suppose I am inclined to believe in all that the Catholic Church teaches. I am accused of being blasphemous, but blasphemy is the comic verse of belief. I am a religious man only when I am sick or up in an aeroplane. On the aeroplane coming over, a nun sat next to me. There were moments when I felt like snatching the Rosary Beads out of her hand and doing a little prayer myself. I like living in Dublin because there my enemies are all about and it's very cosy. I regard the next world as a place full of foreigners.

When asked about Sean O'Casey by Louis Calta of the *New York Times*, he said:

> I think praising O'Casey is like praising the Lakes of Killarney, and praising the plays of O'Neill is like praising Niagara Falls.

He expressed regret that in his 'flaming youth' he had not taken drugs, but that it was too late now. He carefully wore a lapel badge with the legend 'Up Down' on it. This was a souvenir from the All Ireland Football Final in which County Down were playing and which Brendan had shrewdly calculated would appeal to the American public by reason of its Irishism.

On September 27 he went to see the Jackie Gleason Show *Take Me Along*, attended by reporters:

> What I like about Jackie Gleason is that there is a certain amount of sadness of truth about his jokes. Everybody has been so kind to me in America. The head of the King Kong building—I mean the Empire State Building—asked me to come up and look around. I thought I would take him up on it and go to the top just to drop a tear in the memory of good old King Kong. I always thought they took unfair advantage of him, shooting at him with the aeroplane.

Jackie Gleason asked him 'Where are you going to sit? There's a scene in the second act you'll like when I come on drunk. I want to play it right up to you'.

'That's kind of you, certainly', said Brendan sadly. He sat through the whole performance laughing, drinking soda-water and talking.

'Can't you pipe down?' the man at the adjoining table demanded.

'I didn't realize you spoke English', Brendan said as he swaggered out.

On September 10, James Davis in the *Daily News* reported that Brendan had been fitted with a special set of tails for the first night of *The Hostage*. He made one condition only—no British wool was to be used in the making of the suit. The same night he appeared at Harry McGuirke's Jaeger House at 85th Street and Lexington. According to the press he nearly broke the place up with his performance. He sang his uncle's song 'Down by the Glenside' which was referred to in one paper as 'Down by the Landslide', and got the house really going with 'Molly Malone'. Occasionally he would stop in the middle of a song to shout 'Up the Republic', and the audience would roar 'Up the Republic' in reply. Some of the time he spoke in Irish. All this was excellent preparation for the first night, a superb public relations job, with Brendan stage-managing the whole affair.

The Hostage opened on September 20 at the Cort Theatre. Apart from the fact that some of the cast was different, the script had been altered since the play had gone on in London. A number of local jokes were written in and more were to come later on during the run of the play. On the whole, however, it went excellently and was received enthusiastically by the audience who gave it ten curtain calls. Brendan made a quiet speech at the end and then returned to Downey's Restaurant for a party which was being held there in his honour. This was attended by Frederick Boland the Irish Representative of the United Nations, and his wife. 'Your show went well', he said to Brendan. 'Mine went well too. I have just been elected President of the General Assembly of the United Nations.'

Brendan pointed out that he and Mrs Boland once worked together. She had been a well-known artist and was doing a mural for a Dublin bakery at the same time as Brendan was painting the ceiling. Lauren Bacall, Jason Robards and Jackie Gleason were at the party which was given by Jim Downey the owner of the restaurant. As they waited for the notices to come in, Brendan gave his assessment of the power of the reviewers:

If you get six out of six good reviews you can ask the President of the United States to sell you the White House, but I don't think this has ever happened. If you get five good reviews you are doing fairly well, only you have to start worrying about 480 Lexington Avenue, which is the home of Income Tax. If you have four, you can afford to give a party and at least you can afford to attend the party. If you have three good reviews it's time to go home to bed, but if you only get two, stay there the whole of the following day and don't go out until after dark. If you just get one good review, you make an air reservation. But if you get six bad reviews, take sleeping pills.

Later they went to Sardi's where the patrons stood up and applauded Brendan. When the reviews came in they were certainly not the sort that would kill a play. They were critical in parts. They stressed the vitality and comic qualities of the writing. Howard Taubman of the *New York Times* said:

The Hostage is a grab-bag of wonderful dreadful prizes. Organized chaos is the handiest description of it. One calls it organized because Mr Behan claims authorship. Joan Littlewood is identified as director and the improvisations are carefully encouraged if not planned. Even in Mr Behan's undisciplined invention he reveals a flair for drama and a determination to communicate something. There are, of course, some splendid hits in the course of this fusillade, but they are balanced by embarrassing misses. The notion of incorporating illusions to local phenomena like Tim Costelloe or the I.R.A. belong to the misses. The mock sentimentality of the songs which break out periodically ranks with the hits. Miss Littlewood has an abundance of fresh ideas, some excellent and some in poor taste. Like Mr Behan's writing, her staging would not be harmed by discipline. Mr Behan is an original, and so is *The Hostage*. If you are willing to shuttle madly between delight and distaste, you might try dancing to Mr Behan's Irish jig.

John Chapman in the *Daily News* wrote:

Brendan Behan is Ireland's one-man answer to the Katzenjammer Kids. Quite often it was madly funny and was played by a colourful company. But Behan only shows primitive knowledge of the fine craft of the stage. He tosses everything into a theatrical mulligatawny which lacks the tang of a soundly made Irish stew. He is not an original as he thinks he is. Some of the jokes in *Thè Hostage* were old stuff years ago.

The play got rather a rolling from John McClain in the *Journal American*:

Behan has created a play or a travesty about an English soldier held hostage by the Irish in a Dublin hostèl or brothel, or pad (he never makes it quite clear) which almost defies description. In this case there is the philosophic and frequently funny caretaker of what the programme calls 'the lodging house'. His wife, an apparent prostitute, an American Negro prize-fighter, a homosexual or two, a social worker, a Polish sailor, an attractive domestic, and an Officer of the Irish Republican Army. The whole thing revolves around a Cockney who doesn't really know what is going on beyond the fact that he is in trouble and has lost his leave and may be given a bad time because an I.R.A. soldier shot someone in Glasgow. The cast was generally very good. I liked particularly the performances of Maxwell Shaw, Avis Bunnage, Patience Collier, Alfred Lynch, Celia Salkeld and Michael Forrest. The local references were more resented than accepted.

Joan Littlewood's interpolations, besides being noted by Taubman, were slated by other New York critics and were regarded as an attempt to cover up what Taubman called 'the fragile thread of the plot'.

Despite the critical element of the reviews, however, the play immediately began to do well. Later in the week there was a report in the *Daily News* by Leonard Field saying that the provocative content of critical approval, in four out of seven of the notices had tipped the scales. The impresario told reporters: 'I think we have got a hit'. He said that the sales during the week had been excellent and had actually drawn $24,000, despite the Jewish holiday that week. They intended, he said, to continue putting local allusions into the play. Joan Littlewood had been scanning the headlines for new material.

Later in the week, Taubman, writing in the *New York Sunday Times*, was more forthcoming than he had been the first time:

There is a song in *The Hostage*, 'The Laughing Boy'. Brendan too is a rousing laughing boy. If he fails to become a great man of the theatre or a natural successor to Sean O'Casey, it will be because of self-indulgence, not only in laughter, but in over-estimation of any random phrase. At its best

The Hostage is a laughing boy's explosion of earthy vitality, and at its worst it is a descent into the sewer to prove that the laughing boy's stomach can withstand queasiness and his nose can breathe any stench.

He had still some criticism of Joan Littlewood, though he admires the 'freshness of her imagination'.

But like Mr Behan, she is guilty of poor taste. Certain obscene gestures are tolerated beyond endurance. Used sparingly they might seem in character, even if needless and shocking. Repeated incessantly they become nauseating. One wonders were some of these touches added for the special delectation of New York. In the final days of its London run last year *The Hostage* was nothing like its first night here in its blatant vulgarity.

The Hostage was to run at the Cort for three months when it transferred to the Eugene O'Neill Theatre. The following year it was to have an extended run at 1 Sheridan Square, produced by Perry Bruskin.

According to Norman Mailer, the appearance of *The Hostage* on Broadway was a landmark:

New York was dead in those days. It was the end of the Eisenhower regime, a puritan period. Brendan's *Hostage* broke the ice. It was a Catholic Hellzapoppin. It made the beatnik movement—Keruoac, Ginsberg, myself and others—respectable up-town. Before Brendan, we were in exile down in the Village. *The Hostage* was adored because of its outrageousness and its obscenity, and because of Brendan's captivating humour and personality. He was an ice-breaker, and the times needed an icebreaker.

The outstanding effect of *The Hostage*, as far as Brendan was concerned, was that it launched him as a personality on the American scene. He was perfect material for the television age: knowledgeable, witty, down to earth, unpredictable and with that relaxed personality and spontaneous expression that characterizes a successful television personality.

New York, as many people have said, is not America. But in his television appearances between September and December, Brendan was able to project his name from coast to coast. At that time the Jack Paar Show held a position of unprecedented power in the television world. It was an interview show interspersed with music or vaudeville spots. It depended for its effect on the personality of its moderator, Paar, who was loved and hated by probably an equal number of Americans. Witty, hard-hitting, prejudiced, vocal, with a gift of getting right to the heart of the matter under discussion, his programme was discussed next day in coffee houses, at luncheon tables, business meetings and bars. To appear on his Show and be a subject of his scrutiny was a test for any personality. Brendan not only survived it, he came though it with flying colours.

On Brendan's first appearance on the Show on October 10 Paar was away. His substitute was the brilliant actress-interviewer and film star, Arlene Francis. Appearing with Brendan were Constance Cummings, Arthur Schlesinger Jun., and Jimmy Kirkwood Jun. Brendan talked about the New York critics, American politics, Vassar, the duty of a writer to attack his country, smoked a cigar, sang a song and denied he was going to have a contest with Jackie Gleason as to who could drink the most buttermilk.

A week later on *Open End*, compèred by David Susskind, he made a real hit with his ability to discuss intelligently almost any subject and then suddenly bring it down to the ordinary man's level. This time he was appearing with Tony Richardson, Tennessee Williams, Jack Lemmon, Celeste Holm and Anthony Quinn.

Susskind began: 'I understand you hate policemen.'

'I don't hate anyone.'

'You hate constabulary.'

'I have never seen a situation so dismal that a policeman couldn't make it worse.'

After this the talk turned to a discussion on how much sex was permissible on the stage. Brendan was silent as Tennessee Williams, Tony Richardson and Anthony Quinn talked the subject out, Williams maintaining that anything was permissible as art was a mirror of nature. Silent, Brendan was almost as conspicuous as when he was talking. Suddenly he woke up. 'In sex', he said, 'I think anything is all right provided it is done in private and doesn't frighten the horses.'

This line was stolen from Lady Desborough who made the

remark when she was told of Oscar Wilde's conviction. But it made the television audience sit up. With the attention focused on him again, Brendan began to expand. He made some perceptive remarks on the theatre.

Then the talk turned to religion and the distinction between the Catholic and Protestant forms of worship. Brendan had an anecdote to illustrate the difference.

You see, there was this clergyman in the West of Ireland and he was giving out to the local Catholic curate about his Church's narrow-mindedness in keeping the sexes apart at Mass and frowning on dances. The curate replied with an old Irish verse:

> Don't speak of your Protestant Minister,
> Nor of his Church without meaning or faith,
> For the foundation stone of his temple
> Was the bollocks of Henry the Eighth.

For a moment there was stunned silence. Then the audience exploded in an avalanche of laughter. Celeste Holm fell back over her chair with delight. Susskind didn't know what to do. But Brendan's aplomb carried the day. There was no 'incident'. It secured him thousands of television fans who, whenever he appeared on television, would wait to hear what he would say next. (Actually, the verse he quoted had been translated from Gaelic by his friend the Dean of University College, Galway, Monsignor 'Paddy' Browne, Gaelic scholar and poet.)

On the Paar Show on October 31, Brendan was again in full swing. Paar said he left Brendan's show in London because he was hungry. Brendan said his play was doing extremely well because people were walking out. He agreed with Aldous Huxley that people who are shocked are the very people who wanted to be shocked. He pointed out that the Catholic Magazine *Commonweal* had praised him, and reminded Paar that he was as well liked at the Catholic Fordham University as Paar was.

From these television performances Brendan was being recognized in the street and stopped in restaurants for autographs. He liked this publicity for its own sake and, of course, it was helping *The Hostage* tremendously.

Brendan's success in many ways resembles Oscar Wilde's in that, like his fellow Irishman, he became a national figure in the United States in a comparatively short time. But Wilde had ten hard years of public relations work behind him. Brendan rocketed to recognition within a year. The difference between him and Wilde, of course, was that Brendan had television to help him and was a natural performer on it. Through it Brendan could sell himself to 20 million people in one night. Wilde had become famous gradually through the pages of *Punch*, where he featured regularly in Du Maurier's drawings. Then Gilbert and Sullivan immortalized Wilde by modelling the character of Bunthorne in *Patience* on him. The right atmosphere had been created when Wilde arrived in New York ('I have nothing to declare but my genius'), and his gift for publicity plus an eager press did the rest.

Brendan was on the dry these days and enjoyed New York immensely because of it. At the Monterosa restaurant, opposite the Bristol Hotel where he stayed, he would come back in the late night after the shows and drink for hours with the cast and friends. It was always tea he drank. Today in the restaurant there is still a little teapot preserved with the pathetic legend pinned on it: 'Brendan Behan's teapot.'

On the evening of October 26, Brendan and Beatrice had a disagreement in the Monterosa. It was about drinking a bottle of champagne. Beatrice said no, but Brendan insisted. The argument developed until Brendan eventually drank seven bottles. Then he proceeded to the Cort Theatre. In a few minutes he had made his way to the stage. The *Daily News* reported:

Last night Brendan Behan resumed his favourite role. A news reporter saw two burly stagehands restrain Behan from going on stage. Soon afterwards he staggered down the stage door alleyway towards the sidewalk, for a second foray. News cameraman Frank Castrol tried to snap his picture. Perry Bruskin, the Stage Manager, smashed the camera and struck the photographer. Bruskin was arrested on a simple charge of assault. Later, Magistrate Morton R. Tolleris paroled Bruskin. Later Behan successfully brushed past the unaware ticket-collectors at 8.45 p.m. during the second act. From the right aisle front Behan interrupted the action to address the audience in words they were unfortunately unable to hear since the monologue was incoherent. The cast got laughs from the audience and laughs from the author. There came a time when a dozen of the cast were front stage in a row. Brendan indicated that he wanted to join them. An actor gave him a hand on stage. The line moved offstage right, taking Behan with it. In the next episode, the actor Glynn Edwards portraying the owner of a Castle appeared in cloak and white wig. Behan moved in from the wings and joined him. Edwards wrapped his cloak around the author and bundled him off the stage. He permitted himself to be assisted to a dressing room from which his words and songs could be heard by dozens at the front of the house. Act Three came with the curtain call. Brendan joined the cast to receive the audience's applause and made a brief speech.

Beatrice eventually got him home, where he continued to sing until the small hours. Luckily this was an isolated incident and he was back on the wagon next day. The booking, however, didn't seem to have been affected adversely. It continued to go up.

Meanwhile, everything that Brendan did was news. On October 7 he went to Vassar. The fee he was offered was hardly attractive, as such young ladies' institutions consider the honour of addressing them sufficient compensation for the effort involved. What interested Brendan, however, was that the Roosevelt Home at Hyde Park was nearby and he was anxious to visit it and see the mementoes of an American President whom he greatly admired. He was charmed with Vassar and called it Tir na Nog, (Land of Eternal Youth):

> There are many lovely girls there and their manners are so good. I was surprised that so much expense could produce so much cultivation.

He passed the 'No Smoking' sign, smoking a large cigar, and went to see the Dean, Miss Marian Tate. When he came out he announced that he had been swopping bawdy limericks. In the College bookshop he discovered a volume of short stories by Eudora Welty. 'She wrote one of the finest passages in American literature', he said as fifty girls stood around waiting.

'What was it,' the girls asked.

" 'Mrs Fletcher is pregnant.' 'Heck, she don't look it to me.' "

That night he addressed the students and did his usual cabaret performance, a mixture of poetry, mime and singing. He did his take-off of Abbey plays, fishermen, old Canons, ancient house-keepers, and many others. Then he mimed a Beckett play, kneeling behind a chair, pretending he was in a dustbin and asking: 'What is Life?' He finished up by singing an old Irish song, and according to the *New York Times*, it was all quite beautiful and the hall was entirely still. He left what he had termed 'a female academy without punishment cells' to great applause.

At Brynmawr on November 9, he was equally successful. Here he sipped tea. He told the girls:

> The theatre is a good racket. I have an uncle who wrote plays and put on leg shows. Children know more in the United States. They act like teenagers until they are nineteen years of age. The only thing I envy young people is their livers.

By now, Brendan had found that he was completely at home in New York. He even found the skyscrapers homely and reassuring:

> London is a wide flat pile of redbrick suburbs with the West End stuck in the middle like a currant. New York is a huge rich raisin and is the biggest city I can imagine. I'd say it is the friendliest city I know.

He told Leonard Lyons the columnist, who became a close associate of his, that New York reminded him of what Lenin said about Communism.

> Lenin said that Communism is Socialism with electricity. New York is Paris with the English language. A city is a place where you are least likely to be bitten by a wild ass.

New York was for him a sort of Lourdes:

> I go there for spiritual regeneration. When I arrive here from Canada I am so grateful that I am in the United States that even Howard Johnson's architecture in Buffalo cheers me up.

Geographically, Manhattan itself is small. People recognized each other in the streets in a way that could not happen in London or Paris. Athletes like Babe Ruth, Jack Dempsey and Mickey Walker, as well as theatrical stars like Jack May or George Cohan, would be hailed casually by passers-by as they walked down Broadway or Fifth Avenue.

In such an atmosphere, Brendan's sense of gesture and talent for being in the public eye had its effect. The legend of the two-fisted Irishman with the heart of gold, ready wit and a 'wakeness' for the drink, was already established in the American mind. Brendan belonged to its consciousness almost before he arrived there.

Though it is the most polyglot city in the world, the Irish hold a special position in New York. In public life they created a style that the city recognized. Jimmy Walker as Mayor, John McGraw as Manager of the Giants, Father Duffy as Chaplain to the Actors' Guild and the 69th Regiment, had become part of New York legend. In Times Square, the navel of the world, there are only two statues, both of Irish-Americans, a priest and and entertainer.

Through Tammany the Irish kept a grip on politics; through the saloon they became the intermediaries between the ordinary man and the sources of power. Later in the Civil Service they exercised considerable influence. Their position in relation to the ruling W.A.S.P. (White Anglo-Saxon Protestant) elite gave them a more important role than the other immigrant peoples. The Irish were of British Isles stock, spoke English and had an understanding of Anglo-Saxon culture. But they were also Catholic and poor. William Shannon, the author of *The American-Irish* has said 'They were the closest immigrant people to being "in" while still being "out".'

Poles, Lithuanians, Greeks, Italians looked up to them. To this day the Irish in New York are afforded a genial tolerance and warmth enjoyed by no other ethnic group.

Brendan cut down New York to his own size. He could roll into the Irish bars on Third Avenue and establish the same quick familiarity that he had delighted in in Dublin. He had his favourite spots for rambling: he liked the bustle and clash of the Fulton Fish Market, the five-cent ferry to Staten Island, the deserted quays near 77nd Street where he would march off in the bleak winter sun to take a breath of air with his friend, Father Jacob of St Anthony's Church in Greenwich village who was known as the 'Junkies' Priest'.

McSorley's Old Ale House on 7th Street off Cooper Square was a favourite spot. It was a piece of Ireland in New York. There was sawdust on the floor. No women were allowed and, if one slipped in by mistake, a ship's bell was rung and she was removed instantly. In the evenings he went to eat at Tim Costelloe's on Third Avenue, or Downey's on Eighth Avenue and at times felt himself back in Dublin among recent emigrants and visitors from home.

Brendan's repartee was dead on the nail for New York. New York humour is largely an Irish-Jewish creation. Brendan was never funnier than when in New York. It sharpened and brought out the best in him. Once he met Harpo Marx in the elevator. Marx started to tell a story. 'Once when I was playing *A Night at the Opera*—'

Brendan interrupted him: 'Stop that. That's like Leonardo da Vinci saying "Once when I was painting The Last Supper".' This broke Harpo up so much his wig fell off.

While he was sober in New York, Brendan was happier than he had been anywhere else, except Dublin. He found certain literary circles there congenial and less inhibited than in London. The artist seemed to have fewer layers of encrusted social background to break through in order to find himself.

He was delighted to meet Allen Ginsberg, whose work he admired. Brendan was a successful Broadway playwright at the time, while Ginsberg, though well known as a poet, was not well off financially. Brendan asked him to a meal. After the meal he followed Ginsberg outside and asked him, 'Do you have any grass?'

Ginsberg thought Brendan meant marijuana and said no. Brendan took out a $50 bill and said, 'Here man, you need this'.

Norman Mailer took to Behan immediately. Brendan had always wanted to meet him since he had read *The Naked and the Dead*. Both of them had had an odd notoriety in their own country, though Mailer's was earlier than Brendan's and he had been a famous figure in the public eye for a much longer time. He was very impressed by the way Brendan could take over a party. He remembers a particularly posh one where Brendan sang 'I was Lady Chatterley's lover', a ribald composition based on

Lawrence's gamekeeper which Norman Mailet found particularly amusing.

Of course, being Irish in New York had its other side. The Irish tend to dislike success among their own. Bill Slocum echoed the feeling of a section of New York Irish-Americans when he wrote in the *Journal American*:

> I suspect Behan's public displays are closely tied to the state of his box office. Behan is an Irish 'Uncle Tom'. Negro performers use 'Uncle Tom' as a contemptuous description of coloured actors who are over humble, self-serving caricatures of the negro who doesn't read and talks a funny mush-mouth southern-accented drivel. Mr Behan is a caricature of the drunken Irishman. I would happily accept his problem as none of my affair if he would just once get a good spontaneous load on and forget to play 'Paddy the Mick' who hates the English and roars 'Up the I.R.A.'. I am as Irish as Mr Behan and I resent his contrived and profitable playing of an old stereotype character, the drunken Irishman. That role went out with the black-faced comic who got his laughs because he couldn't pronouce a three syllable word, or the bearded Jew who built his act on a non-existent accent and a crooked shrewdness about money. I have seen Mr Behan all over town, dressed in carefully prepared disarray, and as sober as a judge. He moves and bows in other places where alcohol is present with far too much ease, grace and wit, to fit into the picture of a helpless alcoholic.

The type whose opinions Slocum was echoing were, among others, the respectable New York Irish of the sort who rejoiced that Communion Breakfasts had shifted from the bustling Manhattan Hotel to the staid Commodore. Often their parents or grandparents had been immigrants from the old country. They had a sense of insecurity. Brendan reminded them of an image they were trying to live down. The Ireland they had learned of through their parents was largely rural. They missed a lot of Brendan's Dublin wit while reacting against his fairground hurly-burly. He was certainly not a favourite with the Irish County Associations in New York or the Communion Breakfast crew. But Slocum did put his finger on something that many others missed. Brendan *was* playing a part. Sober, he remembered the impression that his drinking escapades had made on the public, and he was not averse to giving the impression from time to time that he had had a few drinks just to live up to his reputation.

Undoubtedly he played 'the broth of a boy'. But he played it brilliantly, and, when he wasn't four sheets in the wind, he was not just a clodhopping Irishman but a clever, witty Dubliner. He was conscious of this gap between himself and some of the Irish-American middle classes who were sometimes reactionaries of the worst type with anti-semitic and anti-negro prejudices. He used to explain it by saying:

> My father's people did not go to America. They were real Dubliners. It is a thing only for country people to do.

On December 6, he had another smash hit on the Paar Show. He was in very good company, including Hermione Gingold and Peter Ustinov. They joked about Churchill's birthday, the American Presidential Campaign, taxes in Ireland, and Brendan said that

> Americans are very different from what they think of themselves. They are hospitable, puritanical, and gentle with women, and they are not always after the dollars.

When Paar asked him was he a religious man, Behan said 'I think so, essentially.'

Brendan talked about Paddy Chayefsky's new play *The Tenth Man*, which was running on Broadway. It had just been done at a Hadassah (Jewish) benefit, and Brendan commented: 'That's not a very fair test. It's just like seeing *National Velvet* done for an audience of jockeys.'

He joked about American women: 'It's the land of permanent waves and unpermanent wives. The sort of man many American women want to marry is the fellow with a will of his own—made out in her favour.'

On December 9 he went to Toronto to deliver a lecture at McGill University. He arrived at the auditorium twenty-five minutes late, with his hair tousled and an open-necked shirt, apparently under the impression that he was addressing a French-Canadian audience. He began his speech with a French-Canadian ballad, an attack on the evils of England, and criticism of France's role in Algeria. This was not a success, most of the audience being British Canadians. He marched out singing 'The Marseillaise', did a jig on the campus, and went off to an all-night party with his friend Eamon Martin. When the students cancelled his next day's performance and wouldn't pay for the one he had given, Brendan retorted, 'I don't care about their five hundred bloody Presbyterian Dollars'.

His experience released a whole lot of anti-Canadian comments from Brendan. 'Canada is barbaric without being picturesque', he told reporters. 'Toronto will be a fine town when it is finished.' Asked how he reacted to the fact that the Americans had just been beaten in the space race by the Russians, he said, 'I'm not a Yank and you're not a Russian. You're a Canadian. Stick to your league—Ice Hockey.'

When told that Canada had a lot of wide open spaces, he replied:

> The only space I am interested in for the rest of my life is that between Father Duffy and George M. Cohan in Times Square.

Leonard Lyons, in New York, had a pathetic telephone call from him:

> Hello, how are you? I'm a lousy, I'm a lousy, I'm drunk and I'm not even happy. I wish to Jaysus I hadn't left New York. Why don't you rescue me? I'm hell-holed in this place. I wish I had never come here. New York is the only place on this Continent where you have an excuse for Behan.

Lyons thought Behan's drink was spiked by reporters looking for a scene. But it is more possible that Brendan, in one of his diabetic fits and over-exhaustion from talk, had just relied on drink to carry him through, with the inevitable result.

Brendan went back to New York, and in a few days was in good shape again. He returned to Ireland on December 24, travelling by ship and disembarking at Cobh.

CHAPTER TWENTY-ONE

BACK in Dublin he managed, on the whole, to maintain the pattern of abstemiousness that he had kept to in the United States. This was to be his test. He had proved he could exercise his gift of an entertainer and wit when he was sober. Could he recapture the writing habit as well?

It was over a year since he had done any serious writing. The previous January he had dictated *Brendan Behan's Island* and had in the first flush of his enthusiasm for the method, produced a dictated draft in Irish, of a one-act play, *A Fine Day in the Graveyard*.[1] He intended now to expand this in English, and called it *Richard's Cork Leg*. The title came from a saying of Joyce's. His play *Exiles*, which had a character called Richard in it, had been turned down by a management and Joyce commented: 'If I'd given Richard a cork leg it might have been accepted.'

[1] While he was dictating *A Fine Day in the Graveyard* Brendan had gone to court to act as bailsman for one of his friends who had opened safes without their owners' permission and removed the contents. Brendan apologized to the Justice for appearing in Court unshaven and without a collar and tie:

> It is not out of disrespect for you, but that I was engaged this morning dictating a new play in Irish, *La Breagh San Reilg* (a fine day in the graveyard) and I did not expect to spend La Breagh San Chuirt (a fine day in the Court).

When he wasn't in the dock facing a charge, but in Court as a law-abiding citizen, Behan was fond of exchanging pleasantries with the Justices, some of whom had written plays or were novelists themselves. In front of Justice Kenneth Reddin once, Brendan was offering to go bail for a friend, when Reddin remarked:

> 'I see; you are going to be "A Hostage" for him.'
> 'I hope he doesn't skip to "Another Shore"' Brendan replied.

Reddin had just written a successful novel called *Another Shore* which was filmed under the title *Gulliver Dreams*.

Though Brendan proposed to work on the original draft with a view to a production by Joan Littlewood in London at Stratford East, he was also to incorporate in it a skeleton plot for a novel that he had done some work on, called *The Catacombs*.

He worked hard over Christmas, and by early January had two full acts completed in draft. Four months later he was to add some material after visiting Forest Lawn cemetery in California, working for ten days on the script in Hollywood. The major part however, he completed between December and June 1960–61.

Richard's Cork Leg was the last piece of written work he was to do. It was never fully finished, for after his work on it in May, Brendan did no more writing. The play is marred by Brendan's obvious desire to reproduce the formula which had made *The Hostage* a success. Topical jokes are brought in *ad nauseam* and there is a reoccurrence of his almost childish obsession with Evelyn Waugh:

> MARIA We have the hammer at home in the cabinet by the bottle of Lourdes water and picture of Blessed Evelyn Waugh.
> ROSE Blessed who?
> MARIA Blessed Evelyn Waugh. She was a young girl that wouldn't marry Henry VIII because he turned Protestant. (*Absently*) Amen.

One of the jokes that had appealed to the French in *The Hostage* (though as far as English and American audiences went, it had verdigris on it) was 'Vat. 69, you know, the Pope's telephone number'. Another version is churned out here:

> MARIA Me French gentlemen friends did everything be numbers. Swassawnt Nuff.
> ROSE What's that?
> MARIA Heads and heels . . . it's very complicated.

Sometimes the humour degenerates to:

> ROSE She's around behind.
> MARIA I know she has, but where is she?

and:

> THE HERO I have a great interest in French life, in the French language and French letters.
> MARIA (*Indignant*) How dare you, how dare you mention such a thing.

But it was obvious that as Brendan applied himself to the play, something more than a collection of music-hall sketches was beginning to emerge.

The story concerns two prostitutes, Rose of Lima and Maria Concepta, who meet every year to say a prayer and sing a hymn in a graveyard near Dublin, for Crystal Clear, a colleague who had been murdered in the Dublin mountains twenty years previously. (Crystal Clear is based on a Dublin prostitute, Honor Bright, whose death became a *cause célèbre* in the 'twenties after she had been found murdered in the mountains, and a senior police officer and a doctor were charged with the crime.)

To the graveyard come two blind men with collection boxes. These are The Hero Hogan and The Leper Cronin, his bodyguard. The Hero has fought in The Spanish Civil War on the Republican side and is coming to the graveyard to break up a meeting of Blueshirts, or Irish Fascists. (The Blueshirts had gone to Spain to fight for Franco.) As in *The Hostage*, a farcical figure is introduced—Bonnie Prince Charlie, a Negro Prince who is in charge of the graveyard and who intends to turn it into another Forest Lawn, with recordings of the Irish, American and Jewish dead, played for the mourners. He is dressed in silk, but when he turns round the words 'Harlem Globe Trotters' are sewn on his back. He guards the Loved One, a corpse in a coffin with 'blue rinse and lipstick'.

The plot is virtually non-existent. After a long discussion in the graveyard, Hogan shoots a Blueshirt, Cronin fails to seduce a girl called Deirdre, and in the last section of the play as written, they all end up with the prostitutes in Deirdre's mother's house, singing 'Lady Chatterley's Lover'. Deirdre's mother is a membe of the Plymouth Brethren. Some of the dialogue however, between the two prostitutes, has an earthy quality and is genuinely Rabelaisian, when it doesn't descend to music-hall jokes.

The character of Cronin is interesting, because it is obviously based on Brendan himself, and Cronin expresses many of Brendan's own views of life. The Hero Hogan character is a satire on the 'hero figures' in recent Irish history—members of the I.R.A., Irish volunteers in the Spanish Civil War and militant socialists. Hogan has fought for the Republicans in Spain, but his aunt is a Belgian whose husband has massacred negroes in the Congo with napalm. Cronin, on the other hand, is a disenchanted drop-out, who refuses to work and only wants to be left alone.

When The Hero says: 'What about the men who gave their lives for the Republic?' Cronin replies: 'They were trying to keep their minds off women; they were all mad with the horn. They couldn't think of anything else.'

There is a long argument between them about involvement and the necessity for Socialism, which taken in conjunction with Brendan's other writing at this time, obviously embodies many of his ideas on the subject.

THE HERO   Of course I have. I worked in the mines in Kilkenny, and I was a hop picker is England.

CRONIN   It was interesting for you. Like me going to a foreign land. And don't give me that old shit about artists working. Everyone knows what they mean when they talk about a working man. Talking about an artist working is like talking about a priest working, like they used to tell us when we were kids. If it's so obvious that a priest is also a worker, why the hell do they have to emphasize it? You don't have to keep rubbing it in that a real worker is a worker. You never heard anyone saying, 'Oh, well a coal miner is a worker, too, you know'.

THE HERO   Well, what about doctors and scientists?

CRONIN   Being a doctor, an artist or a scientist is interesting. Anything that's interesting is not work.

THE HERO   Well, we can't all be artists and doctors and scientists. Someone has to do the ordinary work of the world.

CRONIN   (A little angry). Well, you bloody well do it! Why me? Why not you rather than me?

THE HERO   But surely you want to take part in the world's work?

CRONIN   No. I've resigned. Till they give me automation.

THE HERO   You are an anarchist. I met lots of them in Spain.

CRONIN   Don't call me an anarchist! I won't be insulted. I've a brother that's an anarchist in London.

THE HERO   Pray don't feel insulted. I knew lots of anarchists in Spain, they were great fighting men.

CRONIN   That was Spain. In London it means singing red songs with the amused tolerance of the police. They say, 'He's singing Red songs but he's all right—he's an anarchist. They don't mean no harm'. You can get on the Third Programme, too. Revolutionary, romantic and respectable. That's London anarchism. You can get in with millionaire's

273

daughters, and all. But they're one breed of bastards I don't fancy. They remind me of the Salvation Army.

Later when The Hero says 'Maybe you like the Communist Party?' Cronin replies:

Well, over in Russia, they're never done bloody well talking about work for the working classes, and more production. Everyone wants the poor bloody working class to work. Even members of it like me, I suppose.

THE HERO Now, do not evade the issue. Everyone talks about Russia. What about the Reds here, in Ireland?

CRONIN Oh, I'm all for them here, of course. They frighten the other bastards—the rich bastards and the government. But personally—

THE HERO Yes, I know what you're going to say. You do not approve of their party but you like the men, themselves.

CRONIN On the contrary, I detest the bastards personally, but I like their party, because it's the only one that all the big shots are terrified of. All the big bellied bastards that I hate, hate the Reds. It's the only thing that Catholic Protestant Green Trinity College Ulster Racing Board Civil Liberties ex RIC Conservative New Statesmen, freemasons and Knights of Columbus all hate the Reds, so there must be good in their party somewhere. But the Reds themselves are snobbish and ill-mannered.

THE HERO Snobbish?

CRONIN Sure, they wouldn't give anyone a free trip to Russia, except he had an education and owned an estate in Kilkenny or went to Trinity College. The delegation they sent, was three-quarters well-off Protestants, and the Chinese nearly shot them because they couldn't be kept out of the British legations looking for tea, and a read of the *Daily Mail.* And they're ill-mannered, because if you mooch into a pub on the cripple—on the cripple and crutch—on the touch, with no money, they won't stand a drink. If you are out for the emancipation of the proletariat. . . .

THE HERO Well, at least you favour that.

CRONIN Of course I believe in the emancipation of the working class. I made a good start—I emancipated myself. But if you go into a boozer on a Friday night and they're inside drinking their overtime, they'd nearly get you thrown out because you haven't worked all week and they say you're a parasite. They're like the Irish in America. They say that fellow Behan is a disgrace because he gets drunk on champagne and smokes cigars. They think it's unnatural for a fellow Irishman to live on the fat of the land without getting down into a tunnel with a shovel, along with themselves. The Reds is in the conspiracy to make me work, too.

Later, when he tries to seduce Deirdre, Cronin says:

> Well, if you're not a virgin it's a sin against God, and if you are, it's a sin against man. The sin against man is more important because we see God so seldom. However, if you are not a virgin, the priest can forgive that, and I can remedy the other.

Cronin then explains what he regards as his only vice:

> I don't know whether you do or not, pity anyone. I do. Pity is my vice and my downfall. I pity every sort and size of sinner even the ones that don't fall into any officially approved category of pityees. I have become one myself. I stand by the damned anywhere in this world and in the next. If there are people put out of Heaven, put me out with them.

It is not difficult to see why Joan Littlewood was disappointed with what she read of *Richard's Cork Leg*. There is no plot to speak of. Before *The Hostage* had been transmuted by the Littlewood formula, it had been in its own right an excellent play with strong character, texture and plot.

Richard's Cork Leg was worked from the other direction backwards, from the light, topical touch that Littlewood applied to scripts submitted to her, towards the direction of the plot and dramatic story. The play had not reached the plot stage when Brendan showed it to Littlewood in January, 1961. On the other hand, the draft that survives shows possibilities if the characters of Cronin and Hogan were developed and the plot worked out sufficiently. Then the prostitutes and the light relief would have become an effective Greek chorus, instead of, as now, being the major characters for the centre-piece of the play.

Joan Littlewood had come over to Ireland specially to see *Richard's Cork Leg*. David Nathan had written an account of the play in the *Daily Herald*, after he had spent a night in Dublin, working on the manuscript and making shorthand notes of it. Joan Littlewood's reaction hurt Brendan; it also played on his insecurity as this was to be a test for him whether his ability to write was still in him.

In a fit of pique he rushed down to Gael Linn with *A Fine Day in the Graveyard*, the Irish draft of *Richard's Cork Leg*, which he had dictated into a microphone the previous January.

Though Brendan had worked it up from the dictated draft,

Gael Linn felt unable to accept it. They were reluctant to reject the play as, of course, they were grateful for the prestige that the opportunity of staging *The Hostage* had brought them, but Riobard MacGorain of Gael Linn is quite clear that it was not the bawdy quality of the play that deterred them, but that the work as a whole did not stand up to the test of good drama.

By now, Brendan was really upset. The morning he learnt of Gael Linn's rejection of the play, he became involved in a ferocious maul in a provision shop in Stephen's Green. He went into 'Smyth's of the Green', and ordered four bottles of champagne. For some reason he became livid when he was told that the price of the champagne was 35/- a bottle. He asked for a cheaper brand. When he didn't get it he used obscene language. The police were summoned. Meanwhile Behan was taken to the office. There he attacked the secretary, a young man of slight build named Kenneth Fox-Mills. Though with his fair hair, smooth skin, and slim build, Fox-Mills looked the perfect picture of a polite secretary, he was also a hockey international. Brendan got the worst of the encounter. Later when the police arrived there was more trouble before he was finally taken to the station. On January 7 he was charged in court with damage to the telephone and a watch the property of Thomas Byrne in Smyth's, with assaulting Kenneth Fox-Mills, and also with assaulting the Station Sergeant and two other Guards, and with violent behaviour at College Street police station. He had had to be transferred from one cell to another in College Street where he created a good deal of trouble. Joan Littlewood gave evidence for him: 'I do hope he will be able to go free in order to make use of his genius', she told the Justice.

Justice O'Hagan fined him £30, but didn't give him a jail sentence. This was lenient in view of Behan's previous record. Slumped in the dock, with his face twisted and his eye black, Brendan was a pathetic picture, barely able to speak. Something seemed to have gone out of him. His supporters, Gerry Raffles, Joan Littlewood, and some of the duffle-coated Trinity students and actors, who had come to court did not seem to belong with him. Joan Littlewood's features, pinched and tired, were in striking contrast with the vivid faces of the Dublin working-class women who crowded the court. Some of these were witnesses, some of them were there on charges. They were alive, vital, watchful. 'Puir Brendan', is what one heard them say.

Brendan had now reached a crucial stage. Was he to continue to wallow in his public image or engage in the ruthless search for self-knowledge that it is the artist's role to endure? For millions who had never met him, he had become a symbol of revolt. With his open-necked shirt, his cursing, his drunkenness in public, his contempt for convention, he made an instant appeal to a generation that was attempting to shake off the strait jacket of urban conformity.

He may well have been cast in the role of the precursor of the permissive generation as Wilde epitomized the aesthetic revolution and Scott Fitzgerald the Jazz Age.

Yet in many ways this was a false position.

Because Brendan came from a society which had escaped to a large extent the social stratifications of other countries, he was not truly representative of those who saw in him a reflection of the image they aspired to. In Ireland he was an individual among a society of individuals, whereas elsewhere his individualism gave him a special significance among a generation which had been drained of it.

He was in danger of becoming the victim of his own image. Few can escape the imposition of the mask. The majority are denied self-knowledge and recognize themselves only through the image others have given them of themselves. Carried on the current of time, they have no means by which to fix their identity so that the phantom of memory can be separated from the figment of the future.

The artist alone seeks moments of crisis when he will encounter the enormity of self beneath the mask. To survive, he must resist the mask made by the mob and create his own, as Joyce did by self-withdrawal and Yeats by cultivating the antithesis of his real self. If the mask is the artist's own, it can be slipped aside to contemplate the reality beneath. Plunging then fearlessly into the rushing stream, he will encounter the buried self fixed for an instant in time, unrelated to the past and unencumbered by the future, and bring it into contact with the trivial world for whom he has undertaken the duty of revelation.

But Brendan grasped greedily the mask offered him. He began to play up to the role society demanded with a savage vigour: the working-class revolutionary with a prison record, the slum boy who defied convention. In the end, it had become a convention for him to defy convention, to get drunk when required, to interrupt with violent language when the moment was appropriate. But allowing the self to slip from his grasp and the world to make his mask, he could not complain if the mob then came seeking the price of betrayal.

On February 23, 1961, the *New York Times* announced that Brendan was to appear in a new Broadway revue. It was to have a preview in Toronto at the O'Keeffe Center on March 29. The impresario was Arthur Cohen, who said that the revue would have a theme of its own which Brendan would express. It would be a Jazz Revue, featuring Brendan, Ola Tunzi and his Drums of Passion, Nina Simone, jazz pianist, and Art Blake. Altogether the show was to have 40 different artists, and Brendan went back to America at the beginning of the month to prepare for it.

He intended to march with the Gaelic Society of Fordham, who had made him an honorary member, in the gigantic St Patrick's Day Parade which takes place on March 17 every year in New York. On this occasion Brendan was to come up against the other sort of Irish whose reaction to Brendan had been voiced by Bill Slocum earlier on. Harry Hynes, Chairman of the St Patrick's Day Parade, and Special Sessions Judge Comerford, after a special meeting decided they wouldn't allow Brendan to march in the New York parade. The Gaelic Society of Fordham, therefore, withdrew their support of the celebrations unless Brendan was allowed to go along with them. The Committee, however, were adamant, and in the end neither Brendan nor the Fordham Gaelic Society marched. Immediately the Mayor of Boston asked Brendan to ride with him in his car during the parade in Boston, and the Boston Chamber of Commerce also asked him to go up to their St Patrick's Day celebration. In the meantime the Chairman of the celebrations at New Jersey City, E. J. Carey, had taken the opportunity to invite Brendan to march with them: 'We know he will be welcomed in the spirit of down-to-earth Irishmen. This is no lace curtain Irish celebration. His appearance will enhance our St Patrick's Day parade rather than degrade it.'

On the evening of March 17 Brendan received the key of New Jersey city from Mayor Witkowski. With the key in his hand, he said: 'At one end of the Holland Tunnel lies freedom. I choose it.'

Sid Freelander of the *Daily News* reported what Brendan had to say about being banned from the parade:

His principal target was Judge Comerford. 'Judge Comerford will be remembered', he said with bruised righteousness, 'as the man who kept Brendan Behan out of New York's St Patrick's Day Parade. I recommend the Judge to read Confessions of St Patrick in which he said, "The honest man must walk warily as a deer, not so much for fear of the enemies of Christianity as for the fear of those people who pretended to be greater Christians than the Apostles". I do not set myself up as an Apostle', said Behan, 'but I think I can afford to be more open with my sinfulness than Judge Comerford.'

He said, 'I won't march, but I am going to see the parade. I have never seen one before. I'll take a good look at it.'

'In Ireland', he said, 'it is more of a religious holiday. All the pubs are closed. The only place you can get a drink is at the Dog Show.'

'There are three things I don't like about New York; the water, the buses and the professional Irishman. A professional Irishman,' he said, 'was one who was terribly anxious to pass as a middle-class Englishman.'

This piece of Irish contrariness may have upset him emotionally. Certainly on the opening night of the revue at Toronto on March 21 he appeared unrehearsed and incoordinated. He wandered on and off the stage without much apparent purpose. The revue was a flop and Cohen announced next day that it would not go on to New York. Brendan meanwhile had left the stage and gone off to his hotel room for solace. He was told that he couldn't order liquor there. In the course of an argument the hotel detective, John Mathis, intervened and received a black eye. Then Detective Edward Trevelyan and other police officers arrived at the hotel. Detective Trevelyan found the playwright hurtling along a seventh floor corridor like a wild bull, in shirt sleeves and with one shoe missing. The detective was then hit on the forehead. A frightful row ensued, resulting in Brendan being brought to court next day on two charges of assault, and one of creating a disturbance. He was given bail and told he was being treated like any other Canadian drunk. The bail was $1500. Brendan told the Judge: 'As Napoleon said that every French private carried a baton in his knapsack, so I suppose you think every Canadian drunk carries fifteen hundred dollars in his knapsack.'

He didn't turn up for the next hearing of his case, a warrant was issued for his arrest and the bail was confiscated after Behan's lawyer had stated that Brendan was in Sunnyside Hospital, an alcoholic treatment centre, under the care of a Dr Pratt.

In fact, he was much more seriously ill than usual after this drinking bout. Dr Pratt confided in Beatrice that for a while it was 'touch and go'. However, once the crisis was over he made a rapid recovery, and on April 27 he was well enough to appear in court.

He pleaded guilty to the disorderly charge, but denied assaulting a policeman. He was fined $200. He told columnist Leonard Lyons:

On Monday, Mayor Nathan Phillips gave me a pair of gold cuff-links. On Wednesday they gave me a pair of steel handcuffs. I wonder which of these is the proper credentials for a writer. The cuff-links are an honour. The handcuffs show I'm not a statue yet.

Arthur Cohen, the producer of the Jazz Show, announced meanwhile that he was disposing of Brendan's services. 'When I arranged for Brendan to appear here', he said, 'I was satisfied that his problem was a personal one. But it is not personal any more.'

He had been disappointed, he said, when Brendan went off and slept through the matinée performance of the Jazz Revue. He made no comment when it was suggested to him that Brendan had been appearing at a fee of $3000 a week.

On March 24 he made his last appearance on the Paar Show with Joey Bishop and Phyllis Diller. He let off some steam about the difference between St Patrick's Day in Ireland and St Patrick's Day in New York. He advertised the Revue and insisted, despite lapses, he was really off the booze.

On May 2 *The Hostage* opened in San Francisco. Brendan was present, having come by train from New York. Beatrice, who accompanied him, didn't like flying. Dutifully he poured a bottle of stout over actors and audience, and sang 'I was Lady Chatterly's Lover'. In the course of the play he jumped on the stage, grabbed Louis La Rue, one of the actors, by the arm and took him to the bar. The cast, however, seemed to relish this, and even to have been prepared for it. In San Francisco he met a friend of his Paris days, Milton Machlin, who was out there to publicize the book he had written on the Chessman case. When Machlin went to see Brendan in his room he found an icebox full of Cordon Rouge. Brendan explained that the champagne did not do his diabetes any harm. Brendan was swearing vociferously above the conversation of everyone else, and there were broken glasses all over the floor. He gave Machlin a draft of *Richard's Cork Leg* to look at, and Machlin thought it had a touch of Hemingway's writing about it.

On May 4, after a two-day drunken tour, Brendan entered St Mary's hospital. It was announced that he had gone in for a rest. A week later Mike Thomas of the Monterey *Pen Herald* went to see him there:

You don't interview Behan, you attend him as you attend a performance of *The Hostage* which has been running in San Francisco amid headlines about the playwright's unscheduled appearances on stage, his off-stage champagne sprees and his most recent drying-out period in hospital. When he was looking over the menu Behan sang a song about a town in England where people washed their faces three times a day. He left an impression that for some unaccountable reason he had cleaned up the words a bit. Behan talks mostly in wandering monologues. He starts to answer questions but leads to other topics before he finishes the answer. His wife sits solemnly by most of the time and breaks in quietly on rare occasions to register mild disagreement with something he is saying which nobody else understands well enough to disagree with. Some of the things he said were: 'I've got so many prejudices that one cancels out the other. San Francisco they say is a good place to visit but I wouldn't want to live there. The conversation of the British upper classes is rather shocking to anybody who is not used to it. I like it. I like the little places in England outside London. New York is real. You've got the freedom of the streets all night. I'm a barbarian. I'm open for an offer though. I could become a South Californian phoney, live on black molasses and wind up in Santa Barbara.'

On May 20, 1961, Brendan met someone who was to become a close companion of his for the next three years. He was standing at a swimming pool in Hollywood, when he knocked into a well built fair-haired young man, who remarked: 'Do you have to fall on top of me?'

To his surprise Brendan found that the young man was from Dundalk. His name was Peter Arthurs. He was 26 years old and had been one of the youngest seamen in the American Merchant Navy to get his Mate's ticket. He was a skilled boxer, being a former Irish juvenile champion, but had not been in Ireland since he was twenty. He understood Brendan's character well enough to put up with his idiosyncracies and for the next three years whenever Brendan was in New York, Arthurs acted as bodyguard and companion. He was not impressed by Brendan's television notoriety. He liked him for what he was. One of the things Arthurs remembers most about Brendan in Hollywood is how provocative he could get.

'I understand —— is a fag', he said aggressively to a big butch homosexual in a bar, referring to a well-known Hollywood star, and he would shout across to Arthurs, 'Weren't all great boxers queens?'

Arthurs remembers, too, how in a second Brendan could spot a homosexual, even one whose predilictions had escaped the ladies of the party, usually the best judges of men with unusual sexual tendencies.

Arthurs, Beatrice and Brendan went to Forrest Lawn Cemetery where Brendan went around taking notes from the headstones, presumably for *Richard's Cork Leg*, the play he was currently trying to write. 'Jesus', he said, 'the Americans have banished death.' On the other hand, he was enchanted with Disneyland.

By now Brendan had moved to the Montecito Hotel in Hollywood, where various important locals streamed in and out to see him. Hugo French talked about a screen version of *The Hostage*. Andrew Pollard wanted to do a motion picture of the Irish Rebellion. Mike Todd wanted *Borstal Boy*.

From the Montecito, he wrote to Rory, his brother, in Dublin. He wanted to let Rory know how the early instruction in the arts Rory had given Brendan as a boy had left him with a head start on the avant-garde in Hollywood:

Rory, a chara,

I am having a holiday—from what?—you may well ask—here.

It's a screwy kind of place. Full of good kindly famous people. In Frank Sinatra's nite club they played 'Irish' airs for me when I went in last night and Groucho just rang up to say he's calling for us in the morning.

He and Harpo are friends of ours from New York. Harpo and I (and Harry Truman!) share a new publisher.

We had a great party in New York and Harpo and I were televised and photographed all over the place wearing Harpo wigs. It was in the papers all over, but I don't suppose the Dublin papers had it—they only seem to know when I'm in jail or dying.

One of the reasons I never write letters is that I can get more than a dollar a word for writing and I assure you that nobody else has heard of me at such length; but you are constantly in my mind on Broadway and Sunset Boulevard (which, oddly enough, in its own repulsive way is not unlike Sundrive Rd.! Trees and modern shops but unmitigated by the Floating Ballroom even. I'd think you'd prefer Broadway which, I may tell you, is a great place for a *quiet* piss-up, the secret being to get the newspapermen pissed too.) New York is a real city—Los Angeles has no navel—no Broadway—and nothing to recommend it except the sunshine swimming pools. I just leave my suite and go down in the lift wearing my togs, with the Jews and smart Irish—I don't see why the culchies and fardowners ever go any further than England. If you dig holes in the road, a hole in Lancashire must be as good as a hole in Los Angeles.

The songs I learnt off you such as 'Buddy, can you spare a dime?' (sure—lots of them—take 2 they're small) and 'My Deep Purple' enjoy a great vogue and in California all the Broadway exiles regard me as the only genuine purveyor of the Broadway melody.

I always acknowledge yourself as the source of these anthems—which does not run in our family.

Unfortunately, your course in American culture ceased circa 1938 and I horrified the crowd in Sinatra's (a tenement aristocrat like myself) by announcing that what I most wanted to see in Hollywood was a film of W. C. Fields called *The Bank Dick*—several modern film stars went out, presumably to look for an overdose of sleeping pills—

I have a copy of Harpo's new book autographed with a drawing of himself playing the Harp for you and May, but it's back in N.Y. and I thought this message, particularly the few lines stapled on the front of this address were of more immediate interest. Love to May, Deirdre, Jack, Rory, Og, May Og, Mrs Trimble and Tommy. If a guy wants to get on show business here or on Broadway, you provide a good education. You will be glad to hear that Fred Astaire got an award here recently and still looks a lean forty—we talked about you and me and the Drumcondra cinema and about Waterford.

Best wishes and love to you all from Beatrice.

Yours,

Brendan.

While he was at the Montecito he had a renewed burst of energy. He took out the manuscript of *Richard's Cork Leg* and worked on it for a week, incorporating material which he had picked up on his recent trips to Forest Lawn cemetery and elsewhere.

But after ten days Brendan's good intentions broke down. On May 31 he went to McGoo's bar in Hollywood. When he was refused a beer he became disorderly and two members of the vice-squad were summoned by the manager, Joe Cherry Brentari. Brendan attacked the police and in return got a stout punch up the nose. The owner of the bar, Martin Bryman, kindly bailed Brendan out for $105 pending a court appearance the next day. In court he pleaded guilty to two charges of battery and drunkenness. He paid the $250 fine. He even praised the police who arrested him: 'I was treated fairly', he said.

Later, in the bar, he talked to journalists:

I don't know why people take exception to me. A few weeks ago in Toronto a Canadian said that it was an awful black eye for the yanks that the Russians had put a spaceman up before the Americans. I said to him, 'My friend, Ireland will put up a shillelagh into orbit, Israel will put a matzo ball into orbit, and Lichtenstein will put a postage stamp into orbit before you Canadians ever put up a mouse.' Do you know, he hit me..

Brendan was by now on a ten day drunk. He would lie on the floor of his apartment in the Montecito, half stupefied. He never lost his extraordinary habit of remaining in contact with whoever was in the room with him though apparently semi-conscious. On one occasion, as the morning light was streaming through the window, Peter Arthurs, who had waited up, said to Beatrice, 'What time is it?'

Brendan opened his eyes and said, 'Three-thirty.' He was right.

At the end of June he set out on a tour of Mexico with Arthurs and Beatrice. Arthurs was to drive his car. Ernie Kovacs saw them off. By this time Brendan developed a habit of needling Arthurs. He knew that Arthurs had a mild crush on Kim Novak. Brendan deliberately used foul language about her. Arthurs stopped the car and got out.

'You are on your own now, daddio', he said, livid. He was so mad that he broke the car's headlights. Brendan's only comment was, 'Hem shot himself, so what?'

However, Arthurs got back into the car and they drove off again. As they crossed the border Arthurs remembers another example of Brendan's sharp sense of public relations. Some children had tried to photograph him. Brendan called a police-man and pretended to complain. Then they all had their photo-graphs taken together, and Brendan gave the kids $20. The pictures appeared in some American newspapers next day.

Back in New York, after their Mexican tour, Brendan was due to sail to Ireland on July 28 on the Holland–America steamer. He was found that evening outside the Jersey Medical Center, walking in his socks. Police said he had been wandering aimlessly. He told them that he had taken 'a weak spell', and they had put him into a cell for his own safety. Next day they kindly secured a place for him in the New Jersey State Hospital Psychiatric Ward. Beatrice had no money in her possession at the time but the almoner generously took her word that Brendan would pay by cheque when he got better.

A week later he paid his bill, discharged himself, and they sailed for Ireland.

CHAPTER TWENTY-TWO

BACK in Dublin, Brendan made an attempt to dry out once more.

He announced to the newspapers that he was 'off the gargle, a retired alcoholic'. But Dublin to an alcoholic is like a girls' shower room to a sex maniac. Its atmosphere generates a drinking mood.

Brendan belonged to a generation of Irish writers who plunged themselves recklessly into the lotus-eating atmosphere of Dublin pubbery. Three of his contemporaries—Patrick Kavanagh, Flann O'Brien (*At Swim Two Birds*) and Sean O'Sullivan, the artist—were to die of alcoholic poisoning.

Earlier literary groups had been more abstemious. Yeats, George Russell (Æ), and Synge avoided pub life. Joyce solved the problem by exile, but otherwise would have been ideal material to become just another pregnant Dublin writer, slumped in the corner of a city bar, brooding over the masterpiece he would never produce. In his later Paris years it appears that he was seldom sober after seven o'clock; but Paris was a city where writers worked, and by then Joyce would have completed his day's stint. Such discipline was abhorrent to a dedicated Dublin drinker; by seven o'clock he would still be thinking about the work he had *not* done, and by then the time would have come to join in the nightly revelry.

Talk is the attraction of the Dublin pub—often brilliant, witty, savage, cruising down corridors of the mind, swelled by the euphoria which the chemistry of personality arouses in the Irish imagination. The weakness of the pub is that it can become an emporium of paralysis for a race whose Latin religion has led them to regard work as a necessary evil, and who are already heavily committed to side-stepping the tyranny of fact. The attitude is woven into the tapestry of the city. It glows from the complexions of numerous citizens. There is the claret colour found in golf clubs, the rose-red of the windswept yacht club members, the ivory-white of the professional man, glimpsed over large ones, salvaging his personality from the day's exhaustion; the high glory of the dedicated escapist, the grog-blossomy nose, proclaiming its owner's constant contribution to the upkeep of the spirit trade.

Yeats knew the weakness of the town, its 'daily spite', its malice, its envy. He used this as an astringent to trigger off his creative mechanism—as a gourmet adds tartare sauce to make a dish more palatable. In the atmosphere of the pub, it was less easy to resist this 'daily spite'. It built up on top of one, and the defences were down when it arrived. Brendan feared the envy of Dublin; so did Kavanagh and Flann O'Brien. But they were caught in the siren-lure of its talk and never entirely mastered Yeats's stratagem of using it as an irritant for his art.

Brendan was indulging himself so much, a month after coming back from the United States, that Beatrice wrote in a mood of depression to Rae Jeffs:

September 27, 1961

Dear Rae,

Very many thanks for your kind thoughts, and your letter, which I was very pleased to get. These days, concern about Brendan and myself is a rare thing—I mean genuine and constructive. At the time I received your letter I had just got Brendan into a nursing home by ambulance in a state of complete collapse. He stayed two days—and then did his usual trick of running out behind the doctor's back. Ten days later B.B. is off again on the beer. He is today still bashing away regardless, money flying in all directions. Perhaps if he comes out of this bash—say in about ten days' time, David Astor would write him a letter 'playing it cool' as the Americans say—about considering a cure, or treatment—without directly mentioning it. You know the sort of letter I mean, and as Brendan has I know a high regard for him it might have some effect. I don't really know how to manage him any more. I just leave the house when he starts and live with my parents as much as I can to avoid rows. Then when his friends(?) get tired of him he is sent rolling back to me in a state of collapse.

I hope you will come to Dublin soon. Brendan, I think, intends to head for warmer climes this winter—whether I go or not—depends. My very best love and thanks, from Beatrice.

David Astor did write back, with the result that Brendan agreed to come to London to undergo treatment in a Nursing Home in the East End of London, run by a Dr Glatt.

When he arrived at Euston, Brendan insisted on going first to the York Minster, the 'French pub' in Soho with Rae Jeffs and Beatrice. There, under the influence of a few drinks, his resolution weakened, and after half an hour and a murderous row with Beatrice, he decided not to undergo the treatment after all.

Though he did not enter the Nursing Home, Brendan remained in London for a week, mainly to see the film version of *The Quare Fellow* which was showing at the Rialto Cinema in Leicester Square. The play had been altered in the film treatment and a love scene which was not in the original, between Crimmin the Warder, and the condemned man's wife, had been inserted and interpreted in a way Brendan had not foreseen. Though Brendan was upset by the film and fumed to his friends about it, he kept on a fairly even keel for about a week or so, before returning to Ireland.

He decided meanwhile, that he would edit *Brendan Behan's Island* himself, but the task of working on his own taped conversations proved to be more and more distasteful, and he began to look round for any excuse to avoid it. A telegram from New York provided it. Perry Bruskin said that the off-Broadway production of *The Hostage* which he was directing at the Circle in the Square, was having its premiere on February 5.

In the first week of February, Brendan took a taxi to Shannon airport and hopped on a 'plane to New York. This was to be a short visit lasting less than a month. His return there was something of a triumph as the new production got excellent notices from the papers.

Louis Calta wrote in the *New York Times*:

The Hostage is fortunately back after being reluctantly taken off Broadway because of a Stop-Clause, and it is as irreverent and mirth-provoking as ever.

Another reason Brendan had for going to New York was to see a girl friend whom he had been having an affair with. She was a Dublin girl who had in fact been introduced to him by Beatrice. Beatrice, with her usual innocence, had noticed nothing in the relationship between Brendan and the girl, though the three of them had often been in company together on previous visits to New York.

Later, when Beatrice learnt the real implications of the association, it hurt her deeply—perhaps for the first time in her life with Brendan. He had done many things to her, including beat her, which other people would have considered outrageous. He had even gone round openly with other women. But Beatrice had taken this philosophically as Brendan had not disguised it. However, she felt betrayed and stabbed in the back with the girl in New York.

Because she understood Brendan and had made allowances for him as a writer, recognizing the sensitive poet under the roaring boy, there was a bond between them until this point that only they understood. But now she felt betrayed because not only had a friend behaved treacherously, but Brendan had helped to make her look a fool in front of the very person who had lured him away from her. It was another link gone in the chain that bound Beatrice to Brendan—a link that up to now had prevented him from falling headlong into complete despair and self-destruction.

In March, Brendan returned from America and celebrated his homecoming by going on another drinking bout that landed him in hospital once again. As usual, he recovered quickly and, after drying out, kept himself in good shape until mid-May when he went for a holiday to Carraroe in Galway with Beatrice. It was here that he learnt that *Brendan Behan's Island* had been chosen by the Book Society as their October Choice and that the French Theatre Critics' Association had chosen *The Hostage* as the best play of the season.

He was due to attend a *Yorkshire Post* literary luncheon in the middle of September and appear on *Monitor*, the B.B.C. arts programme, as part of the promotion for the book. When he arrived in London on his way to Harrogate, he was in poor shape as he had been drinking for some time. To add to his troubles, the *Observer*, which had begun to serialize *Brendan Behan's Island*, had been served with a writ arising out of one of Brendan's stories, published on September 2, which was to appear in the book and which it was alleged was libellous.

At the lunch, however, at which Lord Boothby was in the chair and the other speakers were Frank Swinnerton, Ursula Bloom, and Kenneth Allsop, he made an excellent speech and behaved perfectly throughout the function. He was taken on the hop early on by the Bishop of Knaresborough who, when Brendan asked him: 'What's your fucking businesss, Mac?' replied imperturbably:

'Not as profitable as yours, I'm afraid.' Always ready to acknowledge a witty reply, Brendan shook his Lordship warmly by the hand.

By now, however, public appearances imposed a strain on him that left him in a severe state of nervous exhaustion and, on the journey back to London, he got hopelessly drunk. After a week's drinking in London he ended up at his brother-in-law's house. There he had such a fearful attack that Joe Paton drove him straight to Westminster Hospital where he remained in a critical condition for some days.

He recovered and did his old trick of discharging himself without notice late one night. But the next day he agreed to meet David Astor once more to discuss the possibility of a cure.

The patient editor arrived, bringing with him the *Observer* medical correspondent, Dr Abraham Marcus. Dr Marcus told Brendan with commendable frankness that, in his opinion, Brendan would be dead within a year if he did not stop drinking. It was not an answer which was calculated to appeal to Brendan with his morbid fear of death, and he went off into a violent round of abuse at both the doctor and David Astor that made further discussion impossible.

He rushed out into the street where Rae Jeffs and Beatrice managed to steer him into David Astor's chauffeur-driven car and, by various manoeuvres, finally ended up with him again at the Westminster Hospital. However, after no more than an hour there, he discharged himself once more.

A day later, on Sunday, September 30, by an extraordinarily appropriate mistake, he entered a home for alcoholics. He had been looking for a friend's hotel in Victoria when he knocked at the door of a nursing home, believing it was the hotel he was looking for. Seeing his condition, the doctor in charge kept him overnight. It was, in fact, a private nursing home, owned by an eminent London specialist in the field of alcoholism. He himself was away in Rome but, a day or two later, his partner managed to contact Beatrice and proposed to her that Brendan should remain on in the hospital that he had entered so fortuitously and undergo what is known as 'aversion' treatment. This involves giving the patient a drug which if he subsequently touches alcohol, makes him so ill that he may never wish to take it again. Beatrice agreed to the treatment but left Rae Jeffs in charge while she went to Ireland to arrange her household affairs before coming back to stay with Brendan during his cure.

For a week, the treatment seemed to work admirably. Then Brendan developed double vision which the doctor suggested might be due to pressure on the brain, and recommended an operation. Brendan was terrified by this information as he had an obsessive horror of the surgeon's knife and also nourished a secret fear that some day he would lose control of his mental faculties. He refused to have anything to do with the operation whatsoever.

Each day, he was allowed out for a period with his male nurse, Joe McGarrity. He would go round London in his company, visiting the bars and some of his old haunts but always drinking milk or lemonade.

Samuel Beckett and his cousin John Beckett, a close friend of Brendan's, visited him here. Brendan was in bed when they came in. Beckett was distressed at the change that had taken place in him since they had met in Beckett's flat in 1952.

They brought him French cigarettes and this seemed to please him:

'He told us a long story about a drugged greyhound but his mind would wander away and leave the story and then come back. I admired him for his marvellous warmth, but I never really saw him sober. When he went on and on he was impossible.'

Though the libel action against the *Observer* had been a source of worry to him before he went into hospital, he rather enjoyed the subsequent publicity. A High Court Judge in Dublin had given the necessary permission to issue a writ for libel out of the Irish jurisdiction, and a process server was searching London for Brendan. 'He seeks me here. He seeks me there', he boasted to a *People* newspaper interviewer, 'but I'm damned if I know what the fuss is about. I didn't leave Ireland to escape from the law. I came over here to be cured of the drink but I'm going to fight this case tooth and nail.' Assisted no doubt by the publicity given to Brendan's statements, the process server unearthed him a day later and served the writ on him.

During his round of the pubs, his old flair for conversation began to reassert itself. Whenever he met his friends, he would begin to pour out stories which recalled something of his conversational talent before alcoholism had diminished it, in the last year or so. His friends of this period remember his penchant for steering the conversation round to sexual encounters, a subject about which he would expound with a great deal of enthusiasm in compensation, perhaps, for the restraint he was placing on his appetite for drink.

Against the doctor's advice, he decided to finish his treatment by going to visit his old friend, Ralph Cusack, in the South of France. Beatrice was to go ahead while Brendan visited Paris on the way with Joe McGarrity. After extracting £450 from Hutchinson's as an advance for a novel, *The Scarperer*, which he had serialized in the *Irish Times* in 1950, Brendan set out for the Riviera.

Despite 'aversion' pills which McGarrity slipped into his drink, he began again to take occasional glasses of wine while he was staying with the Cusacks, but otherwise the visit was a quiet one.

An invitation to appear as a guest on the Eamonn Andrews television show, *This is Your Life*, gave him an excuse to return to Ireland and also an opportunity to get back to an atmosphere where drinking was regarded as a way of life and not merely as a pastime. The B.B.C. programme was to deal with Stephen Behan's life and Brendan was to appear with Dominic, Brian, Kathleen and other members of the family, in the format familiar to viewers of this programme. Elaborate precautions were taken by the B.B.C. team to keep Brendan sober and he arrived at the studios in good fettle. It was recorded in Dublin and subsequently broadcast from London.

But the effect of Dublin on Brendan could not have been worse. With the knowledge now that two serious attempts to cure himself had failed, he went back on the drink with a vengeance. He began now to sleep out in the houses of drinking companions or in 70 Kildare Road, where his mother never had the heart to refuse him a bed, instead of going home to Anglesea Road where he lived with Beatrice. This meant that her influence on him was lessened.

Always at the back of his mind, Brendan had the hope that he could shake off the whole terrible business of alcoholism by some monumental gesture. Dublin, he thought was killing him.

Could he get away from it? New York again seemed to him to provide the hope of a Promised Land. After all, he had been sober there for nine months in 1960 and so, at the end of February 1963, he telephoned Beatrice's mother from London to say he was going away for the week-end.

Actually he was on his way to New York.

This time he had no excuse for his journey. Like other writers with intimations of death, he was seeking a new world, believing that the cure lay in a change of place and environment rather than within himself.

CHAPTER TWENTY-THREE

For the first week or two, New York exercised its old charm on him. Brendan had discovered that New York could be an intimate city. By now he was a familiar figure in the Third and Second Avenue bars, in the restaurants and the nightspots. Rolling along with a sailor's gait on his small neat feet, he could walk from bar to bar exchanging greetings and conversation as he came and went. He could take the subway down to the Fulton Fish Market and visit Thomas Addis Emmet's grave (brother of Robert Emmet) at nearby Trinity Church, in the same morning.

Wherever he went he was recognized immediately. He was a public figure. People turned their heads in the street cars if his Christian name was mentioned. For the first few weeks after his arrival in New York, Brendan was in great fettle. He was delighted to be back. He sensed the vitality of the city again. But when Beatrice was not with him, he often forgot to take his pills and would neglect his diet. Without these attentions he was in danger of slipping into a diabetic coma. The strain on his nervous system if he did not take the medicine was appalling, which, in turn, led him to drink more.

But in the beginning he was determined to keep fit and make a new start. His sailor friend, Peter Arthurs, was at this time staying in the Chelsea Hotel at 23rd Street. There was a Y.M.C.A. gymnasium across the road and he and Brendan went there regularly for work-outs. Brendan would punch the bag inexpertly but vigorously, do some press-ups and swim interminably up and down the pool. Afterwards he would sweat it out in the steam bath, his eyes lighting up, a member recalls, as he saw young men pass by naked on their way to the shower.

This period of reform lasted no more than a fortnight. Soon

Brendan was on the drink again. His conduct in the Bristol Hotel where he was staying became increasingly worse. If he was thrown out, he would find if difficult to get another hotel, as he had already been expelled from the Algonquin on 45th Street. It was becoming known in the hotel business that he was an undesirable guest.

One night he had a monumental row at the Bristol. He had asked the porter to send out to a nearby restaurant for skishkebab, a favourite dish of his. The manager of the Bristol refused to allow the porter to go out unless Brendan paid for the skishkebab there and then. His credit was not good at the time. Thwarted and hungry, Brendan flew into a rage, cursed and roared, broke up furniture and offended the staff so much that next morning he was asked to leave.

Where was he to go?

By chance, his publisher, Bernard Geis, was able to provide him with alternative accommodation. A week previously Geis had met Brendan and noticed what bad shape he was in. On Sunday, March 10, Brendan had arrived at Geis's apartment in even worse condition. It took a while before Geis realized why Brendan had paid him the compliment of a visit on Sunday morning. The pubs in New York were not open until after one o'clock and he needed a drink badly. When Brendan scuttled off on the dot of one, Geis reckoned that his chances of getting a return on the $10,000 he had advanced Brendan for a book on New York were somewhat slim.

A day or two later Brendan was thrown out of the Bristol Hotel, and arrived at Geis's offices. Katherine Dunham, the dancer and choreographer, happened to be there at the same time. Brendan was dishevelled and drunken when he arrived. Miss Dunham was horrified at the spectacle. She gathered from Geis that he was thinking of having Brendan committed to the Psychiatric Center at Bellevue. Her heart was touched at the sight of a fellow-artist in this predicament. On a sudden impulse she offered to take care of him herself, if Geis would pay the rent, by installing him in her hotel and arranging to have him looked after there by members of her cast. Geis agreed, willing to try any plan that might result in Brendan's producing a book.

Next day, Katherine Dunham installed Brendan on the tenth floor of the Chelsea Hotel in a self-contained suite, from which he could see down over Manhattan. Lucille, one of Miss Dunham's dancers, was to look after him by day, and Ural, one of the male dancers in the troupe, was to watch him at night.

A characteristic of the Chelsea Hotel is its unpretentiousness. A plaque on the wall contains the names of many famous artists and writers who have stayed there—James T. Farrell, Robert Flaherty, O. Henry, Thomas Wolfe, Henry Moore and Edgar Lee Masters. Dylan Thomas had stayed there before he died. Arthur Miller has a permanent suite in the Hotel. Yet there is nothing arty about the Chelsea. It is an enormous turn-of-the-century brownstone building on 23rd Street, with iron-work balconies, and has never tried to change its decor to suit its customers. It is one of those rare places—an hotel with character. The rooms inside are massive, with brass knockers on the doors, high ceilings and heavy Victorian furniture.

Brendan flopped down in the Chelsea with a grateful sigh. Subjected to a careful routine by Katherine Dunham, he began to improve instantly. He confined himself to drinking Guinness. He talked incessantly to Lucille and Ural. Preston, another of Katherine's dancers, who sometimes stood-in for Lucille and Ural, remembers how Brendan would lie on the floor with his fat stomach pointing to the ceiling, talking away nineteen to the dozen.

Brendan enjoyed the company at the Chelsea, where he met Arthur Miller, James Farrell, Agnes Bolton (Eugene O'Neill's wife), and others. It was a congenial atmosphere for him. He was on familiar terms with writers who had been his idols when he had been a young unknown writer in Ireland.

The Chelsea had many delights. On the fifth floor, George

Kleinsinger, the composer, lived. Kleinsinger, best known for his opera *Archie and Mehitabel*, is an entertaining New York eccentric. In his apartment in the Chelsea Hotel, he keeps twenty-seven different types of animals. These include two pythons, six snakes and an iguana. There are many kinds of rare fish in fluorescent-lit aquariums. The walls of the room are lined with tropical plants, many of them imported from Africa. Some of these stretch to the ceiling. In among the plants fly parakeets, finches, canaries, red-plumed Brazilian Cardinals, mynah birds and other breeds.

Kleinsinger's flat became a haven for Brendan. Kleinsinger welcomed him and he would come down and sing there for hours, accompanying himself at the piano. Kleinsinger thought him the last of the troubadors. Brendan was intrigued by the menagerie around him. To have constructed a private zoo in an apartment in the middle of Manhattan seemed to him a splendid feat. The mynah bird and Brendan were soon on hostile terms. Whenever he sang, the bird would interrupt with a piercing shriek at exactly the wrong moment. To make things worse, it would occasionally accompany Brendan in a voice that was sometimes more in key than he was. He had his hour of triumph, however, when the bird was institutionalized for misbehaving himself by scoffing a rare African robin right down to the beak. After this he was kept permanently in his cage. Brendan used to gloat at it, wag his finger and say: 'Now you know what it is like to be in the nick!' In between singing and playing the piano he would talk a lot about his uncle Peadar Kearney, the author of many of the best Irish ballads. He told George Kleinsinger how his uncle had died a pauper although he had composed the Irish National Anthem. One evening, moved by some memory of the past, Brendan sat down at the piano and started to sing the Anthem—'The Soldiers Song'. Kleinsinger managed to switch on a tape recorder and get the microphone in front of him. The tape reveals a good deal about Brendan at this time. His voice is cracked, but he sings with great fervour, as if he was trying to summon up something of the patriotism of his early days to inject into the song. Yet there is something false, almost pathetic about the performance, like an old actor trying to recreate the triumphs of the past, by acting from memory and drawing on an emotion that is not there.

Brendan and George Kleinsinger had long conversations, often arguing into the small hours of the morning. Two things were obsessing him, Kleinsinger remembers, the fear of death and the fear that he was a phoney. He joked about death, calling himself a daylight atheist. But in his dark moods when a depression was on him, he was terrified of it. Brendan was poor suicide material— he wanted to live. When darkness descended, he leaned on the religion of his childhood. Scoffers at religion irritated him. One day Kleinsinger and Brendan were sitting in the restaurant downstairs in the Chelsea listening to a writer who claimed that he had abandoned his religious beliefs. Brendan sneered at him: 'He'll be the first to call for the priest, and I'll be the first to call for the Fire Brigade.' He confided in Kleinsinger that he had an idea that he was a phoney. Would he be found out? This puzzled and worried him as he sat in these indoor zoological gardens, his head sunk in his shoulders, surrounded by tropical birds and reptiles.

Perry Bruskin, who produced the off-Broadway production of *The Hostage* at the Cort Theatre, remembers also that Brendan had become very unsure of his position at this time. He thinks that the term 'frightened to death' was never meaningful until Brendan died. People expected too much of him. Perry Bruskin recalls:

> Idols must be able to do failures like anybody else. Brendan zoomed into the public eye without enough background to support him. He was always afraid of the hard times. He had become afraid of failure. Giving him money to produce a book didn't work. It was like holding him up and shaking the pennies out of him.

He knew that, unless a miracle happened, he would write no more. The energy necessary to concentrate, get words on paper and give them form, was gone. He was like Oscar Wilde in the last years in the Paris cafés, only able to talk, though, like Wilde, his chat was capable of enchanting listeners.

He was alert enough mentally to be able to dictate two more books with Rae Jeffs, *Confessions of an Irish Rebel* and *Brendan*

Behan's New York—the former while he was in New York and the latter after he had returned to Dublin, a few months before his death. The tapings were to Brendan what the café talks were to Wilde and the last shattered recital of *Under Milkwood* to Thomas: an indulgence in reminiscence of the power they enjoyed at the height of their fame.

Brendan and Oscar in their decline were surrendering to the impulse to luxuriate in failure, an instinct rooted in the Irish psyche. The Irish are suspicious of success believing that there is more of the infinite in its opposite. Failure they can offer up to God. Wilde summed it up perfectly near the end of his life:

> The artist's mission is to live the complete life; success, as an episode (which is all it can be); failure, as the real, the final end. Death, analysed to its resultant atoms—what is it but the vindication of failure: the getting rid for ever of powers, desires, appetites, which have been a lifelong embarrassment? The poet's noblest verse, the dramatist's greatest scene, deal always with death; because the highest function of the artist is to make perceived the beauty of failure.

Caught in the sensual music of decline, Brendan assuaged his agony at not being able to create, by dramatizing himself in a tale of sordid and desperate collapse.

His disintegration was astonishingly rapid. Whatever shells of discipline he had imposed on himself swiftly disappeared. The soft core of his Narcissus complex asserted itself. The desire to shine, to be the centre of attention as he has been as a child, became the dominant appetite of his life. By gratifying this desire to talk, he could anaesthetize himself against the knowledge that he could no longer write.

On one occasion before his death, Terence Chapman, his physician, called at the Behan house in Dublin to find him sitting amid scenes of squalor, talking compulsively to a few bored hangers-on. When he noticed the doctor had come in, Brendan took his hand and continued talking, cunningly purchasing Chapman's silence by occasional squeezes, so that he could continue his monologue uninterrupted. This desire to shine became an obsession with him, so that eventually he began to degenerate into a parody of himself.

Had he developed in early life a mental discipline, his collapse would not have been so sudden. But the only discipline he had been subject to was that of prison life, which he would have tended to reject rather than retain. Once he reverted to the dominant impulse of childhood, his collapse was sudden and total.

Pressures were exerting themselves from all sides. At this time he was never sure that some enterprising journalist would not spring the story of his affair in New York. This explanation would be used in Ireland to explain his frequent visits to America. His past homosexual encounters might be raked to the surface. Brendan was still hot news, and any hint of scandal would be amplified a hundred times.

His nervous and physical resources were almost exhausted. Tortured and ill, his mind was prey to strange desires. The presence of a group of Spanish boy dancers in the Chelsea Hotel disturbed him in a way that terrified him. Brendan always had a deep-rooted horror of corrupting children. In *Brendan Behan's New York*, written a few months before he died, he advocated laws which would protect the young from sexual interference. In the slum-ethic of his youth, the primal crime was to molest children. A slum mother who might laugh at a man who had accosted her, would have castrated the same person if she had found him near her children.

This conflict in Brendan was one of the burdens he bore in his last years. When David Astor observed that there seemed to be something deep in Brendan, torturing him, it may have been a desire for youthful sexual companions, and fear of giving in to the appetite. One night in 1962, in a drunken stupor, he had momentarily fondled the head of a young boy at a party and later when he was reminded of the event, became savage in denying that it could ever have taken place. It was as if it was a secret part of himself which he did not want to recognize—or want other people to recognize either. In New York in his last year, he would sometimes ask an acquaintance to arrange a rendezvous with negro youths who took his fancy, but would always fail to turn up himself for the appointment.

Though he fought against these desires, he was mortified that his weary frame should have become prey to emotions like them.

Despite these pressures, under Katherine Dunham's care, Brendan began to make a remarkable recovery. She was herself an artist and she spoke his language. She understood the conflict between the world of imagination and the world of reality and how difficult it was to bring an idea down to earth and clothe it in the permanence art can give it. She was a practical woman. She had had to be, to become an impresario who had created a new movement in the world of dance, the African ballet. She applied her practical flair to Brendan with some success. She took no nonsense from him. For a while he knuckled down and did what she said.

He had improved so much by the middle of April that Bernard Geis persuaded Rae Jeffs to come over and begin taping Brendan's autobiography. Rae Jeffs arrived with her daughter, Diana, on April 13. She checked in at the Governor Clinton Hotel. Presently she went to see Brendan and was delighted to find him dressed in a spotless white shirt and a crease in his trousers. Lucille, Preston and Ural were doing their work well. Brendan was full of enthusiasm for the project they were to undertake together and anxious to get down to work. In the meantime, however, he insisted on taking Rae Jeffs and Diana around New York, exhibiting his usual knowledge of out-of-the-way bits of information about the city.

His work on his autobiography was to exceed everybody's expectations. Despite a bad tape which didn't record a line of his first session with Rae Jeffs, Brendan managed to get 50,000 words of the book done in two weeks. This was a prodigious feat. It left him exhausted mentally and physically. He was to pay the penalty shortly afterwards.

After he had finished recording *Confessions,* Brendan went on another drinking bout. While he was on this bat, Beatrice arrived from Dublin. At Christmas she had refused to accompany Brendan to New York so he had come by himself in February.

Repenting her decision, she had come over now. But something had come between them since their last meeting. From this time on there was to be a change in their relationship with one another.

Neither was to blame.

They were two people caught in a chain of circumstances made inevitable by the life they had chosen to lead together.

For Brendan to have held any grudge against Beatrice was unreasonable. She had behaved with the patience of a Saint since she had married him. He would never have produced the work that he had if it had not been for the care she took to see that everything was directed towards his writing. No trouble had been too much for her when it came to keeping Brendan in shape to ply his pen. She seemed to have inexhaustible tolerance. But, from now on, Beatrice's influence on Brendan was to subside.

His mind at this period was still alert. He talked about his family and his I.R.A. past to Kenneth Allsop, who was visiting New York, with something of his old spirit:

> If you want a professional I.R.A. killer you must look at another set of initials—not the I.R.A. but the B.B.C. There my brother Dominic is shooting Englishmen on the Third Programme at the expense of the British licence-holder. My brother's I.R.A. service is about as existent as my father's writing. The other day my father told a journalist about his writing, and also stated that I am washed up.

Brendan also started to accept invitations to parties again. Once the news got round that he was available, the usual parasites began to gather at his door. Brendan was a valuable property in New York. To be seen with him was to stand a good chance of getting into the newspapers. On one occasion, Peter Arthurs discovered a man he knew smuggling Brendan half drunk out of the Bristol Hotel at one in the morning to bring him to the opening party of a new public house in the hopes that Brendan would create a scene and secure a mention of the place in next day's evening papers.

By the middle of May, Brendan was going on fearful binges. Rae Jeffs had gone home and Beatrice could do nothing about it. She had told him repeatedly that the reason she had come from Ireland was to let him know she was pregnant. But sometimes she wondered as he rolled drunkenly round the room whether he heard her at all or had he taken in what she had said. Katherine Dunham's interest was waning. She had presented Beatrice with an itemized bill for Brendan's expenses at the Chelsea Hotel and Brendan had refused to pay it, claiming it was inaccurate.

Wasting the good work of two months, he gave himself over completely to drink. Now he was to make a bitter discovery: the bars where he had been so popular before, denied him admission. Emil, the foreman of Costello's, finally put Brendan out one night and forebade him to come back again. He had become a menace to the customers, abusing them verbally and physically. Thrown out of bar after bar, all his premonitions of failure seemed to be coming true. Where he had been welcomed like a King, he was now an outcast. Cut off from Beatrice and the influence of Katherine Dunham, he went to pieces almost overnight. One day, he was helping Norman Mailer up the stairs with a heavy load. Mailer, who had just given up cigarettes, was in good shape, but Brendan was puffing and blowing like a man of sixty. Mailer asked him how he was on the drink question. Brendan threw his eyes up to heaven and said with despair: 'I felt I had to go back. I can't cut it out.'

He had left Dublin, the city he loved most, because of its association with his fearful drinking bouts there. Now he was to do the same with New York—soil his memory of it with horror. But at least in Dublin he was close to something with which he could identify. There was a world of Irish music, of ballad singing, unlimited sessions of talk and story-telling. When he felt that his grip on the future was slipping, he could always slide into the past for comfort. With his old I.R.A. friends, he could feel once more that they were part of the struggle to free Ireland from the oppressor.

He could not now find the same reassurance in the Irish bars on Third Avenue. Cut off from this solace, there was no place to retreat from his public image. The public he played up to in New York and London were sceptical and déraciné. They could have no comprehension of Behan's umbilical attachment to Irish Republicanism, Socialism and Catholicism. He had allowed himself to be adopted by an international set who had not examined his credentials for admission. He was a man adrift, clinging desperately to beliefs which had supported him in the past, as a life-belt to keep himself afloat on the unruly flood.

He clung tenaciously to his belief in an after-life. It was the engine which drove his being. Without it, he would have had to reconstruct his relationship to society. It freed him from the slavery of brooding on his dissolution and brought him intimations of an existence which tortured beings use to persuade themselves of the temporary nature of their exile. He turned to God to obtain the impossible because there alone he recognized he could encounter it.[1]

Sometimes in order to prolong his stay in a bar, he would launch into one of the old rebel songs in a terrible cracked tenor. He would rouse himself up and, for a moment, some of the old fury and fire would show itself; but instinctively he knew they were clapping an echo. If they had heard the real thing, they would have clapped just as loudly because the reality of the environment which had bred Brendan was beyond their comprehension. Yet it was they who had made his mask. His sin was that he had accepted it, knowing it to be a false one.

The climax was reached in a dreadful alcoholic seizure, which necessitated Brendan being rushed to hospital.

Beatrice and Rae Jeffs (who had returned to America to tape the proposed book on New York) came back to the hotel one day to find Brendan in bed. At first, everything seemed in order, but it was too quiet to be true. Beatrice noticed a pile of blood-stained newspapers on the floor. Going over to the bed, she found that Brendan was reading from a book which he held upside-down. The symptoms were only too recognizable. He was on the verge of an alcoholic seizure. Dr Max Tasler was called. Hardly had

---

[1] It is ironic that one of the important writers of the century, the Irishman Samuel Beckett, should have conjectured 'I cry, therefore I live', while many of his countrymen would instead exclaim 'I laugh, therefore I shall not die'.

Are the two irreconcilable?

Both have inherent in them the 'zeal for perpetuity' of which Unamuno talks, which confronted with death 'activates the diastole of the soul with rays of dazzling energy'.

The question for conjecture, therefore, is not whether to laugh or cry, but whether either provides a formula for survival.

the doctor entered the room when Brendan went into a series of violent convulsions. His exhausted body was racked with pain, vomiting and retching, till they finally got him to University Hospital in an ambulance. His astounding capacity for rapid recovery soon asserted itself. Next day, he was much better. Even when, by mistake, he drank some vinegar instead of water, he was able to laugh at himself. The doctor who had been responsible for the mistake, laughed and said, 'That would have killed an ordinary man. You mustn't be as bad as you pretend—you can have a glass of beer as a reward for being good'.

But the recovery was deceptive—this time Brendan's mind was affected. He got the idea that somehow he was in Grangegorman, Dublin's mental hospital. Nothing would convince him that he was not in a mad-house. He was given his clothes and allowed to go. This confusion between Dublin and New York had begun to grow in Brendan's mind as long as two years before. One day, he had said to Peter Arthurs, 'I'm going out to get a coat at Burtons'. Arthurs looked at him and it was then that Brendan remembered that Burtons was a Dublin men's clothes shop and, had no connection whatsoever with New York. Earlier in the year when he had started to dictate *Confessions of an Irish Rebel* to Rae Jeffs, for a moment his mind had slipped off and he had begun to dictate a section of *The Catacombs*, his unfinished play.

Norman Mailer remembers Brendan at this time as 'Carrying an incredible fatigue inside him. He was like a giant in chains'. Mailer was almost ashamed to admit it to himself, but, in his heart of hearts, he knew he was glad to see the last of Brendan:

> He was like a steam engine at this time; bang, bang, bang in your ear. He had a need near the end to speak to someone. He wanted to reach you as if he knew he was going to die. He also brought out stingyness in you— you didn't want to involve yourself. I have a theory that when a person is dying and he can have a conversation with you, he won't die. Behan knew he had his death inside him—he knew that he was ill. But his pride was almost unbearable.

When Brendan eventually realized that Mailer did not want to be with him, he turned away with a look in his eyes like a hurt dog.

Beatrice was determined to get him to Dublin as soon as possible—anything seemed better than to have him hanging around New York rudderless and in danger of going suddenly to the bottom.

After some trouble, for Brendan by this time had used up all his advances—even the one he had got for $10,000 to do a book on the Irish Revolution and which he had not done a word of. Beatrice finally produced a cheque for royalties for *The Hostage* which she had kept in her bag against a need such as this, and bought two cabin-class tickets on the Queen Mary for home.

After a press conference in which he abused the New York City Council for its working-class dwellings and bad bus service, Brendan got on the ship and they set off for home. Beatrice and he travelled cabin-class, while Rae Jeff had a first-class berth. It was a troubled journey. But after a few brushes with the captain and crew they finally arrived in Southampton, more or less intact at the end of July, 1963.

Brendan and Beatrice went to London where Brendan went on yet another drinking bout. Somehow or other on his journey through the London bars he acquired a friend called Alan. When they went to board the train for Holyhead, Alan showed that he was not without resource by arriving with a wheel chair so that Brendan, by this time quite unable to walk through drunkenness, was virtually wheeled into the carriage.

CHAPTER TWENTY-FOUR

HORSE Show week in Dublin, at the beginning of August, was not the best time for Brendan to arrive back. His friends among the Anglo-Irish gentry were never adverse to being seen in the company of a famous drunk, a privilege not available to their English counterparts.

Three weeks later, Rae Jeffs arrived in Dublin. She was shocked at the change in him since she had left him in Southampton. The skin was hanging over his cheekbones in flabby folds and he had not eaten for some weeks. But somehow or other, he managed to summon his powers together. In a few days, he told her, he would be ready to start work on taping *Brendan Behan's New York*. In less than two months he had it finished. The final session was on November 22. It was certainly not Brendan's best book, but it is by no means a bad one either. Though it is quite clear that his memory was not as good as it might have been, it shows, despite his awful excesses, that there was still plenty of life in him, at least as regards recording books, if he could only stop his drinking.

But this he could not do. From November to Christmas, there was another sudden and awful degeneration.

He was barely living at this time. Each morning he rose a shattered wreck, with only one idea in mind; to get to a bar in order to recover from his hangover and steady himself long enough to focus on the events of the day. In addition, though he had plenty of available cash, he had developed a neurotic fear of bankruptcy. He was in mortal terror of an income-tax claim which had been served on him. He had never made proper returns over the years and now he had been assessed for over £8,000. He had made large sums of money from *The Hostage* and on the various editions, both paperback and hard-cover, of his best-selling *Borstal Boy*. But he was finding, as many another writer has, that, to continue making a living from literature, you must continue to produce books.[1]

Now that he wasn't throwing his money around, a lot of the crew who had previously surrounded him dropped away. There were still the hangers-on, glad to listen while Brendan bought. But unless he did, even they were not prepared to pay the penalty of listening to his drunken monologues. Groups would dissolve as he peered apprehensively round the door of McDaid's or Davy Byrne's. To make matters worse, a number of Dublin pubs now barred him from drinking on their premises. For the last two months of his life, there were only a few pubs in Dublin where he could be sure of getting a drink—The Bailey, The Harbour Lights of James's Street, Ryan's of Marlborough Street and Daly's of Fitzgibbon Street.

Once he had been king of the Dublin strip—the bars of Grafton Street. Now the only people who stood by him were his friends of the I.R.A. years. Chief amongst these were Eddie Whelan, Charlie Gorman, Mick Murphy, Paddy Kelly and Dick Timmins. They had never followed him for the money he spent on drink. When Brendan was flying, they had not complained when he had forgotten the proprieties. Once they had asked him for tickets for *The Quare Fellow*, offering to pay for them but asking Brendan, through Beatrice, to claim the tickets so that they would not have to queue at the booking office. They had never got their tickets. But theirs was the comradeship of men who had fought together for an ideal. Now they were glad to show when the chips were down that the bond between them was a true one.

Brendan was not always an easy companion to spend an evening with, especially when alcohol had dulled his sensitivity to other people's presence. Paddy Kelly remembers that

[1] When he was in funds his generosity had been remarkable. On impulse he had often given away large sums of money. Garry McElligot, a Dublin journalist, remembers a friend of Brendan's coming into McDaid's Pub and telling Brendan that the scaffolding business he owned was bankrupt. Brendan asked the man how much he would need to set himself up again. The sum required was £250. Brendan went out to the bank and returned to McDaid's in a quarter of an hour with the money in notes which he handed over to the friend.

> Brendan was a good storyteller at this point but he was not a good talker; he couldn't keep to the point of an argument. He had no grasp for deep matters and would go shooting off into some anecdote or wisecrack to avoid getting under the surface.

His old I.R.A. friends did not pay him any special deference because of his literary achievements. They accepted him for what he was.

After the sycophancy and adulation of New York, London and the bars of Dublin, this reaction must have recommended itself to Brendan. Sometimes he forgot where he was and tried to talk them down as he would have done to a group in a New York or London bar. But here he got as good as he gave. 'My God', he said one day to Paddy Kelly after they had just left Eddie Whelan, 'hasn't Whelan a tongue like a fucking hatchet'. Another day Brendan criticized the extreme nationalism of the I.R.A. and the G.A.A. (the G.A.A. is the Gaelic Athletic Association of Ireland). Paddy Kelly turned round and said to Brendan, 'You should be the last man to say that about the G.A.A. or the Republicans, who has prostituted himself by writing for English papers'. Kelly added that he left hurriedly after this statement, because he knew that, weakened and all as Brendan was, he would have an answer for him.

Among these friends, Brendan could be himself for the first time for years. He had no need to put on an act to pretend he was a saint or act the part of a sinner. Occasionally he surprised them by going out into the middle of the floor and kneeling down to say the Angelus. He would not tolerate cheap sneers at religion. One day an aggressive little Socialist started to sing 'The Red Flag' at what Kelly describes as 'a most inopportune moment'. Pope John had just died. Brendan turned on the singer with withering sarcasm: 'This little drummer can't let up for a minute because he's carrying the burden of the Republic on his shoulders.'

They cut him down to size and he accepted their terms. One night on the way to a boozer in Dolphin's Barn, Brendan leaned back grandly in the seat of the taxi and said, 'You know, I don't need friends. I can buy them with this,' and he tapped his wallet. Paddy Kelly and Charlie Gorman who were with him stopped the taxi immediately and got out. Brendan was flabbergasted at their reaction' He had overplayed his hand. He looked out of the window at them in amazement and suddenly, Gorman recalls, the tears started to stream down his cheeks.

> The gas thing about it was that when we got to the pub, his bloody wallet was empty and he hadn't a penny, We had to pay for the drinks after all. He could buy friends—my elbow!

Another friend in whose company he found solace at this time was a Dublin prostitute, Edith. She had met him some years before. Now when he was lonely, ill and suffering from insomnia, she would often meet him in the streets late at night and take him home for a cup of tea and a talk. She was a well-read girl who knew her Joyce and Yeats well, and she found Brendan excellent company when he was by himself and out of the limelight. She says Brendan was never known to 'operate'. Any money he gave the 'girls' was out of the kindness of his heart and not for business purposes. He was a regular client of Dolly Fawcett's, a café in Bolton Street where the girls used to gather in the small hours. At Dolly's you could buy a vile imitation of whiskey after the pubs closed and this was Brendan's main reason for being there, apart from the fact that he enjoyed the company in this last of the Dublin shebeens.

Edith had been at the head of her profession in London earning over £100 a week and living up to every penny of it when she first met Brendan. The first time she saw him was at the opening night of *The Quare Fellow* at the Comedy Theatre in the West End when she noticed him standing in the foyer. She was perceptive enough to see at once the other side of Brendan's personality—this man who the papers of the time had painted as a complete extrovert: 'He was standing in the foyer in an open-necked shirt, alone. I think he used to shut himself off as people were always going up and talking to him.' This impression was confirmed later on when she met him in Dublin. She recognized this other side to him and she respected it. Her recollections of Brendan, which she has kindly written down, are a valuable account, because of its detachment. She took human beings as she found them:

I always got the impression of vagueness from Brendan, that he wasn't listening to me, but this was not so. I remember the way he would burst into song in the middle of a conversation, always songs of a relevant variety. Sometimes I got the impression he was doing things on purpose, like shouting and causing scenes. His wife would sit serene through anything. She never remonstrated and seemed to have a saintly quality. Whenever we would meet he would always stop to have a 'crack' with me. There was no rapport on the surface, but his eyes were alight even when he was drunk.

When he came to my flat I got the impression that he was lonely. He was kind beyond measure. He was always sorry for the girls at Dolly Fawcett's, the down and outs, and used to give them money for lodgings. He was a rabid Dubliner and didn't like people from the country.

He always seemed at heart somehow different. When he was drunk he would swear profusely and when he was very drunk he would mutter to himself. Nevertheless no matter how drunk he was I always got the impression that he knew what was going on all the time. He had absolutely no viciousness. He would never let one see the real Brendan, I felt. He was keeping a lot of the old characters going. Paddy Shannon was getting a pension from Brendan, I believe. He never forgot some of these men. 'Bugler' Burn and an old man called Hyland were two others he helped.

Edith remembers that Brendan was 'always personally very clean contrary to appearances'. Though at this time, certainly, it was becoming increasingly difficult to see the real Brendan beneath the grime and dust. He was seldom at home for Beatrice to take care of him now and his habits were becoming slovenly. Most nights he slept out in the houses of friends. In the weeks before Beatrice went into hospital to have her child, Brendan stayed with Eddie Whelan at Drimnagh, a County Council estate on the city outskirts. But he had recovered sufficiently to be in the hospital when the child was born. It was a girl. 'It's the biggest thing since *The Quare Fellow*', he told the press when they asked him for his comments. At the christening, he was neatly dressed and well behaved. None of the names given to the child at baptism were from Brendan's side of the family. She was called Blanaid Orla Marghead. Blanaid was the name of Beatrice's poetess grandmother.

Shortly after the christening Brendan was back on the drink again. His condition worsened until the inevitable took place.

He was taken once more to the Royal City of Dublin Hospital in a diabetic coma. He was also suffering from hepatitis, a liver complaint. On Christmas Day, he received the Last Sacraments. He had always been most meticulous about having the attentions of the Church at the end:

> When I die I want to die in bed surrounded by fourteen holy nuns with candles. I am a Catholic. A damn bad one according to some. But I have never ridiculed my faith. Even when the drink takes to me I find that when darkness falls I think of my prayers.

But again he rallied with his prodigious energy. The doctor who attended Brendan at this time was of the opinion that he just might have made a complete recovery if he had really buckled down to it and undergone a course of treatment. But the thought of treatment was by now anathema to Brendan. Four days after Christmas, on the plea that he could get no sleep, he discharged himself from the hospital.

Now his Golgotha was to begin.

One night near the end of January, he arrived at his parents' house. He was in bad shape, so they put him to bed. Kathleen watched over him until he had fallen into an uneasy sleep. Next morning, Kathleen and Stephen were woken and told that Brendan had been found lying further down the street in a pool of his own blood. It seemed as if somebody had beaten him up. Though the police were at his bedside in the hospital next day, they were never able to provide an explanation for the incident. Brendan claimed he was too drunk to remember.

Soon he was out of hospital again, sleeping by day and drinking by night. Beatrice and he seemed to have grown apart. She had no power over him any more. He recognized his responsibility in allowing their relationship to degenerate to this state. One night, he suddenly turned with tears in his eyes to Rae Jeffs and said:

> Love is the most damnable emotion of all. Look what I've done to Beatrice. When I married her she was a sweet and gentle person, now she's a tiger. If I had my way, I'd cut it all out and give my head a break for the killer thoughts that are in it.

He sat there, looking at Jeffs, with the tears trickling down his face.

For the next few weeks, he was a spectre in the Dublin pubs.

He would stagger in, his pockets stuffed with bloody tissue paper, which he used to staunch the almost continual bleeding of his nose. When he slept at home, it was in a room in indescribable untidiness and dirt, because he had forbidden Beatrice to do anything, or touch anything in it.

There is a vivid description of Brendan at this period by Max Caulfield, the author and Fleet Street journalist who came over to ghost Brendan for an article in a London newspaper. He tried for three days to unearth him. Finally, one day he knocked on the door to be greeted by Rae Jeffs and Beatrice leaving hurriedly, but giving him an indication that his quarry was upstairs. With horror and pity, Caulfield surveyed the room. It was 'like something out of Gogol's Lower Depths'. On the bed was the human wreck he had come to interview, who greeted him nevertheless with a cheerful oath. Together he and Caulfield made their way to the nearest pub. After a few drinks, they moved on to another pub. Brendan was a trifle taken aback by the fact that when he tried on his knowledge of Dublin topography on Caulfield, he got back as much as he gave. Caulfield had recently written a book on the 1916 Rebellion and was an expert on Dublin's history. As they proceeded from pub to pub, Caulfield became more and more horrified. Twice Brendan got sick in his car—twice it was cleaned out. Caulfield noticed how Brendan would walk into a pub, borrow interminable cigarettes, smoke them for a few puffs and then drop them on the floor. He seemed to be more interested in talking and putting on a show than in drinking, as if he was concerned to prove that the real Brendan Behan had not died yet. But it was only too clear that something in Brendan had died. 'He seemed to be playing the Irishman', Caulfield noted. 'He must have felt that it was expected of him. He might easily, I guess, have hated it'.

Late that night, Caulfield and he ended up at Rory Furlong's house, Brendan's brother. Caulfield had his pen poised to begin the article when Brendan suddenly started to argue about money. He was unable to collect his ideas, and, rather than admit it, he introduced impossible financial conditions which he knew could not be met, and then stumbled off to bed.

That was the end of the article. As Caulfield drove home, he reflected bitterly on a wasted two days:

> I drove towards the Dolphin Hotel, conscious all the way of that great horrible mess swimming on the floor just beside me, desperately trying to pretend to myself that I didn't really care about it, that Behan should have known better. He had talent, the great idiot, and yet I was glad I wasn't him. And I was glad I didn't have whatever was bothering him.

In fact, Brendan had had his last chance of making a recovery when he went to New York in February the previous year. He had thought that the New World might assuage the agony inside him. But the pressures there were too great and his nervous system couldn't take the strain. He seems to have given in about this time. He told his doctor, Terence Chapman: 'Alcoholics die of alcohol'.

CHAPTER TWENTY-FIVE

EARLY in March, 1964, he was in the Harbour Lights Bar with Paddy Kelly and Kathleen. Kathleen had to leave presently, so he remained on with Paddy Kelly. After a while, he told him that he was getting very cold. Kelly wanted to get Brendan a coat. Then Brendan announced that he was getting very warm. A few minutes later, his hands and legs had begun to grow cold. Kelly shoved a whiskey down his throat, and Brendan immediately started to sweat profusely. Suddenly he fell on his knees. Brendan's cousin, Jimmy Bruce, who was present, and Kelly decided that they must get him home. Kelly rang Beatrice who said would they not try bringing him to hospital. They phoned for a taxi and carried Brendan into it. Kelly remembers how, as they carried Brendan to the taxi, he noticed the enormous hernia that Brendan had. They brought him to the Meath Hospital where he was put to bed immediately. He had recovered sufficiently before they left to say to Jimmy Bruce, 'Go away, Jim, I'm in the hands of professionals now, or supposed to be'. He was in great agony for the next few hours. His liver was partially destroyed. His alcoholic condition was complicated by the usual diabetic semi-coma. Yet by the effort of will which he always managed to reserve for occasions like this, he managed to rally a little. The doctor remembers that he was a very good patient. In order to give him blood transfusions and to make tests, various instruments had to be inserted into his body. He never complained, and even managed to make a few jokes with the nurses. Though he was in a coma for some days, by the middle of the week he seemed to be making some progress. Then by a cruel chance of fortune, he got his hands on a bottle of brandy which was brought in by an acquaintance who had come over from England.

On Friday, March 20, the doctors performed a tracheotomy to allow him to breathe more freely. Stephen and Kathleen did alternate three-hour vigils during the day and Beatrice was with him almost continuously. At eight o'clock that evening Kathleen left his bedside as she was feeling unwell.

John Ryan, his friend since the Catacomb days and owner of the Bailey, came to the hospital with Stephen to keep him company. By saying that he was Brendan's brother Rory, who at the time was marooned in Tipperary, Ryan was allowed to go with Stephen to Brendan's bedside. Ryan noticed that Brendan, as he lay dying, seemed extraordinary beautiful. 'Like one of the Caesars in marble. Even his chest seemed to have become full and round again.'

Stephen, Kathleen and John Ryan left.

Beatrice and Brendan were alone for a while.

He turned and looked sadly at her: 'You made one mistake. You married me', he said.

She replied sincerely: 'We saw the two days.'

It was a phrase they had between them for good times and bad. At the funeral, she told a friend she would have married him again that morning if she had been given the chance.

At 8.50 Rory, his brother, arrived at the hospital from Templemore in Tipperary, where he had heard on the radio that Brendan's condition was critical. But Brendan had died ten minutes before. Beatrice was beside him. He had received the Last Sacraments the previous Sunday, though this was one fact not mentioned in the otherwise very full account which the *Daily Worker* gave of his death.

The news of his death made an impact throughout the world. There was hardly a living writer whose death would have met with greater publicity than Brendan's did at this time. In New York, London, Paris, Stockholm, the papers carried large obituary notices. The *New York Times* said:

> To those who regarded him with disdain, he was a stage Irishman, a strange mixture of the naïve and the sophisticated. For those who discounted his public life, he was a writer of immense talent, capable of transferring people live and warm from their natural habitat to the stage or to the printed page.

317

René MacColl in the *Daily Express* wrote:

> What a sad waste of an enormous talent. This was the story of F. Scott Fitzgerald all over again, the story of a brilliant writer who simply couldn't keep off the bottle. If Brendan had slowed down a little, paced his drinking into something approaching the normal intake, he should have been good for another ten or twelve outstanding plays, another five or six absorbing books.
>
> If ever a man did himself in as sure as though he had picked up a revolver and blew his brains out, it was Brendan.
>
> Too young to die, but too drunk to live.

Dagens Nyheter, the Stockholm morning paper wrote:

> We will remember him, the child, his pockets full of explosives, and his heart full of poetry. Behan was the wild son of Ireland, the impossible island. This fate of his will be regarded as a European tragedy for his generation.

Alan Brien commented in the *Daily Telegraph*:

> Everyone follows the torch of his destiny and Brendan's burned bright and quick.
>
> I remember visiting him in hospital in London some years ago when the obituaries then were already in type. 'Brendan', I said, 'do you never think about death?' He heaved his bulk about in silence under the covers like a beached whale.
>
> Then he burst out—'Think about death? Begod, man I'd rather be dead than think about death'.
>
> It was one of the most courageous and honest remarks ever made by a dangerously sick man. I would like to remember it as his epitaph.
>
> The world will be a quieter, duller, and poorer place without him. I lay an Englishman's wreath on his Irishman's head.

Perhaps the most perceptive obituary piece was written by his fellow-Dublin writer, Flann O'Brien, in the *Sunday Telegraph*. O'Brien, like Behan, was an alcoholic who was to die within a few years:

> Brendan will not be replaced in a hurry, or at all. There has been no Irishman quite like him, and his playwriting, which I personally found in parts both crude and offensive as well as entertaining, was only a fraction of his peculiarly complicated personality. He is in fact much more a player than a playwright, or, to use a Dublin saying, 'He was as good as a play'. One can detect some affinity in him with O'Casey, but the pervasive error lies in ranking a delightful rowdy, a wit, a man of action in

many dangerous undertakings where he thought his duty lay, a reckless drinker, a fearless denouncer of humbug and pretence and so a proprietor of the biggest heart that has beaten in Ireland for the past forty years. I know it is only foolishness in my own head, but there are streets in Dublin which seem strangely silent tonight.

The noisy one-time son has gone home this time for good.

Brendan was a popular writer in the sense that no literary personality of his time had been. Thousands who had never read his book felt they knew him intimately from his appearances on television and the reports of his escapades in the newspapers.

With his death, the legend grew. He was to become a symbol for many too young even to have known his name when he was alive.

He has remained in the public mind as an iconoclast who defied convention, a precursor of the permissive society. Of those who manned the barricades in Paris, who sat-in at Berkeley or loved-in in Central Park, there are not a few to whom Brendan has been a father-figure.

Had he chosen it, his role had been a different one. At the back of his mind lurked the image of the eighteenth century Gaelic poets who had beguiled his boyhood; mocking picaresque figures who brought high culture to the hearth, indifferent how they used their bodies in drink, lust, or rage if they caught for a moment in verse, the fine frenzy that overflowed in their imagination.

On March 21 the remains were removed from the Meath Hospital to Donnybrook Church. Just before the hearse moved out, a remarkable event occurred. Jimmy Hiney—a tiny little man with a reedy voice, the last of the wandering ballad singers—held his hand up. He summoned the people who had overflowed into the hospital gardens from the large crowd gathered outside and ordered them to say the Rosary. They knelt down and answered the Responses as he gave out the prayers. There were many 'oul wans' among them, the mothers of Dublin. Brendan had been their 'laughing boy'.

Next day, after the Mass, a Guard of Honour of eight I.R.A. men escorted the coffin from the church past 5 Anglesea Road.

They marched on either side with military exactitude. Among them were his comrades—Cathal Goulding, Mick Murphy, Paddy Kelly, Mick Ryan and Charlie Gorman. As the cortege reached the centre of the city, thousands of people lined the streets. One Irish paper described it as the biggest funeral since those of Michael Collins and Charles Stewart Parnell.

College Green was thronged. The crowd thinned near the middle of O'Connell Street, but thickened again near Parnell Street on the road to Glasnevin cemetery. At O'Connell Bridge a policeman saluted the coffin. It was draped with the Tricolour, a special tribute the I.R.A. always gave to their dead. Three weeks before Brendan died, he had drawn Charlie Gorman aside very seriously and made him promise he would have the Tricolour on his coffin. The I.R.A., in fact, ran the funeral like clockwork. Though they were technically an illegal organization it was recognized that they would not be interfered with on this day. They had come from Cork, Kerry and Belfast for the funeral.

The President of Ireland, Mr de Valera, was represented at the graveside by Commandant R. MacIonnraic, and the Deputy Prime Minister, Mr Sean MacEntee, was also present. Father Ciaran Hoolahan said the prayers over the grave and recited a decade of the Rosary in Irish. A fourteen-year-old bugler from the Fianna, Peter McNulty, sounded the Last Post over the grave.

Mattie O'Neill, an old I.R.A. comrade of Brendan's, spoke the oration. He spoke first in Irish:

> There was life throbbing in every vein of him. It is heart-breaking to see all that gaiety and all that bravery going under the soil of Glasnevin. His memory will be green as long as Dublin lies on the Liffey.

The speaker then went on to talk of his acquaintanceship with Brendan, one which had begun when they had shared the same prison and internment camps together. Others would speak of the complex personality of Behan. He would remember that Dublin wit which had lightened a dark day in the early 'forties.

> A great light has gone out of our lives for ever, and we hear the echoes of that rich baritone voice, singing 'Wrap my green jacket in a brown paper parcel, I'll not need it any more.'

O'Neill ended with a quotation in Irish, from Maurice O'Sullivan's book on the Blasket Islands, *Twenty Years a-Growing:*

Ni fheicfimid a leitheid aris.
(We shall not see his like again.)

Brendan would have been pleased at the tribute implied in the last phrase. In the world of the Gael lay his ancestral self, the source of the poetry that was in him. He had been adopted by an age which was unable to recognize this. He let it be so. Such an indwelling of the spirit comes but once to a man, and if he refuses it, it leaves and takes its abode elsewhere, until finally rejected it broods over the world awaiting the apocalypse.

An hour after the crowd dispersed, a special ceremony took place. The Guard of Honour drew revolvers from their holsters and fired a salute over the grave.

It was the ritual interment of a blood brother.

After the publication of this biography in July 1970, Desmond MacNamara, the sculptor, and a close friend of Brendan Behan's, sent the following letter to the Irish *Times*.

It was in response to a controversy in the Letter Columns of the paper.

The letter was not printed. The Editor of the Irish *Times* in a letter to the author, stated that he could find no trace of the letter being received. Desmond MacNamara is equally adamant that he sent the letter to the paper.

1 Woodchurch Road,
London N.W.6.
4th August 1970.

The Editor,
Irish Times,
Westmorland Street,
Dublin 2.

Dear Sir,

Surely, surely the brouhaha caused by the reaction to a certain phrase of Brendan Behan's sensual development is itself distorting and exaggerating the very complex truth of the matter.

If a face is enlarged from a photograph of a football team or a school group, the result is a lie which interferes with the common process of perception. It can turn a sentient biped into something from a Hammer film production.

Many people must remember Brendan's anecdotes about what he used to describe as his 'Mahaffyism'. Some of them may have been outrageous lies, though they made good telling. Some were more poignant. When he sang about

> 'the brooks too wide for leaping,
> the lightfoot lads are laid,
> And the rose-lipped maids are sleeping
> In fields where the roses fade'

he was singing from the heart.

'You are a man of somewhat Hellenic diversity' observed the original Ginger Man to Brendan in Paris, many years ago.

'I must have caught it off an Angelica Kaufmann in Dominic Street when I was scraping it down for an undercoat,' was the reply. It was hardly a factual statement, but it wasn't an evasion.

The poem by Dominic O'Riordain in last week's Irish Press summed up the whole sad marvellous story, for me, and I dare say for many more. It should be chalked on every blank wall between Parnell Street and Sundrive Road.

Yours etc.

DESMOND MACNAMARA

325